LAND AND POVERTY ALLEVIATION

LAND AND POVERTY ALLEVIATION

Dr P.K. Agrawal

KALPAZ

ISBN: 978-93-5128-101-6

Price : ` 790

First Published, 2015

Published by

Kalpaz Publications
C-30, Satyawati Nagar,
Delhi – 110052
E-mail: kalpaz@hotmail.com Ph.: 9212142040

Laser Typesetting: Gyan Print (AB-I)
Printed at: G. Print Process, Delhi

Cataloging in Publication Data--DK
Courtesy: D.K. Agencies (P) Ltd. <docinfo@dkagencies.com>

Agrawal, P. K., author.
Land and poverty alleviation / P.K. Agrawal.
pages cm
Includes bibliographical references (pages) and index.
ISBN 9789351281016

1. Land reform--India--West Bengal. 2. Poverty--India--West Bengal. I. Title.

DDC 333.3154 23

Contents

Conversion Table for Measurement of Land

1 Hectare	=	2.471 acres = 10,000 sq. metres
1 Acre	=	4,840 sq. yards = 43,560 sq. feet = 100 decimal = 0.405 hectare
1 sq. mile	=	640 acres = 259 hectares (appx)
1 sq. km	=	247.1 acre = 100 hectare
1 sq. metre	=	1.196 sq. yards
1 decimal	=	48.40 sq. yards = 435.60 sq. feet

Preface

After publication of two works on land reforms, titled '*Land Reforms in India*' and '*Land Reforms in States and Union Territories in India'* in 1993 and in 2010 and working in the field for the land poor in West Bengal for about eleven years. During my service period from the year 1980 to 2010, I wished to work for the land poor of the World. The invitation from the World Bank in 2013 to attend World Conference on 'Land and Poverty', and participation in the Conference gave the final impetus to prepare this volume. I am surprised that the World Bank is now vying the same line of thinking which I have been cherishing for so many years since 1980 that land reform is the only way to remove poverty of the last man on the earth.

At least Vox Populi has been finally established by issuance of Voluntary Guidelines on the Responsible Governance Tenure by the Food and Agriculture Organisation of the United Nations in May, 2012 in Rome which *inter alia* for the first time covers urban areas, fisheries and forests within the ambit of land reform. It contains inputs on how improving the governance of tenure can serve to put an end to hunger and poverty.

Increased demand for land because of volatile food availability at the grassroots level and increasing urbanisation need for well-designed land policies and their implementation at the country level to ensure security of long-held rights to land to facilitate increasing land access to the landless or the marginal land-holders. However, this is not an easy job as land tenure is deeply rooted in a country's history and culture and vary from country to country or from province to province within a country implying a need to adopt the type of sequencing of land reforms to country-specific. And all reforms have to keep pace with the stakeholders and can only lead to the extent the reform beneficiaries can assimilate.

Also as land reforms will take time to bear fruits and may be opposed by the vested interests. There is need to identify challenges and meet them with concerted efforts by all stakeholders including government, local bodies, community councils, administration and the deserving land reform beneficiaries, i.e., the landless persons in rural areas and the homeless in the urban areas. Without doing this, the chances of making quick progress are likely to be much reduced. If these reforms are superimposed on them by a proactive or fiery leadership, the result will be bloodshed in which many of the projected beneficiaries will also be killed during the mobilisation or afterwards whenever the vested interests again re-emerge with more legitimate state or lethal power. It is therefore, in the interest of all concerned that the slow moving land reforms are implemented, so that imbalance in the society doesn't break the safety valve.

If one takes the world scenario, the problem of land-reform has been solved by USA, Australia and other developed countries by pushing their indigenous people like the Red Indians into reserved areas and by giving lot of subsidy to the farmers like $ 400 billion subsidy to US farmers. This of course has created discrimination in the marketing of produce of farmers from third world countries. The countries in Latin America are still struggling with land reforms including updating of their land records and to reduce disparities in ownership of land. The African countries still are going with the community and state ownership of land. The communities leaderships so far are objective and impartial but corruption due to influence of outsiders or multi-nationals or transnational corporations is fast creeping into their system. Therefore, so many civil strafes are the order of the day in the African sub-continent. The countries in Central and Western Europe have systematic land records like UK, Germany, Netherlands but the East European countries are not yet able to come out fully after the disbanding of collective farms there. Neither all the lands could be reallotted to their respective owners, nor is the state able to subsidise these farms which they used to do earlier with assistance from the Soviet bloc.

The Soviet Russia has disintegrated and the disintegrated or liberated countries are not self-reliant and in the transition phase, they look for assistance from any side including Russia. The UN bodies like World Bank are trying to sneak into, but it is doubtful how much they can help them to stabilise their land tenure system. In Asia, China and Japan are two most stable and ideal countries as they have achieved more than 90 per cent redistribution of land. Countries like India, Indonesia, Philippines are still struggling. Countries like Pakistan, Iran, Iraq and other middle-east countries have still to wake up whereas countries like Bangladesh has of late, realised their problem through active non-government voluntary organisation. Yet, the country doesn't have enough land nor resources to purchase land and distribute among their vast landless population in rural as well as urban areas. It shows that the land reform cannot be taken as panacea to remove of poverty without an integrated growth or development of the economy of the country as a whole. Many African countries cannot take over surplus land from the big landowners, because they are unable to pay for the expropriated land at the market price, unlike in country like India, where one has to pay only nominal price for the government expropriated land being above ceiling limit which is generally taken at the level of five hectare for irrigated land whereas in case of dryland, it is generally seven hectare.

It has been proved by many researchers, and there is a common agreement that the implementation of land reforms cause increase in production of foodgrains, or vegetables or cereals etc. Even a patch upto 16 decimal of land can save a family from hunger. Thus, earlier theories of minimum economic holding of land is of no relevance now taken the overall scenario of social-economic background of the poorest of the poor in the World, who are still 70 per cent in rural areas, and 60 per cent of them fully depend on agriculture which is sometimes called even gambling in regions depending on monsoon.

'Das Kapital' of Karl Marx is still 'the Bible of the working class' including of peasants though Karl Marx himself is not the votary of land reform and even failed to forecast a revolution in England during his lifetime because of unmanageable unemployment in urban areas. It is then concluded by his colleague Friedrich Engels that 'England is the only country where the inevitable social revolution might be effected entirely by people and legal means. This is the present day truth. People around the world are so much mesmerised with globalisation and consumerism due to deep penetration of media into their psyche that they look for revolution through legitimate democratic means though ultimately that is not the reality.

No amount of globalisation can stabilise their livelihood unless it is based on sound footing of security of tenure of land to them. It is accepted even by the votaries of globalisation that land reform is the long-term basis of globalisation. The actors of globalisation have started working in this direction so that the palaces or prosperous cities built as a result of globalisation are not overrun by the hungry masses from the rural areas duly supported by the homeless people in cities and mega cities. In fact, China, the living socialist country, has been adopting their path and keeping its revolutionary people at peace with the state apparatus by giving them heavy benefits and luxuries after finishing their implementation of land reforms mainly redistribution of landed property.

After failure of collective farming under state patronage in the erstwhile Soviet Russia and success of China in a mixed system of socialist and market-based economy. It is well-established that Egyptian Co-operative system is worth emulating in which the participant farmer keeps his ownership or title of land intact but he shares cultivation and marketing expenses, sale proceeds and even profits with other members of the collective or co-operative farm. It provides requisite motivation to the individual to work on the farm with full vigour and with maximum labour.

In the first chapter, land has been defined in a generalised way what a common man understands. At the same time, the legal facets have been reflected in a lucid style.

Chapter 2 traces historical facts on how the great revolutions like French Revolution or Cultural Revolution of China and other revolts or mobilisations have caused bloodshed to achieve land reforms and is still causing in the form of civil strife, guerrilla warfare and Naxalite movement in India.

The people or nations, who do not learn from history, commit blunders. It will not be excused by the next generations.

Chapter 3 presents, how various forms of utilisation of land exist world over like communal ownership, *haciendas del norte estates*, sharecropping, collective farming, contract farming, etc. It also contains how the problem of transition from state farm system from socialist bloc countries, has not yet been completed.

Chapter 4 attempts to define poverty on internationally recognised parameters like calorie intake and how poverty is directly traceable and relateable to the land. The more the access to land, less is the poverty. For major period of the year, agricultural worker or peasant is unemployed known sometime as disguised unemployment. If he has access to land, he will be more motivated to work and will keep himself and his family gainfully employed on land. As a result, the production will increase giving push to poverty towards the sea.

Chapter 5 examines, how concentration in land and monopolies in forest produce and pisciculture still exist. This stark inequality is not acceptable in the modern-day world in which thinking is at a high pedestal. No right thinking person can agree that unequal distribution of land and properties can cause prosperity in the society. In matter of land, the skewed distribution of land still exists which calls for urgent attention to do away with such discrimination.

In Chapter 6, significance and modern methods of maintenance and updation of land records have been elaborated. Without being close to correct land records, no redistribution of land or other measures of land reforms will be feasible. It also enjoins the need for integration of Land Administration System (LAS) with the Registration Department, so that mutation of names is automatic and this will provide on in-built mechanism of updation of land records. At the same time, it will reduce corruption in LAS to a considerable system. Need for updation of property records in town, cities and mega cities has also been emphasised which can be triggered by having a mandatory legislation for urban local bodies (ULBs) in this regard like in rural areas.

Chapter 7 is the heart of the book. Redistribution of land is the central goal of all land reforms measures in rural areas. At least, a person having a minimum quantum of land, will not die of hunger. Even land upto 16 decimal, can save a family from starvation because the farmer will raise three crops in that small farm size, i.e., vegetables or foodgrains on the surface, fruit bearing orchard at the middle height and timber trees, at the highest level like in Bangladesh as per experiment initiated by Rural Development Institute, USA. The example of the Chinese revolution is given as a case study for forcible taking over and distribution excess vested land. At the same time, the processes of vesting and distribution of ceiling surplus land has been elaborated so that any country or province can follow it.

Chapter 8 deals with an important segment of land reforms, i.e., recording of sharecroppers on land. The success story of West Bengal, India in recording of 1.5 million sharecroppers has been described in details so as to provide practical guidelines in this regard.

President Sukarno in Indonesia and Robert Mugabe, the Prime Minister of Zimbabwe recognised the same and the foreigners had to return much of the lands to its original African inhabitants. Other countries in Africa and Latin America are still struggling how they can ensure security of right of cultivation to the sharecroppers. It is not accomplished just by passing an Act. Similar right of security of tenancy has been discussed how it can be extended to forests, fisheries and in urban areas.

In Chapter 9, the healthy and active institutions of local self-government and peasants' organisations are very essential for successful implementation of land reforms. As the poor persons are not very enlightened and participative, the local government or semi-government units including NGOs, can reach benefits to their door steps. It has been shown how various mobilisation movements whether non-violent or violent in various degrees have helped the poor people to unite and get their rights all over the world at various times. Ultimately, it is the present movement which gets some right to the land poor. In view of historical fact, the writer has concluded that local level conflict situation will always be helpful to the poor persons because the administration will be on its toes to work for them and will not overlook their problems and grievances superficially.

Chapter 10 discovers that the Constitutions of most of the countries provide for livelihood to the poor. It dwells on legal empowerment of women by making them as the first allottee of government vested land along with her husband. The issuance of farmer passbook will help them to protect them from eviction and will be helpful to get Bank's loan and subsidy. Legal aid is generally not available. If it is there, the lawyers, are not reliable and sincere. They may say something before the court which might be against the interest of the client. Bangladesh is the leaders in the field of NGOs providing legal aid to the land poor and spearheading movement to legally empower the landless, *patta*-holders and sharecroppers. The spreading of legal awareness about rights to land can solve many of the complicated problems related to land.

Chapter 11 examines, how employment generating schemes are essential during lean season of agricultural operations. The bank credit will help the poor cultivation to be self-dependent. If a house site or a house is provided to the land poor, he will make efforts to come out of the clutches of landowner, debt-burden of moneylender and morass of poverty. Three best practices in this field have been brought out in cases of a hilly region, plain area and pasture land near sea belt. The new system of informal or loosely joined self-help-groups (SHGs) are bringing about revolution in the lives of rural poor. In urban areas, the lead to provide housing was taken by the Supreme Court of India in the Pavement Dwellers case. Now, right to shelter for slum dwellers is a recognised right. However, social and religious reforms are equally important so that the poor do not spend lavishly on their rituals, daughter's marriage, religious superstitions and they should get rid off alocoholism and gambling. It is also suggested that land acquired by the state as custodian of welfare of its citizens, should acquire only minimum land required for the project. Secondly, due care should be taken for rehabilitation and resettlement of the evicted people. The land evictees should be associated in the project so that the industry also gets local support which will pay heavy dividends in future.

Chapter 12 explores, how the Land Administration System (LAS) can be strengthened at the grassroots level. Firstly, it requires additional manpower and lot of investment. It should have sufficient allocation of fund to update land records and maintain them properly. Corruption is one problem which requires to be tackled in LAS by women even by taking law in their hands. The officials involved in corruption should be publicly insulted and socially boycotted. Along with political will, there should be administrative will to work for the poor and the landless. Delay and indecision should be equally punished along with violation of official rules and regulations. There should be a separate wing only for survey and for preparation and updation of land records or property records in towns, cities and metropolis.

Chapter 13 approaches to measure the extent of land reforms which is otherwise said to be a vague concept and the officials concerned declare no more need of land reform without knowing that land reforms have been implemented whatsoever was to be implemented. Implementation of land reform is a continuous process like the progress of our society. Two concrete approaches in this respect have been discussed and analysed vividly. In fact, most of the informations have been taken from the World Bank publication entitled Land Governance Assessment Framework. Then the factors so established were taken into the arithmetical formula of addition devised by the writer in the book "*Land Reforms in India*" in the year 1992. Ten factors with their relative strength are Employment Generating Schemes (four per cent), Recording of Tenancy or sharecropping (20 per cent), Local Organisations (10 per cent), Distribution of ceiling surplus government land (40 per cent), Maintenance and Updation of Land records (eight per cent), Social and Religious reforms (three per cent), Legal empowerment and legal aid, to the poor (three per cent) Crop Finance or credit availability (five per cent), Co-operative farming (one per cent), Distribution of houses or House sites (10 per cent).

Accordingly, the four countries in four sub-continents were assessed, i.e., Peru in Latin America, Tanzania in Africa, Indonesia in Asia and Australia. The results by the two formulae were on the same wave length.

Thus, both formulae deserve further confirmation from the field and may differ because many of the factors have been assessed on subjective considerations and may differ from time to time and from person to person. But it is a fact that land reform implementation is the poorest in Africa, followed by Latin America and by Asia. So also poverty is directly proportional to the extent of effect of land reforms.

The final chapter simply summarises the discussion in all 13 Chapters, of the book. The conclusion is very clear that though the revolution by the peasants and the homeless is the realty, yet the poor in rural and urban areas cannot wait for long. They being peace-loving and creative people shouldn't be pushed in revolution until they on their own are willing and prepared to adopt the violent path.

Secondly, the lives of land poor and sharecroppers shouldn't be made miserable until the revolution arrives at their doorstep. Therefore, implementation of land reform in rural areas should continue.

The poor migrate from the rural area to the urban areas in search of jobs but when they don't find jobs due to lack of their skill or fierce competition for jobs there, they return dejected to rural areas. Something is required to be done so that the land poor and the other poor have not to move in life like a shuttle having no stability for them and their families in search of food or livelihood. It is only land and land alone which can fasten to them with the stability as land represents the most stable constituent of the globe. No World Bank or IMF assistance or G-7 nations' sympathetic gestures can feed teeming billion of people. They have to be provided with ways and means to stand on their own in life. Availability of land along with security of tenure can accomplish this great obligation of the society or the state towards the poor so that they may not come again and again to ask for alms or government grants or subsidies. The state or system has to ensure them conditions which if are not exploitation fee, is at least congenial for their development by their own efforts. They are given due prices of their agricultural produce or produce from allied sectors like animal husbandry, fisheries or forests. They have a say in this globalisation world and should not be treated as herds driven by the MNCs or Transnational Corporations at the behest of heads of government of some of the most developed countries. None is superior or inferior. All human beings are born equal. There can be no discrimination between two avocations. All jobs are equally important for the society to exist. The lowest person in the society has to be provided with such capacity that he can tide over all ups and downs in life so as not to starve. Famine and hunger are the worst two defamatory words for the modern scientific and IT society. Let us all make sincere efforts to wipe out tears from the last man on this earth by providing him due access to the land and its produce. If states do not control poverty, then poverty will control them. Let the landless in rural areas and the homeless in urban areas unite in the World for a better future of mankind.

This book will prove a change-agent in the field of land reforms and poverty alleviation. It will be an ideological work for academicians and revolutionaries and will be a guide for the legislatures to draft laws relating to land reforms and a hand-book for the some land administrators to implement land reforms in the field. If this book is able to wipe out tears from the eyes of poor man, I shall feel my work done.

I am grateful to my family members who have stood by my side while writing this book.

P.K. Agrawal

1

Land Defined

The universe developed from a very tiny, dense state into ball of mass which ultimately evolved into what it is today. It was at a moment when all the separate forces of the universe became a part of a united force. After it sprawled over a vast area, the area converted into the mass of earth which later on come to be known land having deep attachment with the innermost layer of the earth. In due course of time, it became a reference point for the evolution of world.

Initially there was lot of land but a very few takers. Therefore, people were asked to occupy parcels of land. Whosoever occupied the land first became the proprietor/owner. Thus things which were not already the subject of property became the property of the first occupant. According to the Indian scriptures led by *Manu Smriti*, a field is his who clears of its jungle. The wild animals belong to one who first pierces them. Manu's "Occupation theory" of property corresponds to the doctrine of 'occupation' which echoed in Rome during the seventeenth and eighteenth centuries. Accordingly, "wild beasts, birds, fish and all animals which live either in the sea, the air, or on the earth, so soon as they are taken by anyone, immediately became, by the law of nations, the property of the captor, for natural reason gives to the first occupant that which had no previous owner.[1]

The land is as old as the universe. With the formation of the universe, the land came out for working by the human beings and animals that evolved first. Initially land was large, but there were only a few people to exploit it. Even after a long march of the human beings on earth, the people were forcibly given or allotted land to cultivate so that they may support their livelihood and build this world a better place to live for themselves and others. Thus, labour on land or earth was the driving force to build up this world.

Mohammad Sahab, the great Prophet said, *"Whoever cultivates waste lands does thereby acquire property in them". The Muslim Jurists differ in their interpretations of this 'hadis'. Accordingly to Abu Haneefa, the mere cultivation of waste land is not enough to create a real right in the cultivator, the permission of the State is necessary for the acquisition of proprietary right. But his disciples Abu Yusuf and Abu Mohammad, both of whom were judges under the Khalifa Harun-al-Rashid, maintain that no permission of the State is necessary to make the cultivator the proprietor. They say that waste lands are, "a sort of common goods and became the property of the cultivator by virtue of his being the first possessor, in the same manner as in the case of seizing game or gathering firewood.*[2]

Thus, the state began to recognise the rights of the individual in his dealings with the State in addition to liberty, equality and religious freedom. According to the Bible "After seven years a year of redemption follows when the entire land goes back to the tiller without compensation to the moneylender or land lord during all time in all climatic zone.".

Thus, inequality was recognised as much as inbuilt in the society as equality and liberty.

As the population grew, State came into existence to arbitrate among citizens or persons to avoid violence or bloodshed. Blackstone and Maine simply supported possession which was close to the ownership. Occupancy ripens into ownership because there is no better claimant to the free goods on land (*res nullius*) and became all things were presumed to be somebody's property.

"The concept of property right gained further support from Bentham, Spencer, Kant and Hegel. The term property in its pristine meaning embraced only land but it soon came to mean much more."[3]

Grotius had treated the right as an acquired right and ownership as either serving individual interest or for the public good. According to him, the acquired right had to give way to the eminent domain but there must be public interest and if possible compensation.

Karl Marx recognised system of co-operative or community farming in India during the Vedic times saying, "These small old villages of India, many of which are still existing, had a system-based on joint ownership of land, co-operation in agriculture and crafts and division of labour. Bhragu Samhita laid down that the land shall belong to these who cultivate with their hands.[4]

The Hindu sages and jurists said repeatedly that the State was not the proprietor of the soil. He was entitled to a share of the usufruct of the lands in the occupation of his subjects, not because he was the owner, but because a share was payable to him as the price for the protection afforded to life, liberty and property. Narada expressly says that this one-sixth of the produce was the sovereign's fees for the protection of the subjects.[5]

The famous text from Manu contains that "the sages who know former times ..... pronounce cultivated land to be the property of him who cut away the wood, or who cleared and tilled it".[6]

The right of subject to the ownership of land was universally recognised by ancient Hindu King.[7]

Private Property in land seems to have been recognised as a sacred right, which even the hand of despotism would rarely violate.

In developing countries and undeveloped countries, the major properties are cornered in land or land related properties. People all over the world have very close relationship rather inseparable relationship with land. In India, land is termed as 'mother'.

The evolution of land resolves around management of land parcels which are used by people in their lives universally. Land has both physical and cognitive aspects. Due to increase of population and thereby increase of pressure on land, the significance of land has all of a sudden exploded so much that it has become the most lucrative sector of the economy. Land has been traditionally defined as—

"Land-attached to the earth means:

(a) rooted in the earth, as in the case of trees and shrubs;
(b) imbedded in the earth, as in the case of walls or buildings; or
(c) attached to what is imbedded for the permanent beneficial enjoyment of that to which it is attached.[8]

Thus, definition of land is absolute. In fact, every other thing is defined with reference to the land which is fixed and stable. Commonly land is defined in the dictionary as the part of the earth's surface not covered by water. The Black's Law dictionary defines, land in the most general sense comprehends any ground, soil, or earth whatsoever, including fields, meadows, pastures, woods, moors, waters, marshes and rock. Land includes free or occupied space for an indefinite distance upwards as well as downwards, subject to limitations upon the use of airspace imposed and rights in the use of airspace granted by law. (Calif Civil Code)[9]. The term "land" may be used interchangeability with property and may include anything that may be classified as real estate or real property.

Most societies and individuals within a society use a 'multiple choice' approach. They mix and match concepts of land to suit their changing lifestyles or needs at the moment. What is fanciful according to one set of norms is real and actualised by another. The varieties of concepts of land are unlimited and ever-changing. For example, in Bangladesh, a small plot of land measuring about 400 sq. metres is adequate for a family whereas in USA and Canada, even 4000 sq. metres bungalow is not enough for a family. Similarly, in metro town like Kolkata and Dhaka, people are happy to get one cot to sleep whereas in the Middle East Countries, USA and Canada people have spacious houses bungalows to live. Farm houses and garden houses are not exceptions in land surplus countries. Thus, the concept of land is also subject to the demand and supply cycle.

Thus, land can be termed as the ground on which we live. It is the surface and area upon which life takes place. It cannot be stitched. It includes the entire surface of earth, oceans, mountains, valleys and plains. It is the source of all life and sustainer of a person. Land is a property of the state or individual. It is the basis of production along with labour, capital and management. An industry can only be established on land and not in space.

It is a nature given source of food, fibre, building material, minerals, energy resources and other raw materials used by society. Land is a durable free gift of nature. Land is regarded as capital because funds can be raised using land as collateral. Land is a means for access to sunlight, rainfall, wind, soils and topography. Land is a means to support livelihood. It is a source of wealth, power, status and revenue. In fact, many wars have been fought to control land and a lot of violent and legal battles are ongoing at all times around the land directly or indirectly. The *Mahabharat* (the great battle) in India occurred five thousand years back because the other side even refused to concede five villages to the *Pandavas*.

This fierce war involved almost all important kings and lords. Even the World War I and II and victories by Porus, Napoleon and other emperors were the result of territorial ambitions of the invaders.

Now, this territorial sovereignty has come down to the neo-rich, who want to spend their surplus money to show their superiority by having posh bungalows or villas on sprawling farm houses built on large chunks of lands.

In few societies and communities in Asia and Africa, people even prefer land over their kith and kin because land is a constant source of livelihood. It can neither be blown by the wind nor can it be burnt by the fire. It can be submerged by overflowing water waves but once the water recedes, land reappears in its pristine glory and ensures bounty of crops to its farmers to compensate the loss caused by the natural calamities like earthquake, eruption of volcano, tidal waves or floods or any other natural catastrophe. However, it seems that land only surrenders or succumbs to drought because it can't sustain without its constant companion, i.e., water which has occupied three-fourth of the surface of the globe.

In fact, in the modern age, the revolution will come through land issues in rural areas because the number of have-nots are much more than the haves in the land sector and rural areas will continue to be in vast majority in terms of area and population. The actual tiller to a large extent doesn't enjoy the fruits or production or return on land in the proportion of his labour. Efforts are on in underdeveloped and developing countries to take away excess lands from the large landowners and to distribute among the landless person or land hungry people so that some semblance of equity may be established in the society under the aegis of the state. But these efforts are far from satisfactory and are not successful. In socialist countries like Soviet Russia and China, the experiments were undertaken through co-operative farming but these were not successful in Russia whereas these are still successful in Cuba and China. Therefore, equity through redistribution of land is also a major issue now-a-days.

In cities and megapolis, the prices of land are touching the sky as the craze for land in town, cities and metro towns keep on increasing. Land provides basic security irrespective of market fluctuations. One can live on land by providing some or other crop. It is seen that a person earns from his hard labour just to invest it on land at the fag end of his life. Thus, land and people are intricately linked.

Thus, land is to be defined on a wide dimension which is to some extent is caught/reflected in the following definition,

> "Land means land of every description and includes tank, tank-fisheries, fishery, homestead or land used for the purpose of livestock breeding, poultry farming, dairy or land comprised in tea garden, mill, factory, workshop, orchid, hat, bazaar, ferries, tolls or land having any other public interests and any other land together with all interests and benefits arising out of land and things attached to earth or permanently fastened to anything attached to earth".[10]

UN Guidelines issued by FAO in 2012 has also included forests and pisciculture in the ambit of land because without dealing with lands in forests and pisciculture, one cannot approach these two fields accurately.

Thus, land has played a very important role to shape the evolution of the world and is still a subject to reckon with and continues to find a prime place in the life of people and will continue to occupy the center stage of struggle of man to make his destiny in historical perspective.

References

1. Sandar's Justinian, p. 172 (2nd Ed.).
2. Hamilton's Hedaya, Book XLV, para 3; (Grady's Ed,) 610.
3. Dr. Agrawal P.K., *Land Reforms in India,* published by M.D. Publications, New Delhi -110 002, p. 41, year 1993.
4. Bhatt, S.N., *India Social and Political Way* (Hindi), Saraswati Prakashan Mandir, 69 New Behrana, Allahabad -211 003.
5. Prajapalavetnam, *Narada Smriti*, XVIII-48, *Sacred Books of East*, Vol. XXXIII, p. 221.
6. *Manusmriti*, IX-44.
7. Richard's *India*, Vol. I, p. 282.
8. Section 3 of the Transfer of Property Act, (Bare Act) Legislative

Department, Ministry of Law and Justice, Government of India, New Delhi -110 001.

9. *Black's Law Dictionary*, USA.

10. The West Bengal Land Reforms, 1955: Government of West Bengal, West Bengal Act of 1955, Section 2(7).

2

Land and Conflicts

The Constitution of a country is a basic and organic document which represents the aspirations and vibration of the people. It is the safety valve against the unrest of the people. The Constitution of a country is the main source of law and the end of any law. According to Radbruch, justice is the ideal relation among withering men. Marx propounded the concept of weathering away of the law. It means disappearance of private law by public law. It suggests that law of the past, which was a private possession of individuals, is being superseded by a public law which is more enshrined in the constitution of every country.

Right to property is the most important right because it is directly related to the livelihood of the people at large. According to Locke, private ownership was a law of nature. Henry Maine points out; "The movement of the progressive societies has been a movement from status to contract".

In the Constitution of United States of America, the property right is entrenched as follows; "nor shall any person be deprived of.... property without due process of law".

Article 29 of the Japanese Constitution 1946 contains "the right to own property is inviolable, but the property right shall be defined by law in conformity with the public welfare."

The erstwhile USSR constitution in its Article 6 declared that "the land, its mineral wealth, waters, forests, rainy water and Air Transport, Banks, Communications, large State Organised agricultural enterprises (State Farms, Machine, Tractor, Stations and the like) as well as

Municipal Enterprises and the bulk of the dwelling houses in the cities and Industrial localities are the state property, i.e., belong to the whole people". Section 9(1) of Czechoslovakia Constitution says that "private ownership may only be restricted by law". Side by side, Sub-section (3) lays down that "no person shall misuse the right of property to the detriment of the community."

The draft Indian Constitution considered:

> "The state shall not recognise feudalism in any shape or form and no person shall be entitled within the territory of India to any special rights or interests on the basis of property falling in the category of *Jagirs* or *Muafis*." However, finally adopted Constitution of India recognised right to property by containing in Article 31 (1) that "no person shall be deprived of his property save the authority of law." But the system of law and courts gradually inclined towards the capital. As a result, this fundamental right of the citizens had to be diluted by incorporating it as simple constitutional right in Article 300A. This speaks of volume of struggle which the dumb majority of peasants fought through their spokesmen and sympathisers.

According to Karl Marx, labour produces more than what is needed to maintain labour in the productive process. This surplus is pocketed by the capitalists. In villages, large landowners are the capitalists. Neo capitalists have come up who control agricultural products from the small town to the mega city and in turn are controlled by the multinationals in the world. Therefore, Engel like Marx advocated for abolition of private property. Marx saw the stagnation in the existence of the village community in colonial India in the existence of communal ownership of landed property and a symbiosis of lack of division of labour (caused by the union of peasant and artisan production) and a rigid caste specialised division of labour inhibited any change. Marx has actually described the exploitation of the farmers through so-called people oriented or beneficial legislation in England. "The law to end slavery in England freed the farmers working on land of feudal lords or landlords but the law also freed them from the lands on which they and their families depended. As a result, these thousands of farmers came on the streets in search of bread. They resorted to begging as they could not get any employment. The English Parliament made laws prohibiting beggary. They were sentenced and their bodies were burnt to make identification marks.

Second time, when they were caught begging, they were sentenced for longer periods and more identification marks were forcibly made on their bodies. Third time, when they were caught begging, they were sentenced to death. But the number of beggars did not diminish. If there is a source of criminality in the society, it cannot be cured by making law alone unless its source is tapped or destroyed.

Similarly, in India by law, the cultivation by sharecroppers has been banned in same states but it is day-light fact that cultivation cannot be done only by the labour or machines of the landowners. He has to employ outsiders to work on their fields either on wage system or on the basis of sharing of produce. By banning the sharecropping system, the lawmakers only ensure that the cultivation by the sharecropper is illegal and thus, it goes hiding and becomes fully informal on the basis or oral contract. As a result, the poor sharecropper even loses his right for stable cultivation for a definite period of time peacefully.

Similarly, land is distributed to the landless person making them landowners. But they pledge or mortgage these parcels of land in cases of economic distress in their family or for life saving treatment. Thus, they again, become landless an even lose their eligibility to get further land or assistance from the government.

According to Jawaharlal Nehru, the *Taluqdars* and the big *Zamindars*, the lords of the land have been the spoilt children of the British government. They did nothing at all for their tenancy and became complete parasites on the land and the people.

In Greece also, the landlords used to enjoy their aristocracy at the cost of the agriculture labourers, by not visiting even their fields. Thus, there were mainly three types of exploitation of farmers:

Firstly, the farmers used to cultivate the lands of the feudal lords and big land owners. In return of their services, they were provided a minimal share of produce and rest was expropriated by the landowners or the elite class under various pretexts like spending on cost of cultivation on many undisclosed heads and also to oblige tax collectors. The feudal or elite class used to spend the little portion of it for so-called piety to get appreciation from the society. But they never allowed these farmers to make permanent abodes on their farms and were kept on changing, so that they could neither claim a status as sharecroppers nor could organise among themselves in rebellion against the landowners or the feudal lords.

They were given share of produce whatever their master, i.e., landlord decided. Naturally, during calamities like flood or drought, they had no other way except to starve or die due to malnutrition. This exploitation was further accentuated when they were even denied the minimum wages for their work on field.

Second type of exploitation is the denial of surplus state lands to the landless persons or have nots in land. The state is supposed to ensure and implement equitable distribution of land among all the citizens of the country, as land originally belonged to none or at the most belonged to the state as a representative of the God or King. The state instrument tried this stupendous job. They first acquired the excess land belonging to the landowners over and above the prescribed limit of ceiling. The process of vesting of ceiling surplus land itself could not be completed. Wherever, the cases of ceiling were finally decided, the landowners were given option to release their choicest land. Naturally, they opted only those lands to be vested in the State which were either non-productive or were disputed. As a result, when these parcels of land were allotted to the landless persons, they couldn't till these lands. Secondly, the erstwhile landowners in actual practice, didn't relinquish their possession. Thirdly, these lands were subsequently disposed of informally when the allottee of government land generally known as *pattadar* found himself or his family in dire distress. And as usual, he rejoined the rank and file of the landless or the hungry people.

Third type of exploitation is the peasants came to the town to serve in construction activities run either by the government or the private persons or to serve in mills and factories or in service sector or in governmental activities.

The farmers had no wealth to purchase lands. Therefore, they were compelled to work in the fields of feudal lords or landlords and used to pay revenue or share of produce as per the rates fixed by them. Their produce was sold off at lesser price but they had to purchase goods from the market at higher prices. The prices of essential commodities kept fit on rising but proportionately the prices of agricultural products didn't rise. Thus, this was another form of exploitation of cultivators by the market forces, which is generally not accounted for. Initially the justice by courts was considered as relief but now justice has also become costly due to high rates of court fees or process fee. On the other hand, delay in delivery of justice further blurred the ray of hope. Justice becomes the bonded labour of capitalists through their professional agents hired as lawyers. The courts, thus, proved a further instrument of exploitation of the poor.

The three major blood revolutions in the world, i.e., French Revolution, Russian Revolution and Cultural Revolution of China had one thing in common that one of their major objectives was achieving land reform in the interest of the poor and the landless peasants. The message was very clear that one who tills the land will own the land.

The main cause of the French Revolution was that the peasants were small landholders, or tenant farmers, subject to feudal dues under King Luis XIV to the royal agents who were collecting indirect farming taxes forcibly whereas the absolute monarchy had a blind eye to perpetration of unreasonable and forcible exaction of taxes, fees or other locally coined dues. Backward agricultural methods and internal tariff barriers caused recurrent food shortages, which netted fortune to grain speculators. Rural over population created land hunger. About 50,000 people were killed during the revolution.

The Russian Blood Revolution (1917), introduced co-operative farming which was once considered in the field of land reform as ideal and ultimate reality after large scale land redistribution. In October Revolution, Vladimir Lenin and the workers' Soviets overthrew the Provisional Government in Petrograd. The Bolsheviks appointed themselves as Leaders of various Government ministries and seized control of the countryside. In the rural areas, peasants took over and distributed land. About 25 lakh people were killed during the political upheaval.

An elementary theory of property, believed by many peasants, was that land should belong to those who work on it. At the same time growing city and material goods were creating unrest. The rural agrarian peasants had resented paying redemption payments to the state and demanded communal tender of the land they worked. Increasing peasant disturbances and sometimes actual revolt occurred, with the goal of securing ownership of the land they worked. Russia consisted mainly of poor farming peasants with 1.5 per cent of population owning 25 per cent of land.

Article 39 of the USSR Constitution (1977), also ensured that enjoyment by citizens of their rights and freedoms shall not be to the detriment of the interests of society and state or infringe the rights of other citizens. In erstwhile USSR, co-operative farming was largely successful until the USSR had a jolt of change of system from Soviet Republics to Commonwealth of Independent States in 1991. In Eastern Germany too, after the reunification of Germany in 1990, the large farms are left without help.

Mao Tse Tung imposed a Marxist solution during the Great Cultural Blood Revolution (1946-49), in which about 25 million people were killed. He distributed 300 million acres of land among 400 million people and then collectivised the land. The modern development of China is now solidly based on successful redistribution of land whereas most of the surplus government land has been distributed among 97 per cent landless persons. In many countries, there were protracted and violent struggles. In Colombia, violence has been a focal point since the late 1930s. The temporal link between unequal access to land and open conflict may not be immediate cause. But failure to address them can significantly increase the potential for conflict like in the case of South Africa and Zimbabwe, where some groups have historically been deprived of their land rights.

In South Africa and Zimbabwe, it was anti-apartheid fight against eviction mainly from white commercial farmers. A recent study from Uganda finds that unresolved conflicts reduced output on a plot of land by more than 30 per cent.

In West Africa, the younger generation, especially those unable to find non-agricultural employment, often competes for lands with the descendants of migrants and questions their parents giving away land cheaply to "foreigners", an issue that can easily spill over into inter-community conflict with a potentially far-reaching impact.

In Rwanda during 1988-93, the build up of land issues led to gradual increase in the potential conflict and provided the conditions that finally led to the outbreak of civil war in 1994, which culminated into the worst communal genocide after the Second World War.

Investigators have identified the lack of adequate mechanism for resolving conflicts or clarifying the nature of land transactions as prime reasons for continued ethnic cleavages in Ghana and Ivory Coast.

In Brazil, there were movements against large land owners who under-used their properties. There were occupation of the Fezenda Annoni (1985), and other large-scale land occupations. As a result of constant pressure on government, there was large scale land redistribution in Brazil.

In Kenya, there was Mau Mau Revolt (1952-60) against the ruling British colonial power. Though, the movement was defeated yet there was limited land redistribution.

In the Philippines, there were numerous militant peasant organisations unified under the Peasant Movement of Philippines in 1985 such as United Nationalists Democratic Organisations which arose against Marcos administration. There was *Epifanio de los Santos Uprising* (1986). As a result, there was large scale land redistribution.

In Guatemala communal lands were in effect expropriated in 1879 by a land giving proprietors three months to register land titles after which the land would be declared abandoned. Most of the 'abandoned' lands were then allocated to large coffee growers. Redistribution attempts in 1951-54, were reversed following a military coup in 1954, when all lands were virtually returned to its previous owners and farms expropriated from foreigners were allocated in parcels averaging more than 3000 hectare. Since then, Guatemala has been a repeated pattern of suppression and bloody conflicts. The peace concords require land distribution as a critical element of the post conflict strategy, but progress thus far has been limited and has not always led to the expected improvements in productivity.

Small lands were similarly appropriated in EL Salvador. A 1856 decree stated that all communal land not at least two thirds planted with coffee would be considered underutilised or idle and would revert to the state communal land tenure, was abolished in 1888. Sporadic revolts and counter-measures followed. Areas with severe land pressure emerged as centers of revolt of 1932, during which thousands of peasants were killed. Guerillas promising land and other agricultural reform gained considerable support in rural areas and violence continued to escalate until 1979, when reform-minded officers engineered a coup and introduced land reform. Narrow eligibility rules sharply limited the number of beneficiaries of land reforms and more than a decade of civil war ensued. The 1992 peace accord mandates additional land reform.

"Colombia also demonstrates the bloodshed due to land related tensions. Conflicts over land between tenants and large scale farmers at the frontier escalated from isolated local attacks in the early 1920s to more co-ordinated tenant actions by the late 1920s. While the government considered various kinds of reform legislation during the 1930s, the law finally passed in 1936, vested rights in previously public lands with large landlords rather than with the tenants cultivating the land. A series of tenant evictions followed, leading to a quarter of century violence (1940-65). Land reform legislation in 1961 and 1968 regularised previous land invasions, but did nothing to improve the operational distribution of land holdings and far fewer peasants benefitted from the reforms that had previously been evicted. Peasant land discriminations intensified during the early 1970, leading to the declaration of state of emergency after 1974. The conflict has not yet been resolved because it is basically land reform problem and not a law and order problem"[1].

Thus, most of the civil wars going on or are likely to surface in Africa and some other small countries have in common the problem of land existing for long.

At times this has led to disintegration of the state, for examples, in Barundi, Ivory Coast. EL Salvador, Guatemala, Rwanda, Zimbabwe and even Bangladesh from Pakistan. However, land reform provided solution implemented in time. In Mozambique, the government could only achieve the quick resettlement of about five million people after the peace agreement, because instead of drawing up elaborate plans, it relied on local institutions to mediate and resolve the conflicts that emerged. Similarly, in Ethiopia, the ability to redistribute land quickly made an important contribution to the rapid reintegration of demobilised soldiers into the economy.

In Cambodia, calls for lands users to register their claims resulted in the lodging of almost six million initial claims and the ability to deal with these quickly is an important post-war reconstruction. In contrast, failure to resolve property claims of quickly in Nicaragua, affected productivity and investment and conflicts multiplied causing Nicaragua, in a situation of constant violence.

Let us take up the ongoing Naxalism in India which is rooted in lack of implementation of land reform and calls for immediate land reform measures which may satisfy the Naxalites.

In Naxalite violence in India, more people have been killed than in the Pakistan sponsored terrorism in India. The total death figures reported in twenty four years from 1989 to 2013 were as follows:

1.	Personnel of Police force or para-military force killed	2421
2.	Civilians killed	6615
3.	Naxalites killed/untraceable	3145

Thus, a total of 12,181 people were killed in this violence as per an estimate. This average killing of 508 people is continuing even today. In 2006, Prime Minister Manmohan Singh called the Naxalites the single biggest internal security challenge ever faced by India. In 2011, he said that Development is the master remedy to win over people and said that the development work was in full swing in 60 Maoist affected districts. About one-third of India is afflicted by Naxalism. The Naxalites, show the palpable injustice to the poor people by highlighting more than allowable land occupied and enjoyed by landlords. Even at present about 1.8 million acres of government surplus land is pending for distribution by the powerful landowners in connivance with or inaction of the local revenue or land and police administration at the cost of the landless persons and marginal land holders. Hardly any sharecropper has been recorded in revenue records except in West Bengal. As a strategy, they occupy government vacant land, forest land and *benami* lands. They do not allow sale of these lands. They hold people's courts in villages and settle local disputes amicably. They enroll disgruntled unemployed youths by convincing them about the failures of governments, kidnap officials to pressurise local administration, burn down roadways buses, railway stations or telephone centers or derail trains, i.e., visible government authority, scare away police informers, *zamindars* and contractors, by causing explosions nearby, attack police station, call *bandhs*, or closures or resort to road blockades[2] to show their strength with a purpose to participate in political process ultimately.

But as the hostilities develop, the Naxalites lose sight of their main focus, i.e., distribution of surplus government land and recording of workers on the farms as sharecroppers for a fixed tenure and disposal of disputes among the villagers. They are hounded by the government sponsored forces. As a result, their main focus becomes how to defend themselves from the onslaught of government security forces on them and to start attacks on them as the best defence and sometimes to take revenge of the killings, done by the security forces. The media has already lost track of the main agenda of the Naxalite movement. They only compete among themselves to report violence both ways in an exaggerated manner so as to increase their readership. In government set up too, the policy-makers, and the administrators have lopsided approach and focus on development strategy as positive solution rather than implementation of land reform as the key solution. Thus, both sides have been fighting aimlessly. Such a situation cannot be solved unless good sense prevails in one of the parties. It is fact that effective implementation of land reforms calls for protracted efforts on the part of government machinery which is not forthcoming and they are indulging in fire-fighting solutions. As a result, the Naxalite agitation which had a small beginning in 1967, has now assumed serious proportions. It was noticed that in villages, the punishment by the Naxalites to a corrupt officer or agent of the landowners has more effect than the burning down government buildings or killing innocent personnel of security forces by disfiguring his face or destruction or impairing his any member or jointly has better demonstration effect or looting government treasury or extorting mainly from the government contractors or government officers. Even when the Naxalism has become misdirected, it has not awakened the government from its deep sleep to take urgent steps to implement land reforms in a new environment of methodology based on IT interventions.

Even Karl Marx had wrongly assessed that the Indians will win their first war of independence by winter 1858, but the Indians were defeated. The Indians have the Himalayan patience and more so in case of peasants. The peasant is very happy and satisfied when the seeds sown by him mature in crops which is the satisfaction of creation. In small countries, the revolutions are successful touching land, but in the modern times of powerful states, revolutions will cause bloodshed but it is doubtful that they will be successful in over throwing democratically elected governments. However, small scale hostilities or violence will always, pay to remind the political and administrative executive to perform their duties towards the poor and downtrodden of the society.

But the scenario has changed now. Globalisation has created two classes having glaring inequalities. At the same time, the silver screen has increased the expectations of goods and material of the common man. These unsatisfied consumers may side with the peasants and may explode the bubble of the globalisation. Then, there will be an unprecedented blood bath by the human race much bigger than the two world wars. Few of the ongoing instances cited should be sufficient for an intelligent and public-oriented persons to give due emphasis on implementation of land reforms, so that the land which had to absorb lot of blood of its people may not have to do again and again and land may continue to manufacture blood for its children to see them healthy and happy.

It is a wrong concept that the Marxist revolution will not happen where peasants are involved. Marxists understood this and gave the slogan "unity of workers and peasants, meaning thereby, that the peasantry would play the role of junior partner to the workers. The famous Marxist thinker and leader Narendra Dev made in Gaya Policy statements that in many Asian countries the solid content of the revolution was the agrarian revolution and emphasised the need for an integrating social movements with the agrarian revolution as follows:

> "Small peasants and landless agricultural workers who constitute the bulk of the community are, by the very nature of their economic conditions, a great revolutionary force. Their lot is the hardest of all and they have, therefore, every reason of struggle for a revolutionary transformation of the present economic order".[3]

Narendra Dev claimed that for Marx, violence was purely a means and not an end in itself. In democratic societies, he found it more difficult to achieve blood revolution as a solution to the exploitation of the working class, i.e., workers and peasants. Narendra Dev advocated Marxism to suit Indian temperament. Therefore, he substituted evolution for revolution, constitutional methods for proletarian violence, inevitability of gradualness for suddenness and reform for destruction. Thus, the process of evolution was bound to be slow, and graded though many lives will be lost in the process.

However, some economists differ. Accordingly, the dialectic materialistic theory of Marx will compel even worker or peasant to be hardworking and proactive otherwise he will be left out of the race.

"Needless to assist that the agrarian programme must also take due cognizance of the production principle, in complement to the question of equity. What is equally important, the tenets of alliance between workers and peasants must obtain actual operational signification in the movement towards national democracy.[4]

References

1. Deininger, Klaus: *Land Policies for Growth and Poverty Reduction*, a World Bank Publication, 1818 H. Street, NW, Washington DC 20433, p. 158, 2003.

2. Agrawal, Dr P.K., *Naxalism: Causes and Cure*, Manas Publications 4402/5A, Ansari Road, Daryaganj, New Delhi, p. 85, 2010.
3. Gupta, Asha, *Socialism in Theory and Practice – Narendra Dev's Contribution*, p. 144, published by Gitanjali Publishing House, New Delhi, 1987.
4. Sen, Ashoki, *Das Kapital, Centenary Volume,* ed. Sen, Mohit, Rao, M.B., People's Publishing House (P) Ltd., Delhi, p. 82, 1968.

3

Forms of Utilisation of Land

Land is all pervasive as God. It is multifaceted. At some places, it is called 'mother' whereas at other places, it is the best resource to multiply one's assets. For the poor and heavily populated areas, it is the only source for their livelihood whereas the well-off people keep land-locked in farm houses and entertainment parks for leisure and enjoyment. Now-a-days, it is recommended that the area covered by forests and water should not be lessened for sustainable development and environment protection. For the aboriginal people or forest dwellers, the forest on land is only recourse of their livelihood so also of the wildlife apart from fish resources reared and protected in their tanks, ponds or other land-locked water sources.

Early ancestors of the human race were food gatherers and wanderers. They took for granted that they have exclusive rights to collect food and to hunt in particular areas.

As long as the tribe of forest fellow cultivators had abundant land at its disposal, a family had no particular interests in coming back to precisely the plot that it cultivated on earlier occasions. At least, he could throw some seeds saving from his food and rain god will shower its blessings and he would get at least twenty times the grains, he had sown. Thus, the land was the only last resort he could look for his survival. Other products were not in his control and more intelligent people from outside will snatch away from him. He will not be able to negotiate his agricultural products with the market forces. They will even use sophisticated forces to take away his produce. Therefore, regular land redistribution, empowering and regularisation of workers on the farms and procurement of agricultural surpluses through state trading in food grains are suggested. And to prevent struggle for survivourship, the state came into existence to regulate relationship among communities, individuals and the property land. This also explains emergence of private right of land.

A family who needed to shift to a new plot would find a suitable plot, or have it allocated by the chief of the tribe. The situation is apt to change with increasing population. However, as good plots become somewhat scarce under such conditions, a family would be likely to develop an attachment to particular plots more and more. As land becomes scarcer, general and inheritable, cultivation and grazing rights are complemented by right to resume cultivating specific plots after a fallow period, to inherit specific plots rather than just general cultivation rights, to pledge or rent out the plots, to use them as collateral in informal credit transactions and to sell them within the community. When the right to sell includes sales to members outside the community, the last vestiges of general cultivation and communal rights are lost and private property rights have come in existence. Under the communal system of right in land, the land can be utilised as follows:

(a) Specific plot or plots of land are assigned temporarily or permanently to members for family cultivation. Other areas are held in common for pasture, forestry, collection of wild plants and games or for community activities.

(b) Sales to non-community members or non-tribes are forbidden or subject to community approval which is the final authority. However, the sales among the members of the same community are allowed.

(c) The chief of the tribe or community can allot or lease out the community sparable land for industry or mining purpose provided the members of the tribe or community are in a dominant position in the company or firm.

However, world over the lands owned by the communal tribes have been gradually encroached upon by the outsiders, firstly because they were superior in arms, or militant strength, and secondly, they cleverly and diligently occupied their lands. As a result, the state has to intervene to protect their ethnic and cultural rights apart from their traditional rights in land. The Indian Constitution grants them special status such as the areas in the North Eastern States and other pockets like in Assam so that they can preserve their traditional rights in land and can continue with their traditional and cultural life style. Even the aboriginal tribes, the Red Indians of the Northern America now USA were pushed in reserve forests like special species being preserved in protected or reserved forest areas on the pretext that there were frequent skirmishes or clashes between the Red Indians and the emigrant mainland inhabitants. Therefore, to protect these tribals from violence, the government in USA adopted their evasive or cowardice path.

Similarly, in rich Australia, the few left out aboriginal inhabitants of the lands are locked in the large forests. They are neither exposed to good life style of modern times nor can they live their traditional way of life.

Their voice doesn't echo in the Australian Parliament because they have hardly any legislative representative. So also in USA, the fate of the Red Indians as original proprietors or cultivators, is a bygone case and is a matter of history. In Asian, African and South American countries, wherever the tribals are in sizeable majority, the tribal chiefs or feuded landlords who receive tributes, taxes or rent from the cultivators, exploit them.

In Mozambique during the colonial era, peasants escaped from forced cultivation, vagrancy laws and forced labourers to inaccessible rural areas. Some of these also were centres of support for the Frelimo (Liberation Front of Mozambique) guerrillas from 1961 until independence in 1975. Land reforms that were initiated after independence, however, resulted in highly mechanised collective farms. The Frelimo government did little to address the problems of the free peasant sector. The counter-revolutionary Renamo (Mozambican National Resistance Party) movement in turn took advantage of the resulting peasant discontent. Peace was not achieved until about 1990.

In Guatemala, communal lands in effect were expropriated in 1879 by a law giving proprietors three months to register land titles, after which lands were declared abandoned. Most of such abandoned land was then allocated to large coffee growers, who evicted traditional right holders. Peasants protested against their exploitation and Guerilla Army of the poor was formed which kept on disturbing peace for 50 years until early 1990s.

In Colombia, conflicts over land between tenants and large scale farmers at the frontier escalated. A series of tenant evictions followed, leading to a quarter century of violence (1940-65), during which guerrillas recruited supported from peasants groups. Peasant movements intensified during the early 1970, leading to the declaration of a state of emergency after 1974. Regional mobilisations, strikes and blockades flared up again in 1984. Indeed, violence and conflict, partly fuelled by the unresolved land questions, continue today. Thus, state should be very cautious to play with communal rights in lands unless it has the capacity and will to implement the community rights in the new circumstances.

Much of the rural support of the Shining Path guerrillas in Peru can be traced to the exclusion of most of the highland Indians from agricultural benefits and the benefits of the agrarian reform in 1973, which helped primarily the relatively few workers in the coastal area. Poor economic management during the 1980s, and continued activity by Shining Path have led to capital flight and economy into decline. It was only under the Fijimore regime that the power of the Shining Path was broken.

That is the reason Marx didn't believe that state can do any good for the peasantry or labour class. He found that the blood revolution was the only solution. But at the time of his writing his theory, Marx didn't have much idea that the state can be so powerful especially in countries like India and China that they can suppress any civilian uprising. Violence by the state on Lenin Square in Russia and Tinamann Square in China are the best examples. In such a situation, Marx would have been happy if the lands continued with the community because at least community leaders are answerable on the ground whereas the bureaucrats are not accountable to anybody. They turn blind eye after they leave their places of postings, along with the booty they earned as corrupt money. In democratic set up, in non-tribal areas the local panchayats are the elected bodies, who can perform the same job which the communal leaders used to perform provided the elected representatives get away from their local affiliations and biases which they had, before being elected to the Panchayat bodies and can work for the real person or deserving person in the village.

Second form of utilisation of farms are owner operated farms who have unrestricted right to sell land. In one case, known as Manorial System, the cultivation of large farms is done by the owner himself and by the tenant employed to help him with a promise to pay contracted wages or production. This is the common type of cultivation all over the world except in Africa where Hacienda or Junker estates are more in vogue.

"When a labour supply becomes available, large landowners can organise their operations either as Junker estate or landlord estates, which the entire estate cultivated by tenanted peasants, or as Hacienda estates, with workers cultivating portions of the Hacienda for their own subsistence as tenants or holders of usufruct rights and providing unpaid labour to cultivate the home farm of the owner. Landlord estates were prevalent in China, Egypt, Ethiopia, Eastern India, Iran, Japan, Korea and Pakistan. Haciendas emerged as the predominant form of manorial estates in Algeria, Egypt, Kenya, South Africa and Zimbabwe, in Bolivia, Chile, Honduras, Mexico, Nicaragua, Peru and other countries in Latin America, the Philippines and in Prussia and other parts of Eastern Europe".[1]

In all types of farms, exploitation remained unabated. Where the land was cultivated by the tenant or sharecropper on the promise of giving a due share of product to him, he was not given due share of produce. On the other hand, he had to do lot of 'begar' for his landlord in the form of taxes in various names recognised or unrecognised. Even he and his family had to work as domestic help of the landlord free of cost as overhead of his permission to cultivate the land of the owner. The "begar' in India means the taking forced labour from the tenant along with taking of a premium, tribute (*nazrana*) for the admission of the tenant and realising more rent what was paid by the landlord to the government.

The Hacienda tenants were not treated as tenant cultivators. They were hailed as serf cultivators. To bypass the permanent right or status to the tenants or cultivators, the landlords adopted many via media or tactics and clever strategies. They adopted the cultivation through them as hired daily labourers and provided them house or garden plots, so that they are always available to them on their bacon call without any statutory liability. Their poverty was blackmailed and they were made to work beyond the prescribed hours of work for a daily labourer. As a result, the peasants or cultivators across the globe got united and they found their supporters in intellectuals, administrators and social workers.

In countries like Russia the then Soviet Union, East European countries and China, the collective farming came into existence as one of the solution. In some countries, these collective and state farms were controlled by the proletariat governments and whereas in some other countries, the state's intervention ceased to exist and these were operated as large commercial mechanised farms. In other countries, these were operated as family operated by the owner himself through advanced equipment. In another set of countries, the farms were collectively operated but the individual owner had his realistic ownership kept intact and well defined. Thus, this structure helped both sides. Production was optimum as the cultivators had their motivation as owner and collectivisation procured them state help for mechanisation and marketing. Of course, in all farms, this was the best form.

This was successfully implemented in the Communist Soviet Russia (USSR) until USSR had a jolt of change of system from Soviet Republic to Commonwealth of Independent States in 1991. In Eastern Germany after the reunification of Germany in 1990, the large farms are left without help like in USSR." German form lobby has a strong ally in German government which supports farmers' demand fully. Farm votes are the main support base for the present German government. But European farmers are facing competition from US farmers, who dominate the world food market by exporting farm products at competitive prices. Of the once 4,000 co-operative farmers in East Germany, 1800 are threatened with bankruptcy. Many are still repaying debts dating back to socialism where they were not a problem.

"Once, you really got into trouble, the state helped-out. The socialist state took pride in its party. State runs mostly co-operative farming system. East Germany was self-sufficient but this had a price. Even poor soils were cultivated using huge amounts of fertilisers and other chemicals and by far more personnel than other countries. While in the US, 100 hectare land being tilled by two people, East Germany employed upto 12 and West Germany needs five to six quite logically. East German farms proved uncompetitive after unification. And with an annual grain surplus of over two million tonnes, it is extremely hard to sell grain in Germany anyway. Hence, co-operative farms are either struggling to survive or being disbanded. Employment figures in agriculture are going down dramatically. Only 300,000 of the once 900,000 job will survive and there are regions in the East of Germany where unemployment has reached the 50 per cent mark".[2]

In Czechoslovakia, even the wind of change has not affected the spirit behind co-operative farms. The Mexico system has a minimum of

20 individuals eligible to receive land, usually heads of families, may form an *ejido*. The members receive wages for work in the first period and in the second period crops they actually produce. In Egypt, all beneficiaries of the land of redistribution programmes were required to join the integrated co-operative societies. The activities of these societies range from the supply of inputs, rural extension, credit and marketing to joint-farming. They have an average about 300 farmers as members for about 68 hectares of lands. Farmers work collectively in ploughing, applying fertilisers and pesticides, watering and harvesting while each cultivator is responsible for his own piece of land in sowing, weeding, hoeing and daily care. Crops are marketed partly by the society and partly by the farmers themselves.

Israel has also no co-operative farming but these are organised largely on voluntary basis having no dependence on government. They have strong communal bonds and are quite successful.

In some places, the small and marginal holdings have not become viable as there is highly commercial and mechanised capital intensive farming. Even if the surplus land is distributed among the poor, the land will shift to the medium and large owners through the land lease system. Similar is the reason or the decline in share cropping. In view of cropping intensity, the time involved in the completion of a particular operation has been reduced, with which the sharecroppers cannot cope. Contract farming is in vogue in production of vegetable, fruits, medicinal plants, pulses, oil seeds, fish production and minor cash crops. The multinational corporations have entered into the field of tea and coffee plantation, where it involves lot of investments. In India, states of Punjab, Haryana and Karnataka are witnessing emergence of contract farming but it doesn't provide declared benefits to the small and marginal farmers whose lands they acquire for contract farming. Their interests should be safeguarded by the state apparatus.

Similarly, in farming areas in fringes of cities and metro or mega towns, sudden surge in prosperity of small and marginal farmers has been seen by way of getting compensation for acquisition of their lands for industrial or real estate purposes either by the government or the industrialists directly at exorbitant rates whereas in earlier times, their lands were acquired at throw away prices on the ground of public interest exercising the power of eminent domain by the government. Here, the government is required to see that the landlords or owners whose lands are acquired are rehabilitated at somewhere else in the same profession as they have acquired expertise by cultivating land for generations and to see that they do not become pauper against after exhausting the sale consideration in luxurious or ostentatious living for short time.

Thus, we have surveyed various types of utilisation of land in foregoing discussions. In spite of unprecedented advances in the sectors of manufacturing and service and gradual reduction of contribution of the agriculture sector in the gross domestic production or total economy of a country, the agriculture sector is the one which will sustain the world when there are unprecedented losses in the commercial world or failure of government exchequer or banks. People look for agriculture sector which can at least make available foodgrains for the survival of the large population specially the poor people. Therefore, there is a fierce competition among the neo-rich around the world to monopolise the land also. But this sector should be saved from the clutches of capital because lands should belong to one who tills the land. Land is the last resort at least to the poor in the world.

References

1. Benswonger, Hans P., M Khize and Deininger Klaus: *History of Land Concentration and Redistributive Land Reforms in Agricultural Land,* Redistribution, ed. Benswanger, Hans P., M Khize, Bourguignou, Camille, Brink, Rogiervanden, The World Bank, Washington, D.C. USA, 2009, p. 57.
2. Agrawal, Dr. P.K., *Land Reforms in India*, M.D. Publications Pvt. Ltd., New Delhi, p. 226, 1993.

4

Poverty Revisited

The story of progress of mankind starts from the dependence on land. As the human race advanced gradually, this dependence got reduced. Still most of the countries and most of the people depend on land and they look forward to solve problems through land either by production on land or by selling or exchanging land. Land at one place is the only asset of the poor man as that is always in front of him and an outsider cannot easily evict him from his possession or ownership of land. On the other hand, society lives on the production on land. Now-a-days, land also includes pisciculture resources and forests.

Therefore, all and sundry agree that the basic objective is to have maximum production from land. Institutional structure may change or may readjust so that the society as a whole may be benefitted from the optimum production in land. Second objective is to do away with the exploitation in landed properties as maximum wealth is parked in land. Third objective is to tackle poverty through land as an instrument because it provides the easiest and long-term solution.

Karl Marx, the messiah of the poor observed that the laws regarding industrial development applied to agricultural holding also. Engels assumes that in earlier periods of human history, land was a common property. When this form began to depress production, land became private property. This change favoured the development of productive forces upto a point. Then the call emerged to transfer the land again into common property now of higher quality.

Marx suggested following course of action subject to local variation:

1. Abolition of private property in land and application of all rents of land to public purpose.
2. A heavy progressive or graduated income tax.
3. Abolition of all rights of inheritance.
4. Confiscation of the property of all emigrants and rebels.
5. Centralisation of credit in the hands of the state, by means of a national bank with state capital and an exclusive monopoly.
6. The bringing into cultivation of waste lands and the improvements of the soil generally in accordance with a common plan.
7. Establishment of agrarian armies.
8. Combination of agriculture with manufacturing industries, gradual abolition of distinction between town and country, by a more equitable distribution of the population over the country.
9. Free education for all children in public school, combination of education with industrial production.
10. Centralisation of the means of communication and transport in the hands of the state.

These basic points included in the Communist manifesto still hold good broadly. It is a common fact that land is scarce but whatever land is there with the state or government, as public land or ceiling surplus land, the same is not being managed efficiently giving rise to rent seeking and corruption and lost revenue opportunities in many countries. Leases in the name of third party, are of much shorter period with no clear procedure for renewal resulting in undermining incentives for long-term improvements. Under the law, priority of land access to be given to women, the poor and other disadvantaged groups. As a result, a lot of land were allotted to local elites.

The poverty line is based on per capita daily intake of 2400 calories in rural areas and 2100 calories for urban areas.

And if we take 2250 calories as the desired minimum level of nutrition, a farmer will require at least 518 gm food grains per day to eat.

Martin Ravallion and Shaohua Chen of the World Bank have updated the World Bank poverty line of $ 1.08 per person per day at 1993 purchasing power parity dollars with a new international poverty line of $ 1.25 per person per day for 2005, based on the new PPP prices for 2005, replacing those of 1993. Similarly, population below $ 1.00 a day in 41.3

per cent in Bangladesh, 24.1 per cent in Nepal, 17 per cent in Pakistan and 9.9 per cent in China followed by Brazil 7.5 per cent. As a consequence 41.8 per cent of India's population was below the international poverty line in 2005. This implies that 469 million persons were living in poverty as per the revised estimate—a huge number indeed. If we take minimum consumption of $ 2.00 per day, 84 per cent of Bangladesh population, 80.4 per cent of India, 73.6 per cent of Pakistan and 41.6 per cent of Sri Lanka, 52.4 per cent of Indonesia and 43.9 per cent of China's population will be below consumption index.

The $ 2.00 a day poverty line takes into account besides food, other items as cloth, education, health or other minimum needs for life which is described 'basic needs line'. $ 1.00 a day poverty line is called 'starvation line' whereas $ 2.00 a day is treated as 'basic needs poverty line'.

"Dr Gaurav Datta of the World Bank in his article "*Has Poverty Declined since Economic Reforms in India*" has found that the urban sector seems to have continued its march of poverty reduction in the process of growth, rural poverty reduction was choked off by lack of rural growth. Dr Gaurav Datt has identified stagnation in rural growth as the basic cause of slowdown in poverty reduction. This naturally puts a question mark on the very nature of reform process in terms of rural welfare."[1]

In a predominantly agriculture economy, liberalisation should precede implementation of land reforms. The World Bank Study (1997), reveals that India has the largest number of rural poor as well as landless households in the world. The two are intrinsically related, i.e., landlessness. Landlessness is more related to poverty than to either the caste or illiteracy. It is the best indicator of rural poverty in India.

No globalisation to reduce poverty can reach the rural areas unless land is made productive because everything else centers around the land in respect of the rural poor. They can not take advantage of a government scheme enriching them because they do not own any land. Without land, they cannot establish their identity. Their only identity is the record of rights of the land owned or cultivated by them which is recognised by all the financial institutions, including banks.

They cultivate lands of other persons, but they are not recorded as sharecroppers on these lands to give them fixity of tenure. They will be evicted if they show eagerness to record themselves as tenants or sharecroppers. How can an unstable person contribute properly to the production? Many landless poor do not have even homestead plots. They reside on lands of others specially landlords without any right on titles. They face eviction if they and their families refuse to be exploited by the landowners on whose lands they reside.

Many rural poor who either own land or have been allotted land, have no means to make their land productive. Therefore, despite possessing the assets, they are not able to make use of these. This being the factual situation, we shall examine how the poverty is related to land apart from based on historically developed economic and political relations.

This World has 70 per cent population in rural areas. In the World, Asia has 60 per cent of global population. Asia has great majority of World's poor next to Africa only. They mostly live in rural areas. Most rural poor are either landless or have highly insecure land rights. Majority of them work as tenant on other's land including land of the government or state or the community. Tenancy is the condition of a tenant; the temporary possession of what belongs to another by his consent. Thus, so far landowner is happy a tenant can cultivate the land. He is terminated on the whims and fancies of the landowner. Many a times, the cause of termination of tenancy is not related to his cultivation job. If the tenant doesn't work at the residence of the landowner or he is not able to satisfy the landowner, his services as a tenant are terminated. As a result, he wanders for search of another job of cultivation as he knows no other avocation or profession. As he is a daily bread earner, he and his family have to starve during this gap period. Therefore, security of tenure has been established as the most important factor if these people of vulnerable sections are to be ensured minimum livelihood or meal or foodgrains to meet his requirement of food twice a day.

Apart from security of tenure on agriculture land, the tenure arrangements in the case of fisheries are equally important. So, also forests are important resources for livelihood of the poor which are controlled by the state. Recognising and securing tenure rights of forest dependent people, including indigenous people known as tribals in India is fundamental for securing livelihoods in forest communities.

Forests and other common property resources contribute significantly to people's welfare, especially of the poor. In Africa and Asia poor people in marginal areas often derive 30 to 40 per cent of their consumption from common property resources. In Latin America, the indigenous population amounts to about 50 million people, or about 10.5 per cent of the total population and many more people are dependent on forest resources. Furthermore, indigenous people are highly concentrated in specific countries such as Bolivia where 71 per cent of national population is indigenous, Guatemala (66 per cent), Peru (47 per cent) and Ecquador (43 per cent). These four countries and Mexico (14 per cent) account for almost 90 per cent of Latin America's indigenous population. About 100 million people in India and some 120 million people (or 30 per cent of the population) in South East Asia are classified as forest dependent. A growing number of countries recognise indigenous land rights in principle and allow for their internal management by the community. For example, in the Philippines the 1997 Indigenous People's Rights Act recognises promoters and protects the rights of indigenous people and provides rights to ancestral domains rights to transfer lands and exemption from property taxes.

Pastoral communities are widespread in the marginal areas of Sahel, the Middle East and North Africa, East Africa and Central Asia. Access to common agricultural resources was in many cases unproblematic under conditions of low population density, but is becoming contested with the expansion of crop agriculture and often constitutes a source of conflict between nomadic and settled communities.

The communities which don't have the recorded land in their names will always be uncertain about their right of cultivation. A better off person in the society will drive him out of his long cultivated land either by force or through legal process which is also inclined towards haves in the society. Thus, recording of names of poor persons and giving them the record of rights will provide him stability in his occupation of cultivation and will ensure his survival in spite of all odds being faced by him on all his other resources. Similarly, if public land or government surplus land is allotted in the name of the female member of the family along with the male member, the basic needs of the family will be better served because traditionally women have sacrificed more than the men for the rearing and preservation of the family specially children. A male member spends more on his drink or other vices, whereas a female member is very particular to give priority to the food needs of her family. Land will provide her long-term safety net more than jewelry or cash in her name because it cannot be sold as per stipulation of allotment by the government. Therefore, name of female member of the family should be invariably incorporated in their land settlement document known as *patta* or record of right. The interest of the poor is sometimes best protected by putting such restrictions on his right to dispose of or sell government land.

If such restrictions are liberalised, the poor person has his number of more pressing needs like health or medical needs, education need or need for organising wedding of his son or daughter. But his only perennial source of survival is his only small parcel of land. Therefore, it should be protected in his possession at all costs and all the time so that he and his family at least survive to tackle other serious problems. For the urgent medical needs, he is sometime allowed to mortgage his government allotted land as an exception but only after permission from the local government functionary.

When we talk of poverty, other factors contribute like onset of a long- term and expensive illness, a disaster such as a flood or earthquake or unprecedented drought or typhoon or overflowing sea waves, a failed crop or failed investment or policy change that leads to loss of livelihood or reduction in income including large scale acquisition of agriculture lands for other purposes like industries. There are some communities, tribes or castes that have traditionally been in the grip of poverty due to their social history and social factors like discrimination practised based on caste, creed, race or religion. As a result, many of these tribes or indigenous people have renounced the mainstream of habitation and have retired in forest or in some other secluded places or habitations where there are no basic facilities available for cultivation, production, drinking water or shelter. These tribes or castes in some countries have been well-identified. Generally, they are also have nots as far as land resources are concerned. Even governmental support has not been able to bring them at par with other castes or communities. In India, two such tribe and caste are known as Scheduled Tribes and Scheduled Castes which constitute about 24.40 per cent of India's population as per 2001 census. During the British Rule in India, it was difficult to identify the poor through scientific survey, census or economic identification. Even the land records were never complete as it took about twenty years for one-round of preparation and updating of land records in rural India. Therefore, classification of poor on the basis of community or caste was the best thumb rule a bad bargain which still holds the field, though the apex court of the country has upheld to exclude the creamy layers of these tribes and caste from the government grants or bonanza but these creamy layers could still not be identified. It is suggested that at least the serving persons belonging to these classes especially in government jobs should be excluded from the beneficiary lists of anti-poverty programmes undertaken by the government.

"Poverty reduction requires that the earnings of the poor increase, either through productivity or through income transfers. If the options for improving income are either weak or absent, poverty will persist. When there are opportunities, through access to decent work or skills, combined with higher wages, transfer of income generating assets, and if the increase in earnings is significant, the poor may escape from poverty. When shocks occur that lead to a decline in income levels, for instance crop failures, ill-health, disabling accidents or other disasters, the number of people who are poor will increase."[2]

The establishment of protected areas is also one of the tools to keep away the poor people living in those rich eco-systems from exploitation by the outsiders in the garb of investment or to bring them into the mainstreams. As a result, their mineral wealth is depleted and forests are degraded . Results show that deforestation and disturbance are lower within protected areas and poverty is not exacerbated in surrounding communities.

The tribals have emotional, psychological and cultural attachments with forests, because they mostly live in forest areas. They collect woodlots and fallen leaves for fuel purposes and collect forest fruits or other produce as their subsidiary food items. They collect flowers and other waste things from the forests and sell them in local *haats* or markets to purchase consumption goods to support their families. In return they protect forests from outsiders and poachers. They are thereby mostly living traditionally, peacefully with the wild life thereby creating a balancing cycle of the nature. The forest officials cannot see eye to eye with them and treat them like thieves or encroachers, apprehend them and file numerous criminal cases against these poor people whose livelihood depends on forests.

It is estimated that in the mid-1980s, there were as many as 817 million small land holders and landless rural labourers in Asia, Africa and Latin America (FAO, 1987). According to another sources, during the same period there were 180 million rural landless in India, 24 million in Pakistan, 12 million in the Philippines, eight million in Brazil and even 324 million in only 64 developing countries (Jazairy *et al.*, 1992).

The forest officials overlook the fact that no forest can survive or flourish without the support of its dwellers, or its fringe people. The livelihood needs of the tribals or forest dwellers assist the forest to keep it clear of weed so as to grow healthy. Therefore, the forest officials are required to give lease or license of lands, they traditionally live on and grant them permission to collect fire wood, dry leave and minor forest produce without hindrance from government officials and their touts. This measure will at least ensure them basic livelihood and they will not die of starvation. Similarly, in cases of fisheries, the fishermen should be allowed to grow fish on their own accord and should be permitted to fish or cultivate fish resources in their water resources, tanks, or reservoir which belong to the public or government and shouldn't be allowed to be cornered by the outsiders, middlemen or the contractors or the multinational companies. Their marketing deficiencies should be made good by farming informal groups among them or co-operative societies so that they may get remunerative prices and should get easy loans to invest in pisciculture. What is happening is that the big houses or companies forcefully push water into the farms of the small and marginal farmers and they are compelled to fall in line to cultivate fish for them. Similarly, tidal saline waves are forcibly allowed to enter into the fields of the poor farmers and they are compelled to work as workers in employment of those companies, who grow prawn and other high varieties of fish. In fact, the profit is pocketed by very few persons and their agents and poor farmers lose their lands forever because as a result of pisciculture, their farms become unfit for agriculture and they lose their last resort to produce food grains at least for their annual requirement which will provide them safety valve from death due to hunger.

Thus, landlessness is the greatest curse on the earth. Even in urban areas, an urban poor throughout his life, aspires to own a plot of land to live peacefully but his dream or ambition is never fulfilled. If he gets the house, he will never get the title for it. A rural poor sometimes gets a parcel of land from the government on paper but he hardly gets its possession to cultivate the land. If he anyhow gets the land title and possession, the land, he gets is unfit for cultivation. The anti-poverty schemes at the grassroots level, hardly take care of the fact that the waste or unfit lands should be made productive first so that the productivity goes up ensuring food security to the society or the nation which is the first aim and priority of everybody and every scheme. If he raises, the production on his government allotted land, he is exploited by the middlemen as regards rates of his farm produce because being a small grower of food grains, vegetables, etc., he cannot hire a vehicle and sell his produce outside his village *haat*, *mandi* or the market. Thus, a rural poor continues in continuous poverty. Landless is one of the first and foremost indications of the one's poverty. If one has sufficient land beyond an economic holding, he will not be poor.

Thus, land and poverty are closely related which has of late been realised by the World Bank, and thc World Bank has now taken an optimistic campaign to remove poverty from the face of the last man on the earth through optimum distribution and management of land resources in the world. It is an accepted fact that land belongs to none. Therefore, the persons who have lands beyond the ceiling limit, should give away their lands through the state instrumentality, so as to reach into the hands of the real poor who are ready and willing to make this earth a better place for living by raising production through their hard labour.

Agriculture remains a fundamental source of livelihood, subsistence and food security for rural people. It is a basis for economic growth in developing countries. In this context, secure land tenure for rural people is also extremely important. Radical efforts are also needed to make land available and affordable in urban, peri-urban and rural areas for expanding populations.

The example of China clearly elucidates how poverty is co-related with the land. "In the 1950s, the collective farming system introduced in China reduced sharp historical inequalities in land ownership, preventing the re-emergence of famine after the Second World War. However, collective farming restricted individual household's security of tenure and incentives to invest in the land, impeding agricultural growth. Since the 1980s, and particularly since 1990, the gradual introduction of more secure land use rights has contributed to dramatic increases in agricultural productivity and reductions in rural poverty.

Under a 1980 scheme, households acquired rights over land and were allowed to retain any increase in farm revenues, leading to higher productivity and poverty reduction. However, Village Committees continued regular redistribution in response to change in population and family sizes, discouraging household investment in land improvement. The 1998 land management law has since provided households with greater tenure security. However, uncertain and insecure land rights remain an issue for women, who are dependent on male relatives for land access, as a result of discrimination due to customary inheritance practice and Village Committee."[3]

The case study of state of West Bengal in India also reiterates the experiment of China. It is now accepted fact that implementation of land reforms in West Bengal during the Communist rule from 1977 to 2010 has resulted into higher productivity of food grains in West Bengal through votaries of economic size of holdings would not agree with this proven fact. It is a fact that farm size below a certain optimum limit, will not provide full food security to the land holder, yet it will not allow him to die also. At the same time, his and his family involvement in cultivation over his small size will have record production which will in turn, will contribute higher production of food grains to the society. Wherever, government or community surplus land is not available for distribution among the landless persons, it should be procured or purchased by government and should be handed over to the landless persons, who are ready and willing to cultivate the land.

"In India, the proportion between landless people and the limited number of available land plots makes large plot distribution schemes financially and politically impractical. West Bengal's distribution of 1.64 million acres to 2.54 million land poor households has had a positive impact on livelihood opportunities, even though many received only 0.07 to 0.38 acre.

In Pakistan and Bangladesh, ownership of even relatively small plots of land is associated with significant reduction in poverty. Data for 1999-2000 show that in India, small improvements in land ownership were associated with five to nine per cent reductions in the incidence of poverty. This is because small plots provide a supplementary source of income and food to the poor, as part of diversified livelihood strategies that also include work as wage labourers, trade or cottage industries and remittances. Small plots can also function as sources of credit, social status and security in times of crisis."[4]

Conclusion

It is well-established fact that land is intimately linked with the incidents of poverty. It is a reality that the poor men gradually lose his land due to medical distress, accidents and other natural calamities. But it is the responsibility of the state or the local self-governance units to provide them land because they are prepared to put their devotion and hard work on the land. If a single factor of land is taken into consideration and none is left landless, none will die due to starvation. Thus, the reduction in poverty in rural areas and peri urban areas is very much dependent on land.

References

1. Datta,Gaurav and Mahajan Ashwani: *Indian Economy*, S. Chand and Company Ltd., Ram Nagar, New Delhi, p. 378, 2011 (62nd edition).
2. Mehta, A.K., Shepherd Andrew, Bhide, S., Shah, Anita and Kumar Anand (ed.) - India Chronic Poverty Report: Towards Solutions and New Concepts in a Dynamic Context, IIPA, IP Estate, Ring Road, New Delhi, pp. 5-6, 2011.
3: UN-Habitat: Secure Land Rights for All, Global Land Tool Network, UN-Habitat, PO Box 30030, GPO Nairobi, Kenya, p. 20, 2008.
4. Hanstad, T., Nielson, R., Bown, J. *Ibid.,* 3, p. 19, *Land and Livelihood Making Land Rights Real for India's Rural Poor*, 2004.

5

Concentration of Land and Poverty

The notion of poverty is intricately connected with the idea of inequality. The distribution of income in the agricultural sector and the standard of living of the majority of the rural population are greatly affected by the degree of land concentration. In India 7.5 per cent of the households owned 51 per cent of the nation's land. In Iran one per cent of the rural population possessed about 60 per cent of the available land. In Pakistan, 15 per cent of the land was shared by 65 per cent of the owners. In the Philippines, about three per cent of the land owners owned 42 per cent of land. In Colombia, 0.07 per cent land owners owned 30 per cent of the country's farm land. In Mexico, one per cent of the population owned 97 per cent of the land, whereas 96 per cent of the population owned one per cent of the land.

This results into absentee land ownership. The *Zamindari* systems of India and Pakistan provide notable examples. As a result, *zamindars* and the middlemen neither did any agriculture work nor lived on their farms. In Egypt, almost all the big landowners resided or settled in the towns. Therefore, there was not proper investment in land. As a result, production suffered and the persons or workers working on land-owner's fields got less share of produce and their poverty became more critical. Naturally, a person working without any fixity of tenure on somebody else land would not cultivate land with that hard work and sincerity which he would have done on his own. Thus, the interest of the community or society suffered. On the other hand, the exploitation of the general mass of the peasant remained unabated. They were compelled to work forcefully and in return got penny. As a result they and their families suffered. They had to even face starvation. There were famines few of which were created by hoarding jointly by the big landowners, middlemen and their counterpart in cities as traders and wholesalers. The large land owners enjoyed the life of luxury and ostentatious living whereas workers on their farm were just begging for their livelihood. But in return they were beaten by sticks, confined to black dark rooms, were employed as yoke and honour of their women was outraged. It was more than what Marx noticed during annals of history in respect of industrial workers.

"Take the example of Algeria. Before Algeria obtained her independence, there were 2203 agricultural exploitations, encompassing 2,726,700 hectares, that belonged to French settler. The 22,000 European settlers completely dominated the 6,30,000 Muslim agricultural producers. The European accounted for 60 per cent of gross agriculture and revenue. Their profits alone were 53 per cent of total net agricultural revenue. The profits of this minority which represented less than four per cent of agricultural population were equivalent to at least 12-15 per cent of the national income."[1] It will not be in appropriate that the dreaded terrorist Bin Laden was a product of this exploitation.

In Morocco, the bottom 40 per cent of the income distribution is concentrated in agriculture. Information on income distribution in fragmentary, but it seems likely that four-fifth of the lower four deciles would be found in rural areas. Secondly, the agriculture, forestry and fishing account for less than a third of the national income though nearly two-thirds of the populations are located in rural areas and over half the employed force depend directly on farming and livestock for a livelihood. Similarly, the average consumption per head in urban areas is 2.2 times that in rural areas. A very large section of the rural community is sinking ever deeper into poverty. One of the reasons has been that agricultural investment has been concentrated on large dams intended to irrigate the best lands which belonged to mainly rich and large landowners. The landowners surrender only those lands under the government ceiling laws which are dry and unproductive. Dry farming, livestock and small scale irrigation facilities have been woefully neglected.

"The great majority of the poorest lived in rural areas, and the acute poverty they experienced was largely the result of the high-degree of inequality in the distribution of land ownership that characterises the region. Indeed, despite the reforms that have been introduced in some countries, land concentration in much of Latin America is far more pronounced than elsewhere. This certainly is true in the countries like Colombia, Guatemala and Ecuador."[2]

The distribution of land in Guatemala is highly uneven. For the nation as a whole, 88.4 per cent of the landowners possess 14.3 per cent of the land, while at the other extreme of spectrum, 2.1 per cent of land owners control 72.2 per cent of land. If one looks not at the distribution of land among landowners but at the distribution of land among those active in agriculture, one finds that 1.2 per cent of families active in agriculture monopolise 72.2 per cent of land. Moreover, the average quality of land in large holdings is undoubtedly superior to the quality elsewhere. The monopolisation of the most important agricultural resources, in combination with the paucity of employment opportunities in the urban areas, enables the large landowners to acquire a strong bargaining position in the labour market as well."[3]

"In mid-1960s, largely in response to the 1964 agrarian reform law, the Church became interested in increasing the welfare of Campesinos, i.e., about 88 per cent of the rural labour force out of which 30 per cent are landless labourers. They organised the sale of four haciendas totaling 5000 – 6000 hectares at low prices to about 2000 families. Later on, the Church ceased to be interested in its 'land reform' and became interested in real estate in urban areas. However, these organised Campesinos were recognised as trade union. The police and armed force, have intervened repeatedly in dispute over land, invariably on the side of the land-owners. Campesinos frequently have been killed by the police, e.g., in the course of ejecting them from land which they had allegedly invaded. There is no known instance of the police shooting land-owners. If the poor are not to be allowed to help themselves, the government must alter the systems of labour control which contribute to the perpetration of poverty".[4]

India is no exception to concentration of land among large landowners and adjoining poverty among their agricultural workers and landless persons using unscrupulous methods, such as *benamidar* collusion with revenue officials and politicians, coupled with their social status and power. The *ex-zamindars* of Bihar succeeded; by and large in protecting their class interest. The *ex-zamindari* of Darbhanga, Hathwa, Dumraon and Ramgarh still own large tracts of lands. Even tenure holders under them, like Raghubans Narain Singh of Kursela, happens to be a big landowner. Maul Babu, who once provided himself of being a modest *raiyat* of Darbhanga Kingdom, now possesses around 18,000 acres of land and an airstrip. In UP District Deoria, tehsil Pandrauna, the Raja of Pandrauna, had about 7000 acres of surplus land which was protected by his gangs of musclemen. The Supreme Court in Banwari Seva Ashram case (3 RD, 1988 p. 168) through Maheshwar Prasad Committee found unauthorised occupation of roughly 1 lakh 80 thousand acres of land in the Mirzapur and Sonbhadra Districts of Uttar Pradesh. Many other committees pointed out many big landholders possessing thousands of acres of land in almost all districts of Uttar Pradesh. Like tea gardens in Darjeeling and *tarai* region of West Bengal and Munar in Kerala, Coffee plantation in Karnataka, a lot of lands are locked in sugar factories in UP which need to be enquired whether all the lands are being properly utilised and are required. Similarly, Jagannathji Religious and Charitable trusts like thousands of other religious and charitable trusts spread over throughout India, have lakhs of acres of land in many districts. The landless persons are the greatest devotees of Lord Jagannath ji. But it is still awaited when they will get their names recorded as tenants or as sharecroppers on those lands to provide them peace of mind and stability in life. The great Mahant Kesava Nanda Bharathi of Kerala professing his life and organisation (Mutt) devoted to the welfare of the downtrodden in the society challenged the Kerala Agrarian Relations Act which sought to acquire his large estate held as lease from the state under the Pandaravake Verumpattim and Puravaka tenures. The apex court rejected this argument as it was a part of social welfare legislation and therefore enjoyed the umbrella of the Ninth Schedule of the Constitution of India. Under Nizam of Hyderabad, the village landlords were driven away from their houses. Their lands were seized by the peasantry. The people of 10,000 villages organised 2000 guerrilla squads against attack of the Nizam Police. In the same vein, ex-King Shankari Prasad Singh Deo of Panchkotraj, Purulia who owned the best coal mines in eastern India alongwith others, went to the Supreme Court to challenge the acquisition or vesting his surplus land in the State. As a result, the Union Government had to pass First Constitutional Amendment Act, 1951 which was supported by the Supreme Court of India. Even the lands acquired by the state for public purposes under its power of 'eminent domain' were not acquired keeping an eye on the welfare, settlement and rehabilitation of the poor persons, who were rendered landless, after the industrial units came into existence, which a mark of prosperity in the area. For example, National Thermal Power

Corporation of India and other state and Central government bodies acquired more land than what was required in Mirzapur district displacing the tribals and it has been reported that the excess lands in those acquired lands have been leased out to persons from outside which are creating problems in running those industries as lot of anti-social activities and mafia got generated around these excess lands. The land acquisition fiasco in Singoor in West Bengal is a living example. The farmers opposed the acquisition of the excess and fertile land by the Government of West Bengal through its statutory undertaking, the West Bengal Industrial Development Corporation by 1/3rd of the total quantum. Similarly, farmers of Nandigram opposed acquisition of lands by the Haldia Development Authority in East Midnapore district of West Bengal to set up unspecified industries. The development authorities all over India like Noida, Greater Noida in NCR Delhi have become neo-*zamindars* by acquiring land at the lower cost from farmers in the name of industrial and urban housing development as a part of globalisation. The farmers who though received handsome compensation, became landless and homeless in long-run in the absence of their long-term settlements and rehabilitation policy which now the government of India has implemented through an Act, i.e., "The Right to Fair Compensation and Transparency in Land Acquisition, Rehabilitation and Resettlement Act, 2013".

Thus, a balance has to be drawn where the community interest will be served along with the interest of land evictees. It will save valuable surplus land from clutches of industrialisation and commercialisation of agriculture for ulterior motive. Similarly, in the garb of contract farming and agro-based industries, lot of lands are being acquired and purchased from free market by the industrialists, who render many of the farmers poor for generations. Many co-operative farms hold hundreds of acres of land in states denying rights to sharecroppers and the landless. An insight into their working reveals the usufructs or productions of those farms are being taken away by the landlord or person in command with the help of local influential persons backed by hired local criminals who treat cultivators of those lands as bonded labourers. "Begar" is taken from them and their women are exploited. In urban areas also, lot of land is being used for farm houses and government bungalows whereas houseless persons live on streets. In rural, semi-urban and urban areas both, lot of agricultural land is kept beyond the purview of land reforms laws by getting it recorded as non-agricultural land in connivance with revenue officials. Lot of government or public land lies unattended. Any land which is not allotted to the beneficiary will be encroached upon. Somebody or the other will utilise it. It is also a crime to leave the land fallow against the society. Thus, government as the biggest land owners or *Zamindar* is responsible for maximum contribution towards poverty among its vulnerable sections of the public.

It is equally applicable in urban areas where land issues are more neglected than in rural areas. Some innovative measures have been taken in various countries to reduce coincidence of poverty. Temporary Occupation Licenses (TOLs) were introduced by Nairobi City Council to promote efficient use of idle public land in strategic locations, e.g., street inter-sections, road reserves in the high density neighbourhoods and open land on the urban fringe. Under a TOL, the local authority allocates land for a productive use while retaining long-term control. Since the license is renewable annually and the licensee is allowed to build semi-permanent structures, low income communities in Bangkok have evolved a practical arrangement with land owners to enable them to live in areas with affordable access to livelihood opportunities. The poor look out for owners waiting for their land further to gain in value before developing it, they afford to rent the land on a short to medium-term lease, paying what they can afford. Land owners favour this as a defence against third party invasion of their land. As urban growth brings livelihood opportunities to other locations, so the poor can move with the flow and negotiate a similar arrangement with another land owner.

In Bangladesh, pro-poor NGOs such as Samata and Nijera Kori facilitate poor people's access to public (*Khas*) land. In Bangladesh, 3.3 million hectares of lands have been illegally occupied. These NGOs are up against the local elite, who control public land through political, administrative and judicial links as well as organised violence and intimidation. Those NGOs promoting land rights provide services to farmers and poor people's networks and help them gain access to land. They also help the poor to engage with private landlords and the land administration.

Monopolies of Land in Forests and Fisheries

Forests are often owned and controlled by the state. In the Philippines, major portion of land is recorded as forests and is under control of the government. Similarly, in African countries, sizeable land stands recorded as forests. About 33 per cent of earth's cover should be forest. Then only this earth can have sustainable environment. Lot of minor forests produce, timber, leaves, etc. are produced automatically in forests. Who are enjoying these resources?

Legally, the people living inside forests or in the fringe areas are not entitled for these natural usufructs. These are used at the sweet mercy of forest officials of the government. They are thus the biggest landlords under government patronage. Therefore, there is a need for great transparency and reduced corruption in forest management. At present, the middlemen, government or forest contractors, smugglers and poachers of wild life in connivance with forest officials of government smuggle lot of timber from the forests to urban areas and to rich countries around the world. These are readymade luxurious items of the elite households, hotels, offices and other high profile venues. Even today, wood is taken out from the forests for cooking food and other fuel purposes unauthorisedly. There is hardly any law enforcement machinery. Even all forest lands are not properly recorded and demarcated. In the process, the poor tribals or forest dwellers are harassed by the forest officials in connivance with the local police. The local police are bound to act on the complaint of a senior official of the forest department. Thus, the exploitation of long users of forests goes on unabated. Some states, have taken steps to regularise them. But one can't say about the time-frame.

Similarly, livelihoods of tens of millions of people who depend on marine are inland capture fisheries. Even saline water fisheries are very important resources. The livelihood of many of the rural poor are diversified and are dependent on access to various resources including fishing, livestock and grazing and on cottage industries. In inland water fishing, a lot of multinational companies have entered. They have the cold chains. As a result, loss of fish can be saved. Like big landlords elsewhere, the fishery field is also being dominated by fish-mafia.

The fishermen traditionally are the poorest of the poor in the society. Their avocation and professional requirement keep them away from the mainstream of the society. They are for most of the day either inside the water or around the water. They are mostly illiterate. As a result, they can neither keep track of their tanks or other water reservoirs. Traditionally, large water reservoirs belong to the big landowners of the area. Lot of investment is required to develop these water reservoirs as fish production centres. They only work as daily labourers on these fish farms running in hundreds of hectares. These farms produce exotic varieties of fish which are mostly exported. Thus, these fish farms become beyond the reach of participation of local fishermen. However, in fish production, marketing is very important. This can only be sorted out if government arranges for proper marketing yards or centres known as '*Mandis*' in India. This is not ensured that the fishermen whose lands are within these farms get a share of profit from these farms or tanks. Similar is the case where government grants fishing contracts to the fishermen's co-operative society for large reservoirs of irrigation dams. Ultimately, contractors become active behind the functioning of these societies and pocket most of the profits from the output of fish from these reservoirs or lakes because they manage the marketing of fish-production.

The story of public grazing ground or pasture is no different. Lot of lands is earmarked in every village for the grazing of the cattle because cattle are the sources of subsidiary income from milk or meat. It is a part of agricultural operation and is known as allied sector. Most of these grazing grounds were left under control of the local self-government units functioning under various names in different countries. These local self-government units or community chiefs couldn't protect these lands in long run. One of the reasons is that the vested interest grew among the functionaries of these local supervisory units to control these pasture for self-interest. And then many powerful people encroached upon their grazing plots or parcels leaving no grazing ground for the cattle. Then these cattle become stray cattles and cause nuisance in and around the village. In India, these village pasture lands have been allotted to real estate developers near cities and mega cities. In India many charitable trusts got exemption of thousands of hectares of lands in the garb of serving the cow, a revered animal in India. But these lands have not been properly utilised to serve the cause of the cow or society in general. In the Western countries, especially Europe, North America, Canada and Australia, there are large pastures for the cattle and large cattle farms where the cattle are grown to send or to sell to the slaughter houses to meet the food need of the non-vegetarian people who are a majority in the world. Thus, the land is the most vital resource for production of meat. As the business of meat is quite capital intensive, this is captured by the capitalists and grazing boys, men or women are just daily wage labourers who look for their survival towards their cattle farm owners or to the middlemen or slaughter house owners. The pasture lands sometimes become unfit for agriculture which can however, be made fit for agriculture through proper schemes. Therefore, it is very important that efforts should always be there to reserve maximum land for agriculture so that the local rural populace dependent on agriculture, can at least live without outside support or supplies because market, forces are very complex and cruel having no human vibrations. Maximisation of profits is the sole aim of the market forces.

Another fall out of the concentration is that the sons and daughters of large farmers, and the poorest agricultural labour tend to migrate to cities or to developed countries. If the maxim is implemented that land should belong to those who till the land, the rich farmers will stay in the rural areas or near their farms and will add to the development of the areas. They will not indulge into fomenting terrorist movements based on religion or race or creed. Secondly, the migrant labourers will not have to leave their home and hearth in search of seasonal employment where they are exploited places in foreign land. There is none to see that they get their due wages and they have proper place to stay along with their children and women. Sometimes, their women are outraged and children are subjected to all types of diseases apart from malnutrition. Thus, concentration of land is an important factor of poverty in rural and urban areas.

In urban areas, the lowest income groups are virtually shut out of the land market. Those shut out of the land market are generally called squatters although each country has its own descriptive term, e.g., *Colonias Proletarias* in Mexico, *Publiacones*, *Cellampas* in Chile, *Villas miseria* in Argentina, *favelas* in Brazil, *Jhuggis* and *bastis* in India, *bidonvillas* in Casablanca and Daher. These very poorest families will not be able to afford land on terms acceptable both to them and to sellers. For these families land should be virtually free in monetary terms at the same site where they had found their work or job for livelihood.

They live in ramshackle, very densely populated dirty and badly laid out squattered colonies. It is very difficult to address the need of land for the poor in urban areas as only limited land is available in urban areas. Therefore, they are provided only multistoried housing. Efforts were made in few countries like India to implement land ceiling in urban cities and large urban agglomeration. But these were more failures than success. Firstly, the plots acquired or vested by the governmental authorities were scattered here and there and couldn't be joined for any worthwhile or feasible scheme by the government. Thus, the poverty on land front in urban areas has to be treated differently as concentration of land is not so acute there what is there in rural areas.

Laski had rightly said that "so long as there is inequality, there cannot be liberty." Engel advocated for abolition of private property. It weakens the system because the have nots in majority get discouraged and demotivated. As a whole, there is cultural and development lag. Labour produces surplus. It is advocated by the votaries of globalisation that when this surplus will be distributed in the forms of taxes and revenue among the needy, the whole society will shine up. The multinational corporations cannot keep surplus with them. This is not true. The capitalists have unquenched thirst for gulping the surplus. It results into more hiatus between the rich and poor. Ultimately, the poor after getting no support from the state or society, leave hope and live on fate. Thus, poverty continuously increases. They gradually isolate themselves and escape to their camps of poverty in the forms of indigenous villages or sub-villages/settlement or *jhuggi/basti* in rural and urban areas respectively. The people who have excess of land, gradually acquire political power and do everything to perpetuate the monopoly of land and see that land reforms are not implemented. If the organisation of the poor men can create a sense of insecurity among them regarding title or ownership of land, they will go back to their lands, exercise better supervision, invest more funds and will arrange for better marketing. It will ultimately add to more production of food grains and more availability of foodgrains in urban areas which is the aim of every system of polity in the world.

References

1. Griffin, Keith: *Land Concentration and Rural Poverty*, the Macmillan Press Ltd., London, Madras, 1976, pp. 26-27.
2. *Ibid.,* 1, p. 119.
3. *Ibid.,* 1, pp. 161-62.
4. *Ibid.,* 1, pp. 212-13.

6

Security of Title Through Maintenance and Updation of Land Records

Information about land is a major role of government and is essential to avoid conflict in the society. Territorial sovereignty has been the undisputed primary source of wealth and power. Maximum conflicts arose due to disputes in the land. The land use maps provided important tools to settle land related dispute, in the society. The land use maps include demarcation, surveying on the basis of geodetic controls, recording the persons in possession and preparation of maps or base maps with demarcation of boundaries of private and public or state lands. Each land parcel is systematically identified on the ground in the presence of an owner, lessee or person in possession and adjoining owners or ncighbourers, usually with some independent local person, like a village chief or mayor, overseeing the process. The parcel boundaries are physically marked and all land parcel and ownership possession data for the parcel is collected including copies of any documentation that confirm the interests of owners or persons' possession or lessees.

These land records when finally made, are converted into records-of-right. These are considered as presumptive land titles. If these can be classified or recognised land titles, a major cause of conflict and bloodshed in the society can be avoided.

The land records as these exists today all over the world represent mostly possession conclusively, because the officials or the technical teams which visit the field record what they find on the spot. Of course, they also verify the transfer deeds but persons concerned may conceal the documents which may go against them and opposite side, may not appear either due to lack of information or due to sheer callousness on their part. However, they are further given opportunity of hearing once or twice and sometime thrice. But many of the genuine land owners don't even appear on the third occasion as they are mostly absentee landowners. Therefore, the land records as finalised will not represent the correct legal position on the field but officials will certainly record correct persons in possession due to local evidence and witnesses or local representatives of public, i.e., community leaders, panchayat representatives, ward-members, etc.

The government officials or the technical teams who visit the village for survey and settlement of land records or property records don't have that acumen in legal aspects so as to arrive at correct judgments. Sometimes, these officials and now even the members of the so-called technical teams are corruptible. In that situation, it will be a blunder if they are given full authority to decide and record conclusive titles or ownership.

They mostly record possession. Possession is not the same as ownership. It is said that possession is nine-tenth of the law. This phrase suggests that someone, who possesses an object or land is most likely its owner. The idea of possession is as old as the related concepts of private property and ownership. The modern possession laws, originated in the ancient Roman doctrine of '*possessio*'. English Natural Law inherited most of the Roman possession ideas and later the British brought their law of possession to the American colonies. Following the war of independence in USA, state and federal courts continued to use and expand upon the historical notions of possession.

Possession may be actual, ostensible, constructive, adverse, conscious, exclusive, illegal, joint, legal, physical, sole or criminal possession. Actual possession, also sometime called possession in fact, is used to describe immediate physical contact. When the real owner, by his conduct, allows the world at large that he has no right in the property in fact, was not in possession of the property, the ostensible owner has lot of probability to be recorded in records of rights. Similarly, constructive possession also sometimes called possession in law, exists where a person has knowledge of land or property plus the ability to control the same.

If a purchaser ascertains, that his vendor is in possession and is entered in the property or land records, he gets some protection but that does not dispense with the duty to make the usual inquiry into title.

The title may be so clear that no particular inquiry is called for, which is called due diligence. In a case in India, Chief Justice Stanley said:

> "We think that where a person is found in possession of property and is recorded as owner and holds the title deeds of the property and deals with a third party in respect of it, there is nothing to suggest a want of good faith in such third party in dealing with him in respect of the property."[1]

Therefore, if government machinery can hold due diligence in case of all properties for updation of their records, there is nothing better than this.

Perhaps this mammoth job can't be handled by government agency within a reasonable time. They take lot of time at present. By the time, new and updated records become final, these become many years old and lose their correctness and reliability in actual practice.

Five core tenure processes common to the most nations are:

1. Transferring land by agreements (buying, selling, mortgaging and leasing).
2. Transferring land by social or family events (death, birth, marriage divorce and exclusion and inclusion among the managing groups like tribal chief).
3. Farming new interests in the cadastre, generally new land parcels or properties (sub-division and consolidation).
4. Determining boundaries.
5. Formally titling land.

The last one is very important and is the culmination point and should be considered an ideal for all land administrative systems of all countries.

The 'title' means and constitutes the legal ownership, a right to possession and interest in the property. To derive a single meaning as for title, the title holder should have not only the ownership but possession of the property which he can freely transfer to any person.

The title is the *prima facie* proof of ownership, constituting the legal right to control and dispose of property; the legal link between a person who owns property and the property itself.

The land title means that the State guarantees the title to this so-called recorded owner of land and appurtenant to land through the land administration system.

The land administration system (LAS) provides a country with the infrastructure to implement land related polices and land management strategies. The definite land titling system in advance ensures primary protection of the State for the possession or use of that property.

It is also support for governance and rule of law, alleviation of poverty, security of tenure, support for formal land markets, security for credit, support for land and property taxation, protection of state lands, management of resources and environment, management of information and statistical data.

It is therefore, essential that popular governments must provide well-defined titles to their citizens through government records. It is the irony of the situation that information about land in the government records is not available properly though it is also a major asset of the government. Many countries, including Indonesia, Malaysia, Laos and China, regard maps and plans as quasi-military information and impose substantial restrictions on their availability. Another group, including the United States and New Zealand, make land and spatial information, including digital maps, generally available at little or no cost to stimulate the economy. And still another group, including Australia and European countries, generally adopt cost recovery path and relies on the primary audience for land information to pay an estimated price reflecting the cost of maintenance and sometimes cost of data collection. In African countries, the land records either are non-existent or they are in a preliminary stage. In countries like India, Bangladesh, Pakistan and Middle East countries, the land records are not updated and the major portion of the land is with resourceful landowners.

Methodology

Preparation of proper records of rights involve following steps:

1. Traverse survey,
2. Cadastral survey,
3. Scrutiny of record of rights by giving opportunity of hearing to all interested parties.

4. Preparation of the village/city maps and area and boundary comparisons.

However, under the new gigantic information technology, many technologies have developed whereby the time consuming survey work of area can be simplified by way of existing area survey with the help of modern sophisticated instruments, satellite imaginary methods, aerial survey, Electronic Total Station (ETS) and Global Positioning System (GPS).

"Total station is basically a combination of Theodolite, EDM and a microprocessor which computes rectangular co-ordinates of the survey stations in the field with the data of angular measurements taken by the Theodolite, distance measurements by EDM and the initial bearing of the survey line.

The global positioning system is a state of the art equipment for providing ground control with the help of a system of 24 satellites, called Navstar, of which at least four should be available for tracking to give better results. The difficult hilly regions or the riverine areas can be measured with the help of GPS. The accuracy factor has greatly increased in the last couple of years with the introduction of Differential GPS which is a combination of one static receiver with the precisely known location and another as a rover and which should operate within a radius of 10 km of the static receiver.

In Aerial Survey, generally aerial photographs in 1:10,000 scale are obtained to prepare cadastral maps as 1:3960 scale."[2]

In the second stage, it is confirmed and corrected through traverse survey of a very high degree of accuracy (1:20,000) for providing ground control for rectification and enlargement of the aerial photographs to 1:3960 scale of village map is a tedious and time consuming process. Survey operations once begun never tend to get completed leading to time and hence, cost escalation. In some countries, cost of or partial cost of survey and land record operations are realised from the landholders.

Technology: There are three generations of survey technologies available. First is the conventional technology of diagonal/offset and the plane table method. Indian and other countries have been using this technology for more than a century now. It is a people-friendly technology as few generations, have the experience of the same, which can help to protect the interest of the landowner or *raiyat* being recorded in records-of-right. Secondly, in this technology, the plane table is there in the village until the work is completed. The villagers or the inhabitants accompany the surveyors and keep watch on day to day basis. Thirdly, the very presence of the plane table and the team in the area is notice enough to every landowner or sharecropper to come at the plane table and put his grievance before them at any time either in open or confidentially. Thus, in this methodology, proper opportunity of hearing is automatically ensured as right of natural justice. This is also not very expensive as the officials appointed for this job are there for decades and they are not fit for any other sophisticated job.

However, in this age of information technology, this methodology is conservative and outdated as none has patience so long for getting the record of his ownership. It is still good for African countries.

The second is intermediate technology which is represented by the use of more efficient instruments like Theodolite and the EDM. These help in survey work but land plot/parcel-wise physical enumeration is a must to verify against the tentative field map prepared on the basis of advanced equipments. The latter phase is the real time consuming process as it is more than judicial process giving opportunity of hearing to the affected persons on more than two occasions.

Then after preparation of final register of land parcels or property parcels in a given area or village, it is published as draft record. Then public objections are invited, heard and disposed of like court and then only final records of right come in shape.

The third, state of the art technology, comprises any of the three modes photogrammetry (through aerial survey) with Rectification, Global Positioning System (GPS) and the Satellite Imagery System.

The survey operations or record preparation operations comprise six distinct stages in India:

(i) Kishtwar involving the correction of the existing village maps;

(ii) Khanapuri involving the correction of the record-of-rights;

(iii) Attestation, wherein the entries are explained to and confirmed by the landholders;

(iv) *Objection:* wherein the objections to the draft record-of-rights raised by the landholders are dealt with;

(v) Appeal, involving disposal of appeals against the orders made at the initial stage;

(vi) And final publication of the record-of-rights.

These stages were alright when the population was scattered and land was in abundance. Therefore, there was less number of disputes. Now, the situation is reversed. Now-a-days, objections are received in large number. Against one parcel of land, there might be objections ranging from five to ten in number from his co-sharers, heirs, purchasers, sharecroppers, neighbours or somebody imposter producing a fake transfer for deed of the property in his favour from the collector or government or local body. Therefore, it is essential to compress various stages. It is feasible to combine Khanapuri with attestation and objections.

The effort should be at maximising the level of accuracy at the initial stage so that the subsequent stages do not prove burdensome.

The most appropriate and updated technology used in India is known as Angul-Nalco Project, which combines the best portions and least time consuming process from each technology including going around the area with the plane table. "The technology primarily uses a combination of stereo-photogrammetry which leads to the generation of digital co-ordinates of rectified mapping and the concept of geographic information system (GIS). This technology includes, obtaining fresh aerial photography of a revenue unit area on a suitably large scale providing some ground control points using electronic distance measurement and stereo-digitisation in three dimension using high precision analogue photogrammetric machines fitted with PCEK22 system; processing of captured parcel co-ordinator in workstations for mapping of a village; sending the maps on a 1:2000 scale for Kistwar operation for field updating of the digital database using the field measurement book (FMB) procedure and the Field Correction Module (FCM) software; preparation of plot-maps and index-maps for *khanapuri* operation; re-visiting the field parcel-wise for further corrections as per records/ground position shown is each base after *khanapuri,* using the Parcel Edit Module (PEM) software. In this process, digitally corrected and updated village revenue maps (not in the final maps) for 'attestation' and 'objection' hearing are brought out before going for final publication".[3]

The system of survey and preparation of land records is similar in all countries. A land parcel is normally understood as a single piece of land that is determined geographically by its boundaries and held under relatively homogeneous property rights. A property is normally understood as a legally defined terms for ownership of land units. A property may consist of one or several land parcels and each parcel may consist of several plots, where a plot is something that can be plotted on a map and is often equivalent to the way in which the land is used or managed. Each parcel needs a unique identification number so that data concerning the parcel can be given an exclusive reference. The form of this reference or its terminology varies from country to country, and is rooted in the country's cultural heritage. Therefore, the land book, or land register and cadastral systems reflecting historical and customary practices cannot be easily changed. Thailand has almost all stages in final preparation of records of rights as described above. In Vietnam, the borrower for cultivation goes to the distinct bank branch and applies for loan approval. When the Chairman Commune People's Committee, approves the mortgage, credit officer disburses the loan. When the mortgage loan is repaid and the bank returns the hypothecation paper to the borrower.

In Australia, vendor prepares the details of property. The buyer investigates the property and if found proper, arranges for finances. Then transfer deed is executed. The buyer pays the remaining consideration and stamp duty. Thereafter, it is registered and then it is sent to the local Council for approval.

In Western countries, tenure processes are robust supported by technology and flexible enough to meet local conditions and policies. These create initial data that is build the ownership and cadastral records from a land titling process. Reform of the processes typically involves projects to automate a land title register or to move a hard copy base map into digital environment. These records permit access, inter-operability and multipurpose use of the data along with maintenance. This is known as Torren System. German is the leader in the Torren System. Many developed countries including Great Britain and large parts of the sub-Saharan Africa and practically the whole of the South Eastern Asia have switched over to the Torren System under which each item of immoveable property is backed by title documents. Asian countries like Thailand and Malaysia have been the latest converts to this system. The Torren System started in 1970, is spreading gradually.

Most countries using the French/Latin approach make only a loose connection between the cadastre and deeds registries and in many, the two activities are completely distinct and separate. In some countries, the registry functions are carried out in the private sector.

Many countries lack the capacity to build even rudimentary systems and others in response to massive and uncontrolled urban expansion Cities like Jakarta in Indonesia, Lagos in Nigeria, Kabul in Afghanistan, Manila in the Philippines, Mexico City in Mexico, Sao Paulo in Brazil and others illustrate situations, where administrative capacity lags well behind need. For example in Indonesia, while 70 per cent is zoned as forest land, only 14 per cent of that has been mapped, surveyed and specifically designated as "forest estate". Of the 30 per cent of land area, only 10 per cent land of agricultural area is now administered by the National Land Agency (BPN) white rest of non-forest land areas are controlled by military, police and various other government institutions. Of the 10 of land area formally under the BPN's authority, only about 1/3rd of non-forest land parcels are formally registered under BPN. This is also situation in undeveloped African and Latin American countries and is a great challenge to remove the poverty from the planet earth.

The modern technology has come to the rescue and there is a possibility for early solution of the long standing problem.

China, the neo-rich country now is trying to activate a nationwide farm-land registration system involving important factors as political leadership, legislation, administrative planning and system design, financial resources mobilisation, access to international comparative experience as well as public participation, women's empowerment and education on farm land registration.

However, in other comparatively poor countries, researches and efforts are going on like in Kenya, Rwanda, Ethiopia and Austria to reduce the cost and time of cadastral activities using simpler processes, reducing required expertise and using cheaper technological approaches. The various multinationals involved in this neo-developing field can perform the job by employing new and latest sophisticated technologies based on computerisation, yet their employees deployed from other countries will not be able to establish that rapport to hear and dispose of objections from the local population. Therefore, in spite of high technological application, the ultimate product will suffer from this basic infirmity. It is doubted that in spite of spending colossal sums, the object will be achieved to have acceptable land records by the majority of people.

There is a growing need all over the world for land information as a basis for planning, development and control of land resources. Security of title is a pre-requisite for a functioning land market. Real property right must be registered and the ownership information should be easily accessible. The authorities should guarantee the content and transparency of the register. This register has found constitutional recognition for the first time in the Constitution of Republic of Kosovo 2008, Kosovo is one the erstwhile USSR's states. The law on cadastre No. 04/L-013 regulates the registration of immoveable property, national and cadastral surveys, geodetic and cadastral works as well as acquisition, keeping, maintenance and use of cadastral data.

In Ukraine, the National Cadastral System (NCS) was launched in January, 2013 for completely automated electronic system for registration and cadastral operations. NCS was developed within the co-operation between Ukraine and the World Bank. For the first time in history of the country, the information about all land parcels became public and was shown on a on-line public cadastral map. In Romania, the National Agency for Cadastre and Land Registration is implementing the project CESAR. The main objective of the Project is to develop systematic registration of properties in 91 communes. During the project implementation in 19 pilot communes, it was discovered that in all pilot communes, the contractors of works were not interested in vulnerable groups. Practically, the workers, technicians or officials of survey and record works stay in accommodations provided by the big landowners of the village or area and vulnerable people either by force or show of fear, are not allowed to appear before the survey team. As a result, the recording is done one-sided and the fact of cultivation by vulnerable sections of people or sharecroppers is not recorded by the team. Secondly, women also do not come forward to record their name as owner, or cultivator, or tenure holders though for most of the time, they only work in the field specially in tribal or hilly areas. These vulnerable sections have possession of land with them which also doesn't get reflected in finally published records.

Thus, the very purpose of updation of land records is defeated. It is a different story that they will not be able to defend or secure their title at the adjudication tribunal or court. By the time, they try to procure a copy of records-of-right in their favour other party will have an *ex-parte* order in their favour. Therefore, it is essential that the recording of title is done in a just and objective manner to ensure justice to the tiller of the land.

In China and India, emphasis is also being given for recording of tenure on forest land. The persons who have been living now for generation on forest fringe lands, can manage forest land better as they are the biggest stake-holders in protection and preservation of forests. Their livelihood is based on forests. Therefore, they are empowered by legal certification and stronger tenure security. However, establishment of protected areas do not increase poverty around as well as deforestation. This is a misconception spread by the vested interests. In Peruvian Amazon, more than 1200 native communities were given title over 11 million hectare of the degraded forest land. Between 2000 and 2005, an increase of forest cover by 40-60 per cent was observed through high resolution satellite images.

In India, Government of India, through Department of Land Resources, Ministry of Rural Development, has come out with a solution through computerisation of Land Records after the manual system of land records management came under huge pressure to incorporate 103.5 million e-transactions in India every month in Revenue and Registration Departments. The National e-Governance Plan has been launched. Its main components are; common service centre, State Wide Area Network, State Data Centers and State Portals along with State Service Delivery Gateway. Like the above, there are many success stories. But the problem is huge. The resources available cannot match with the requirement. There is deficiency in capacity of number of personnel and their quality and motivation of working. Thirdly, the customer, client or consumer is not very vigilant as regards his right to the service.

"The following figures may be noticed:

Country	*No. of land parcels (in million)*	*Land parcel per 1 million population*	*No. of land title*	*Land records per million population*
China	246.5	205,400	188 m	156,700
India	210	205,500	41 m	39,900
Australia	10.2	531,300	750,000	39,100
Germany	61.2	745,500	14 m	169,700
Japan	200	1,575,500	0	0
Indonesia	84.5	361,100	3,000	13
Turkey	35	516,200	10 m	147,500"[4]

Thus, the job of management of large number of land records is huge. Its maintenance itself is huge and its updation will be even more stupendous. In India, the land records are known as Khatian like the bank account in the name of the owner of the money and is known as records-of-right ROR in English language.

In urban areas, the problem is more acute as land parcels are very small, congested and disputed. It is difficult to subdivide rights of many people in a multistoried complex so far as plinth area or land is concerned. Therefore, the simplest solution is to provide identity cards to each tenure holder, or landowner in the urban areas. But this is also a huge size of problem.

The government in various countries could not complete proper land records. No other land records for agricultural land in rural areas are available. At the same time, proper titling in urban areas in municipalities and in large corporations has attained serious problem. At present, under the auspices of the World Bank, FAO and other international organisations, the titling system in urban area is being emphasised for updation of land records along with rural areas due to economic and social necessity. The Voluntary Guidelines issued by FAO, United Nations makes it obligatory on all countries to provide definite records of right as follows:

"Recognise and respect all legitimate tenure right holders and their rights. They should take reasonable measures to identify, record and respect legitimate tenure right holders and their rights, whether formally recorded or not; to refrain from infringement of tenure rights of others and to meet the duties associated with tenure rights."

It is hoped that all countries in Asia, Africa and Latin America will follow these guidelines as sacrosanct.

At present, in municipalities, town or metro areas the records of properties are not available except in very advanced countries like USA, Germany, Japan, UK, Netherlands etc. The urban local bodies (ULBs) or Municipal Corporations are interested to maintain records for purpose of collection of property tax, water tax, sewerage tax or sanitation tax etc. It was earlier the case in rural areas. There is no statutory mandate or backing to maintain and update property or title records of urban properties. This should be done urgently so that a process may be initiated for maintenance and updation of urban property records. As the survey and land record machinery in rural areas has acquired lot of experience and expertise over centuries in this job, the same machinery may be employed to start with. Later on rural machinery can be withdrawn when the staff or technical set-up of the urban local body is duly trained and acquires confidence in this job which is a pious obligation of every state. "It is surprising that Australia has 3500 land surveyors, Germany – 23,000, Japan 201,351 whereas large countries India and China have 30,000 land surveyors which is very low proportionate to the population."[5] This clearly indicates that State's resources have to be considerably increased in the job to securing land titles or land records to the persons. "At present, the policies and tools for land administration and management are often developed with an exclusive, top-down approach that does not involve the grassroots communities that these tools are meant to serve them. Likewise, implementation may be conceived as a top-down process. Without the active participation of grassroots communities, implementation is done without the wealth of knowledge of local conditions that these people possess and without them defining their own needs and priorities. In treating communities as passive beneficiaries, implementing authorities fail to recognise how much the communities themselves can do to overcome problems and to contribute to governmental efforts. Indeed, without these communities actively creating pressure for implementation that addresses their needs, it may not happen at all".[6]

If existing land rights are unclear or weak, using a sporadic or an on-demand approach for the first time, registration of rights can carry a significant risk of land being concentrated in the hands of well-connected and powerful elite. The powerful elite do not allow registration of allottees of government lands in government records because those lands have generally been taken away from them as ceiling surplus land under the measure of equitable legislation by government. They continue to get these cultivated by their own men or want to continue with those lands either by force or in connivance with government records officials. The powerful landowners never want that the sharecroppers or lessees cultivating or staying on their land be recorded in government land registers because then they will have some semblance of security and it will be difficult to evict them from those lands. Similarly, squatters in rural areas and in urban slums are opposed to be recorded because then the people exploiting them, will not be able to exploit them any further. They do not want to consider that government land records recognise and register only long-term unchallenged possession in respect of public and private land, although different rules may apply. And they have always recourse to the battle in court if they otherwise have legal title. In the remarks column, it is specifically mentioned that the possession is as per contract/agreement between the landowner and the sharecropper in rural areas and between the lessor and lessee in urban areas for a limited period even referring the date of deed. Bangladesh has even allowed sharecropping for five years in one go. Even that is being opposed by the landowners. Such negative approaches without any legal justification will give rise to peasants' rebellion in which the landlords will be murdered, their lands will be snatched away and their families will be banished from the place where their land parcels are situated.

Simplification of change of title and classification of land by integration of land records department (LAS) with the Registration Department

The mutation of names from one owner to another owner takes lot of time after the transfer of property through the office of the Registrar. It is suggested that maximum period should be prescribed within which the application of mutation is either cleared or rejected. Similarly, there should be well laid down procedure backed by rules under which change of character of land like from agriculture to industry should be allowed or disallowed. Prescription of maximum period for mutation and conversion will reduce lot of corruption and delay in the procedures. Mutation can be an automatic process if there is integration between the LAS and the Registry offices as below:

The registration is being done after 'no objection' or after seeing updated record of rights maintained by the land record department or local revenue authority (LAS) by the sub-Registrar's office on line. As a result, lot of requirement of paper is reduced and corruption is almost eliminated.

After integration, the mutation by the land record department of the government (LAS) is done automatically after transfer deed is registered. Thus record of rights is updated automatically and lot of paper work is reduced. However, the mutation is carried on cautiously as per rules in complicated cases. The concerned authority of land record wing is free to give notice to the person transferring the property to the person buying the property who is more interested in mutation or to both. This experiment is successfully going on in Andhra Pradesh and Karnataka in

India and in many EEC countries. It has resulted in reduction and simplification of work in both wings of the government.

Suggestions

As updation of land records is a stupendous task. World Bank can come forward to assist the underdeveloped countries to properly maintain and update the land records of their citizens. The World Bank or NGOs can develop simple technologies for the poor countries according to their local adaptability. The developing countries can be assisted for their capacity-building through training and mutual exchange through the world bodies African and Latin American countries are no longer intellectually backward. They only require fund push. On the other hand:

1. Registration Act should be amended integrating them with the Land Administration System or Urban Local Body so as to facilitate automatic mutation.
2. There should be simplified procedure of mutation and conversion by the Land Administration System even providing for deemed mutation or conversion within a prescribed time limit after submission of application, if no objection is received by the Land Administration System within the prescribed time.
3. In case of urban properties, the mandatory requirement should be incorporated in all statutes governing the functioning of the Urban Local Bodies that they will maintain and update the records of properties within their jurisdiction.
4. The names of the allottees of government land should be reflected in the record of rights. The names of sharecroppers should also be recorded in the record-of-rights maintained by the Land Administration System depending upon the period of contract of cultivation under the existing land reforms statutes.

It is amply proved through experience of various conflicts world over that many of the bloody conflicts can be avoided if there are correct land/property records in place after going through proper transparent procedure. The poor are the greatest sufferers in any conflict. Thus, the firmed up land records will be close to the conclusive proofs of titles of ownership not only of possession. This will not only infuse more equity in the society but will also ensure more peace and tranquility in rural and urban areas.

References

1. Khwaja Mohammad V. Muhnammad Ibrahim (1904), ILR 26 ALL 490, pp. 493-61. Ramsaran V. Harihar Prasad (1961) ILR AP 314.
2. Das, C.R., *Modern Technology in Survey and Settlement Operations in West Bengal*, *Land Reforms in India*, Vol. 10, ed. Wajahat Habibullah and Manoj Ahuja, Sage Publication, pp. 256-265.
3. Dhal, N., *Land Reforms in India, an unfinished Agenda*, Vol. 5, ed. by Sinha B.K. and Pushpendra, Sage Publications India Pvt. Ltd., New Delhi, p. 108, 2000.
4. Williamson, Ene Mark, Wallace, Rajabifard. *Land Administration for Sustainable Development*, ESRI Pressi Academic, USA, California, pp. 278-79, 2009.
5. *Ibid.,* 4, pp. 287-88.
6. Bending, Tim, *Tapping the Potential: The Role of Grassroots in Land Policy Implementation, United Nations Human Settlements Programme* UN-Habitat, 2012, p. 2.

7

Land Distribution as a Tool of Poverty Reduction

Distribution of land and property has been the mainstay of the human race since its origin. They were at the heart of the Prophet of Islam, the Roman Empire and the Chinese dynasties. Inequity has never been an acceptable principle of the human race but inequity continuously flourished in societies.

The concentration of ownership in land and the rights over land historically around the world were outgrowths of power relationship. Land owning groups used coercion and distortions in land, labour, credit and market mechanism, patronage from the kings, emperors and the state and even from the religion, extraction of exploitative rents from the land, from peasants and workers or sharecroppers and more recently from urban settlers or squatters.

The consequences of failing to undertake redistribution measure have been loss of dignity or requisite development of the majority of population, i.e., farmers, losses in productivity of food grains which is central to every society, as well as peasant revolts, revolutions and civil wars or conflicts and bloody violence. Redistribution of land has been central to the land reform. Demands for land to the tiller has been an old recognised demand. But this is yet to be realised through the instrument of land reforms. To implement land reforms, there have been revolts in Bolivia, revolutions in Chile, China, Cuba, El Salvador, Mexico, Nicaragua and Russia, conquests of Japan and Taiwan (China), the end of colonial rule in India, Kenya, Mozambique, Vietnam, Zimbabwe and the end of major rulers in Hungary and many of the Eastern European countries. Attempts at land reform without massive political upheaval or political commitment or political will have rarely succeeded in transferring much of a country's land to the landless peasants or agricultural workers. Since the end of World War II landlord estates in Bolivia, large areas of China, Eastern India, Ethiopia, Iran, Japan, Korea and Taiwan (China) have been transferred to tenants in the course of successful land reforms. This also serves the purpose of land to the tiller as the tenants on lands had security of tenure on those lands, they had been cultivating for long. Collective farming was also introduced in a number of countries based on well-calculated belief in the productive superiority of large farms. For example, landlord estates in China, the former Soviet Union and Vietnam were initially converted into family farms. The redistributed farm lands were later consolidated into collectives, in which land is owned and operated jointly under a single management having government support and backing.

In China, the process of consolidation started with setting up of the Kuomintang leadership but the political, judicial and economic power in the country side continued in the hands of the land owning class and its intermediaries. In the matters most directly affecting the peasants–like the administration of their villages or the amount of taxes they had to pay, the Kuomintong could enforce neither efficiency nor justice. Growth of population, the declining individual share of cultivable land, its unequal distribution, high rents and still higher interest rates collected by the money-lenders, maintained the majority of peasants as prisoners of an informal cycle barely above the subsistence level, without any margin of safety. Drought or flood brought tragedy. Exorbitant rents and interest rates spread insecurity and that merely helped to drive interest rates and rents still higher. Yet after a bad harvest the farmer was driven to the money-lender, to place his land under mortgage and to accept such high interest rates that he would never finish paying off the loan and would ultimately lose his land.

All this, together with high taxation by local regimes, particularly in areas under war-lords, put the majority of farmers under intolerable pressure. That dangerous explosive forces were thus created, or that change was needed, was generally admitted. But how to proceed was less easy to decide. Some of the more far-sighted counsellors of the Kuomintang were urging the government to act. But political power was in the hands of the landlords who were often also the money lenders. Even the most generous compensatory scheme would have been against their immediate interests. Yet in the early 1930s, there was some hesitation in view of the urgency of the problem. At one stage a pilot scheme was envisaged in the province of Kiangsi to try out agrarian reform on a limited scale. In 1934 a group of experts of the League of Nations were invited to help draw up the detailed land reform programme. But this, as many other projects of a similar nature, never got beyond the stage of intentions.

Instead, the more convenient method was resorted to of passing apparently satisfactory legislation which was never seriously enforced. This way a law was passed ordering the lowering of farm rents to 37.5 per cent of the crop yield and the abolition of sub-tenancy and the right of perpetual lease. It remained on paper. The landlords continued to collect rents going from a half to over two thirds of the harvest. Interest rates were never controlled and there was no alternative cheap rural credit. Not infrequently, after payment of his rent, his interest rates and of his taxes, the cultivator was left with no more than a fifty, or perhaps even less, of the fruit of his labour.

Evidently, injustice on such a monumental scale could not be lasting. But there was no philosophy or theory of reform to inspire change. Nationalism alone was not enough. His over-estimation of the importance of financial power as the expression of the established order went together with indifference to public opinion or to the need for reform and social change. And that obsession accompanied him like a shadow from canton to the Shanghai massacres and from his alliance with the bankers and industrialists right to the strategic conception of the wars he was to conduct.[1] As a reaction and influence of success of communism in Russia under Stalin, the Chinese Red Army emerged as the Communist military force. The communists organised insurrections in the countryside. Mao Tse-Tung had been sent to his native Hunan province to organise peasant disturbance there. He was chased and he withdrew to the mountainous border. At the same time, Peng Pai managed to form a peasant militia and to establish the first Chinese Soviet Government in the sparsely populated Haifeng and Lafeng areas not far away. Throughout the scattered rural Soviets, Chinese communism was beginning to acquire a modest territorial base. The small Red Armies adopted guerrilla tactics and they started getting conquests. Mao Tse-tung emerged as the foremost leader. The Shanghai Control Committee couldn't overlook or brush aside the emergence of Mao Tse-tung in spite of their reservations. In 1931 November, Mao Tse-tung was chosen as uncontested leader the first Chairman of the 'Provisional Government, born in 1893, Mao Tse-Tung was one of the four sons of a peasant. Later, he founded the Chinese Communist Party at Peking in the age of 28. He carried popular quotation and colourful images which sprinkle his writings and speeches and which provided him with a natural bridge to the minds of the Chinese people. He made a passionate plea: "The force for the peasantry is like that of the raging winds and driving rain. It is rapidly increasing in violence. No force can stand in its way. The peasantry will tear apart all nets which bind it and hasten along the road to liberation. They will bury beneath them all forces of imperialism, militarism, corrupt officialdom, village bosses and evil gentry. The democratic forces in the village have arisen to overthrow the feudal forces in the village."[2] He convinced every one that unlike in Marxism, the peasantry was not the reactionary force. He established the peasantry's role as the main force of revolution. He knew that no Chinese peasant rising had ever succeeded without leadership by the scholar–officials. The Kuomintang's police and armed might under Chiangkai-Shek couldn't make much headway against the rebel communist regime as their forces receded and dissolved before the attacker, only to re-appear in some fresh sector of armed strength. Corruption was threatening the vitals of the regime like a cancerous growth. The highest dignitaries were turning to profiteering and graft and were amassing fabulous fortunes. While most people had to put up with great hardships and suffered from shortages of even essential goods, members of the government and high officials lived in safety and in comfort, thereby further contributing to the sagging morale of the population as a whole. The communists were steadily extending their influence and rivalry was increasing for power between them and the Kuomintang. The Red Army was incorporated partially into the Nationalist armies, received a monetary subsidy as well as a small allotment of ammunition. Chou En-Lai was recognised as their principal delegate in the capital. Even after the Japanese had over-run many areas, they couldn't occupy more than the big cities and the main lines of communications. The policy of the communists was to infiltrate into these regions and to set up local administrations within them through guerrilla units. The Kiangsi method of the expropriation of landlords now gave way to a more selective process whereby only the absentee landlords' holdings were confiscated while in the case of cultivating landowners, only rents were reduced by the reduction of the proportion of the crop they exacted from the sharecroppers. Similarly, rather than to abolish debts, interest rates were controlled. The expropriated land among the landless, were redistributed among the landless, by the organisations of local Soviets, Councils or rural co-operatives. Thus with the energies and enthusiasm generated in villages, the original Shensi army of 30,000 men in 1935 developed into a force of one million, composed mainly of peasants and supported by a militia of nearly twice that size. In 1940, Mao Tse-tung's essay On New Democracy established a new Marxist-Leninist theory which based revolution on peasants rather than industrial workers. He even admitted small landowners and nationalists capitalists to the broad national front. The Americans, being great supporter of democracy around the world didn't support Kuomintang as Mao Tse-tung was leading China to a people's democracy.

In 1948, the major Nationalist garrisons, containing the government's best armies had been isolated. The Communists closed in on Manchuria and established its hold. Mukden and other big cities surrendered gradually. Within four and half months from the beginning of the Manchurian collapse to the occupation of Peking, the Nationalist armies had lost over a million men. Most of them defected to the communists, taking with them over half a million rifles and huge quantities of other modern equipments, most of it American.

Flushed with success and with complete victory within sight, there was a significant shift in communist propaganda. On 21st January, 1949, the Generalissimo announced his decision to withdraw. Chiangkai-Shek fled and took refuge on the island of Formosa. On 21st October, 1949, Mao Tse-tung, proclaimed the People's Republic of China and became the first Chairman of the Republic. This was the end of the Chinese Revolution but was the beginning of implementation of land reforms by the new communist regime.

However, taking the clue from the peasants' revolution of China, there were many conflicts and agitations around the world and there are still many movements including violent ones are going on. One of these is Naxalism movement in India. The Naxalite agitation still couldn't succeed because the State is very powerful now-a-days with very sophisticated weapons. As a result, the revolutionaries take refuge in jungles or forests and are unable to show their *bona fide* by even symbolic achievements to the suffering peasantry and they only indulge in guerrilla warfare against the salaried armed forces, who are sent to fight against them without much of moral or motivation dose. Thus, these movements are only playing hide and seek games with no results forthcoming for the teeming millions. In the process, the main issue of implementation of land reforms including equitable distribution of land goes in oblivion. There are many lessons to be learnt from the Great Chinese Revolution, so that land may become conduit to reduce poverty in the society. This was also done successfully in Brazil through the Rural Landless Workers' Movement (MST) within the ambit of the Constitution of Brazil. The militant members used to enter the property or land late at night and they erected temporary barracks out of heavy plastic sheets and woods. Then the negotiation with landowners and government would go on and on. Even unproductive land was also included for expropriation and distribution among the landless squatters to fulfil the 'social function'.

"The initial phase of China's high and sustained growth and poverty reduction spurt clearly was linked to its 1979 change from collective large scale farms to small family farms. When collective production was abandoned and key agricultural markets were liberalised, China's peasant sector initiated rapid economic growth that dramatically reduced poverty. Equity in land distribution is associated also with overall high economic growth (Deininger and Squire 1998, Deininger and Olinto 2000)"[3].

"Table 7.1 shows how the main component of land reforms, e.g., distribution of Government vested land or surplus arable land distributed is directly proportional to the economic growth of a country because Japan, Taiwan, South Korea and China are economic tigers in Asia now-a-days whereas India is lagging behind on both counts.

Table 7.1: Percentage of Distributed Arable Land in Japan, Taiwan, South Korea, China and India

Country	*Percentage arable land distributed*	*Percentage of landless household receiving lands*
Japan	41	81
Taiwan	44	100
South Korea	33	64
China	90	<90
India	~5	<28

The equitable distribution of land will ensure a peaceful foundation of the polity on which any industrialisation or technological advancement can take off without any turmoil in future. In fact, in times of crisis in economy, agriculture sector through its production had saved many countries from collapse on many occasions. No country can depend on uncertain imports of foodgrains totally during the crisis like war, civil wars and specially during globalisation where market forces are ruling the roost.

On the other hand, it will not be an exaggeration to state that Pakistan was dismembered in Pakistan and Bangladesh, because the Pakistan dictatorial rulers enhanced ceiling limit in Bangladesh up to 120 acres to woo the middle class and big landlords. In India, three new states in India, i.e., Chhattisgarh, Jharkhand and Uttarakhand were separated from erstwhile Madhya Pradesh, Bihar and UP because these regions were also neglected by their parent states from the point of view of redistribution of vested land.

The United Nations' Fourth Report (1970) says that "the redistribution of land can lead to the spread of national consciousness which is pre-condition for popular national government. On the other hand, lack of land reforms, high mechanism, capital and intensive agriculture can cause agitation".

Methodology of Distribution of Land

To distribute surplus arable land among the landless farmers, government must have sufficient bank/stock of surplus agricultural land with them. The government gets the land vested in excess of the ceiling limit prescribed by the statute.

Identification of Ceiling Surplus Land

For this purpose government machinery or officials of Land Administration System should identify the excess land with the landowners, who are given options to retain land within the ceiling and allow the LAS to take possession of the other parcels of land belonging to him subject to payment of compensation in due course of time. Thus, the distribution of agricultural land involves following broad steps:

Firstly, the excess land has to be identified. For that purpose, the landowners, possessing land above the ceiling area on a prescribed data have to submit returns to the LAS. Then, the prescribed authority examines his return and statements and decides after enquiry from his departmental officials, if the landowner has no other excess, quantum of land to be vested in government. Here the option is given generally to the landowner to keep better land with him and leave the unproductive or infertile lands for the government. The prescribed authority also provides opportunity of hearing whose land is likely to be vested in government. If a landowner doesn't submit the return and he holds land in excess of the prescribed limit, the prescribed authority shall serve a notice on the landowner calling upon him to appear before him. The prescribed authority may make such further enquiry as it may think necessary to detect the surplus land. The authority will also decide whether more area for ceiling is to be allowed in view of the size of the family or it is in the nature of charitable trust or endowment or specified cash crop or crops like tea or coffee cultivation to be exempted from ceiling. After the land in excess of ceiling limit is determined, it is taken over through possession by an officer of LAS, and the land is entered as public or government land available for distribution among the landless or have nots eligible persons as per extant rules or practice.

However, lot of parcels of land still lie outside the net of vesting as these lands generally belong to influential persons of ruling political party or chiefs of local community, so-called religious and charitable organisations or big moneylenders or landowners of large estates. Even initiation of process of detection of *benami* lands in the names of their dogs, cats or servants or non-existent relatives will not be successful because they will take help of battery of lawyers and politicians and even musclemen. The only way out is to get occupied their *benami* lands forcefully by the really deserving landless persons who have nothing to lose. The key indicator in detection *benami* land is whether the production or usufruct from that land is going to the influential person or big landowner.

Preparation of Lists of Beneficiaries

This is the most ticklish and difficult job. The demand is more than the supply. Therefore, the priority among the landless persons has to be fixed with lot of caution. The best way is to entrust this job to the local elected body whose representatives have a lot of knowledge of the grass-roots people. The bureaucrats have also to be associated so that party or community colour doesn't influence the decision of the locally elected body known as 'panchayat' in India, Bangladesh, Nepal etc. The local revenue or land reform officials prepare the preliminary lists which are finalised by the Land Sthayee Samiti or the full body of local council or panchayat. Generally persons holding one acre (0.4047 ha) land or above will be excluded from such lists. Secondly, he will personally cultivate land which is not made transferable and is only heritable. A preference is given to indigenous people in allotment who are also landless.

Distribution of Government Vested Land

After the lists of beneficiaries have been prepared objectively without any discrimination, the long-term lease deeds known as *pattas* are prepared in their favour by departmental or LAS officials. A poor is a poor. There cannot be a dispute between the two poor. A comparative landless person and poorer will get the priority. Then the distribution of these surplus arable vested land should be taken up in a drive method so that land titles actually reach them without delay and free of corruption. The government land distribution camps or land distribution programmes are generally attended by State or District VIP. Some leases or *pattas* are distributed from the dias and the rest of *pattas* are distributed from various counters made for this occasion.

The beneficiaries or *pattadars* are given advice that they should preserve the *patta* or lease documents with full safety and security like their own mother as land is mother. They should not mortgage this land whatsoever adverse situation arises except mortgaging for bank or co-operative loan or for joint or co-operative farming. They should cultivate land themselves or through members of their family. Even banks are invited, who get the applications for loans filled in by the new assignees of the vested land for bank loan at a minimum rate of interest of about four per cent. Without bank linkage, they will not be able to utilise the allotted land property as their traditional link with the village landowner is scrapped and usual flow of credit to him is barred.

The real problem arises to put the allottees in possession of these newly-allotted lands as because someone or the other has been cultivating the land. For this purpose, apart from peasants' help of power of the state or police force, the help of local peasants' organisations should be taken. In these programmes, if land is allotted to an ineligible beneficiary, other allottees or a person who has been denied his right to get an allotment due to ulterior motive by the LAS machinery take objections. Later, some developmental schemes especially labour intensive schemes may be implemented to make these allotted land more productive. Some of the leased out lands can be joined together and can be jointly developed by creating water source or storage on one of the parcels because without availability of irrigation the lands will not be productive. Lastly, after few years of continuous cultivation personally by the allottees of government lands, their names can be recorded as landowners in the remark column keeping government as overall owner.

Similarly, homeless or houseless persons in the rural areas can be allotted homestead land just to erect their *kutcha* or *pucca* house out of the available non-agricultural land in the village up to 1/16th of an acre or even less so that they may not be evicted and made refugees in their own village or habitat by the local influential persons now and then. Secondly, they will also be able to keep their cattle adjoining their hut or *kutcha* house and can grow vegetables or seasonal crops for their survival. Even agricultural land can be allotted for homestead purpose after conversion of the classification, because need for home is equally important. In these leases from government, the name of wife should appear first as first allottee of state, so that male beneficiary may not mortgage or transfer leased land due to debt, drinking habit, gambling etc. Women are more cautious to run the family than their male counterpart. Self-help groups can be formed so that they may get credit from banks and may purchase high cost equipments like tractors, harvesters, etc. centrally and also arrange for marketing of products centrally. Thus, co-operative farming can be promoted among government allottees of land keeping their individual ownership intact. If no land is left for distribution, government should purchase the land from the open market in nearby areas of the landless persons below poverty line and distribute them up to 16 decimal of land to construct their homestead and for garden/crop cultivation. It is upon the government to arrange finance to pay compensation to the owner of ceiling surplus land and cost of purchase of land if land is not available as surplus. The World Bodies can come forward in this venture. Or the States can acquire more lands by lowering the ceiling limit which is now five hectare per family on an average and differ from country to country and state to state.

Earlier, there was an hypothesis established that not less than two hectare plot of land will be economically viable for agriculture purpose.

But it has now been established that in Russia, three per cent of arable land contributed 25-30 per cent of value of agricultural production. Similarly in China, private plots during collective era of five per cent of arable land contributed more than 20 per cent of value of agricultural production. So also is the case in point in India. In the field of agriculture, every member of the small plot holder works in the farm. As a result, the production increases. The economists rightly calculate their labour in terms of cost. Therefore, the small farms do not become economically viable. But the fact is very clear. There is no alternative employment for these people either in their own villages or in nearby areas. This is disguised unemployment. As a result of intense hard work and sincerity, the production on small parcels of land substantially increases. The members in turn keep guard to the farm or crop. As a result, these small plots become ideal units of food grains production.

It is estimated that nearly 500 million rural people are directly dependent on forest resources for their livelihood. Many more extract food, raises animals, fish, collect wood and medicinal plants and so forth, on a regular basis. Also most of these resources are renewable. It is therefore essential that the common property resources should also be earmarked if not distributed.

In the case of forest land, the whole of the forest cannot be allotted to the fringe people living around the forests as there might be a danger of usurpation of forests or at least degradation. As preservation of environment is more important, the tribals are given lease on very limited and degraded fringe area of forests and they are allowed rights of gathering minor forest produce or fuel wood for their own livelihood. The local elected bodies like PRIs (Panchayat Raj Institutions) are associated to verify the field situation so as to recognise the right of the long settler on the land. One such Act was enacted in India titled 'The Schedule Tribes (Recognition of Forest Rights) Act 2005.' Other countries can follow it with local variations. In case of tank fisheries, lakes or pisciculture, the land has to be jointly allotted because none can control movement of fish and other marine resources to move inside the water resources. And they can run the water resources on co-operative basis like unsuccessful co-operative farming system in Russia minus shortcomings noticed during their operation in the past.

Redistribution Programmes Implemented

Broader entitlement approaches commonly used to redistribute land to the landless and the land poor have been introduced in many countries including Brazil, Kenya, Malawi, Namibia, the Philippines, South Africa and Zimbabwe. In some countries like Brazil and Zimbabwe, programmes targetting different groups are run in parallel. In other countries, such as South Africa, India, a single programme is designed to benefit various groups. Albania and the Commonwealth of Independent States countries opted for distributing land to the workers. Most countries in Central and Eastern Europe and the Baltic States took the restitution route, whereas Hungary and Romania used a mixed strategy. A ceiling capping the quantum of land one can own often is defined by law and all agricultural land above the ceiling that is rented out or has been occupied peacefully for a long time is targetted for distribution like in Brazil, Colombia, India, the Philippines. The Brazilian and Colombian programmes also focus on underused or poorly used land, partly because land is abundant and much of it is under-utilised. In Kenya and Zimbabwe, land re-distribution focussed on white-owned farms and exempted black owners from expropriation. Another mechanism of land acquisition is outright confiscation or seizure of land for the poor and the landless.

This occurred in the revolutionary land reforms of France, Russia, Eastern Europe, China, Cuba and other Communist countries. Extreme rural poverty had virtually been eliminated in Cuba after the land reforms. Australia, Canada, New Zealand and the United States have introduced land restitution schemes either to restitute property or to provide fair compensation to individuals or communities unfairly dispossessed.

The State's role in land re-distribution is very important. Even after forcible occupation of lands of large landholders, the State instrument has to recognise and protect the possession of the poor persons on land. It sometimes promoted reform, sometimes prevented it, sometimes reversed it and sometime diverted it to benefit other groups than the rural poor. A primary mission of the state was usually to protect the status quo in this respect, as it traditionally derived its power primarily from support of the properties classes. The changes in state policies leading to or accompanying land reform can be explained ex-post facto by the emergence of new influential social actors such as organised peasants and workers together with power allies in other sectors of society.

But in the state itself, there are some conscious bureaucrats and political executives, who have successfully implemented re-distribution programmes of land in their limited sphere of influence. Political parties also played important roles. Regimes which came to power as a result of political upheavals like in independent India, Mexico, Bolivia, Nicaragua, Cuba, China and Vietnam had mandate to implement land redistribution measures and they did a bit from their end. So far the slogan of land distribution helps them more than anything to win votes they will adopt the same tactics. International Organisations like the World Bank, FAO and ILO promoted land redistribution programmes. At least progressive NGOs and committed international organisations can play important roles as catalysts in helping grassroots peasants and landless movements to organise and pass their demands for lands. In India, one political-cum-saint leader Vinoba Bhave collected lakhs of hectare land in donation and distributed among the landless and the most needed persons who would cultivate the land personally.

The advantages of land redistribution programme are as follows:

1. For rural households, land is an effective instrument to accumulate wealth and to transfer wealth to the next generation.
2. Land ownership is a source of self-insurance and old-age and all weather social security. Land can be sold, rented out, or pawned for consumption smoothing in response to shocks and life cycle stages.
3. Land ownership is a source of security in continued access to the same plot of land, offering the possibility of capitalising in long-term investments and a source of local social capital and credit from banks and other financial institutions or local moneylenders.
4. Land ownership is a source of social status and bargaining power.[4]

Feasibility of Land Redistribution Programme in Urban Areas and in Peri-urban Areas

The guiding principle for distributive equity in landed properties in rural and urban areas is that "the ownership and control of the material resources of the community are so distributed as best to subserve the common good and the operation of the economic system does not result in the concentration of wealth and means of production to the common detriment."[5] To achieve this purpose, no person in urban area should be entitled to hold urban land in urban and urban agglomeration beyond a limit. Private dealing in urban land in recent years led to much speculation and profiteering. It has also been noticed in recent years that large palatial buildings with show of luxury have come up on extensive areas comprised therein. This is one way of investment adopted by wealthy persons not only for convenience and comfort but for a vulgar display of their wealth. This generates the feeling of helplessness and inferiority among the majority urban poor and ignites the spirit of dissatisfaction and revolt. None can justify the purchase of large villas by industrialist Laxmi Mittal in London for more than $ 100 million and by celebrities like Football legend David Beckham for $ 50 million and by Hollywood movie stars.

This is not good for a stable society. On the other hand, every citizen has a right to a residential plot of land or at least a residence. It is attractive from an equity perspective but is difficult to apply because land is not available. Thus, squatting is encouraged. It is therefore imperative, that the urban poor is at least given a shelter so that he can earn his food and clothes to wear. The urban poor is more interested in finding a job rather than finding a plot whereas in rural areas, land is the only way for livelihood and to protect the poor from starvation or hunger.

The urban poor enjoy a better life because poor slums are adjacent to a rich neighbourhood and they find easy jobs in domestic chores of the rich people. The farthest out are squatter settlements which are next to the poorest groups but not the poorest. The poorest are interspersed in slums all over or even sleep on the streets as in Kolkata. The rich occupy the areas with the highest amenities qualities. Good scenic areas, access, locations with good views, etc. are occupied by the high income groups. The poor are relegated to the most inhospitable terrain like steep slopes and marshes. Their primary interest is in land as shelter and security. Even then, last two decades have seen an explosive growth in the size of cities in almost all developing countries. This growth can in large measure be attributed to rural-urban migration reacting to poor condition in the country side or expectation of higher income in the city. Therefore, there has to be an expansion of the supply of urban land and more intensive use of existing land. While the supply of all land is not like rubber which can be stretched, the supply of urban land can be stretched. Conversion of rural land to urban use, release of undeveloped lands in urban areas or better use of public land and housing or accommodation of more people in a given space constitute increases in the effective supply of urban land.

The Philippine urbanisation presents a good example. Out of total 92 million population, 63 per cent live in urban areas. Unregulated urban growth and acute poverty have resulted in severe housing problems. Of the roughly 10 million Filipino families living in cities today, an estimated 3.1 million lack security of tenure with 2.7 informal settler households in Metro and capital Manila alone according to data from the National Housing Authority in 2007. The government and the private sector deliver housing services with the participation of several public and private institutions. Private developer producing and selling social housing units are becoming increasingly important actors in the social housing sector.

This is also true in India. Much more is being done by the private builders than the government agencies or authorities. In cities, there is no other alternative except to arrange large scale housing facilities for the urban poor. An experiment was done in India by enforcing the Urban Land (Ceiling and Regulation) Act, 1976 on the pattern of acquisition of land through ceiling in rural areas.

The Act is intended to achieve the following objectives:

1. To prevent concentration of urban property in the hands of a few persons and speculation and profiteering therein;
2. To bring about socialisation of urban land in urban agglomerations to subserve the common good by ensuring its equitable distribution;
3. To discourage construction of luxury housing leading to conspicuous consumption of scarce building materials and to ensure the equitable utilisation of such materials, and
4. To secure orderly urbanisation.

The Act mainly provided for the following:

(i) Imposition of a ceiling on both ownership and possession of vacant land in urban agglomerations, the ceiling being on a graded basis according to the classification of the urban agglomeration;

(ii) Acquisition of the excess vacant land by the state governments with powers to dispose of the vacant land to subserve the common good;

(iii) Payment of an amount for the acquisition of the excess vacant land, in cash and in bonds;

(iv) Granting exemptions in respect of certain specific categories of vacant land;

(v) Regulating the transfer of vacant land within the ceiling limit;

(vi) Regulating the transfer of urban or urbanisable land with any building (whether constructed before or after the commencement of the proposed legislation) for a period of 10 years from the commencement of the legislation or the construction of the building, whichever is later;

(vii) Restricting the plinth area for the construction of future residential buildings;

Let us examine how this experiment has shown results in India. The Act failed to achieve its purpose because of following reasons:

(i) The process of disposal of cases under the Act was very tedious and tardy. As a result, only few lands could be vested much below the target.

(ii) The patches of lands acquired in between large bungalows or vacant lands which could not be allotted for any fruitful use.

(iii) The property tax, water and sewerage taxes are so high that the urban poor cannot afford. Even they cannot afford huge cost of construction. As a result, they only take land to sell it immediately as they get huge price and then they again become homeless forever.

(iv) There were legal hurdles even the courts did not agree with such a discriminative ceiling law at the same place against the right to property. The administering department was busier in pursuing court cases rather than vesting *benami* lands of the big houses.

(v) The investment in urban areas fell down considerably in all sectors including housing. The government had no parallel solution for public investment in place of private investment.

(vi) The state didn't have funds to provide huge compensation cost to the owners.

(vii) Ultimately on suggestions of many state governments. Government of India brought in the Urban Land (Ceiling and Regulation) Repeal Act, 1999 repealing the earlier Act giving options to state government to continue with the Act. Only two states opted to continue with the Act to avoid backlash of vote bank of the urban poor without cogent development cause.

Concluding Remarks

It is clear that the land redistribution will certainly save the rural poor, who are also land poor or the landless from starvation. After allocation of land at least for their subsistence, the responsibility is shifted to them to work hard on mother earth and earn their livelihood. The state's responsibility to the extent of keeping them away from hunger will be over. However, this solution is not effective in the same way in urban areas. In urban areas, more important issues are employment and housing. But in every house allotted, the urban poor should have proportionate ownership of land of the group housing.

However, title of land or house would enable the allottee to access credit market. Thus, they can themselves try to come out poverty trap. The poor fail to get out of poverty not because they are unproductive or lack skills, but because, due to credit market imperfections, they never get the opportunity to utilise their innate ability. However, neither the rural poor nor the urban poor should be allowed to sell off such assets allotted to them by the government or state or by the community because the poor have unlimited number of problems which are equally very pressing. To safeguard them from temptation of either mortgaging or orally handing over the possession of their land asset, they should have social and personal security and insurance at least against serious diseases or lethal ailments if not against crop failure. In any way, the redistribution of land and urban housing are great steps forward to alleviate poverty from the mother earth.

References

1. Mende, Tibar, *The Geat Revolutions: The Chinese Revolution,* Thames and Hudson, London, pp. 95-96, 1961.
2. *Ibid.,* p. 104.
3. Mkhije-Hans P. Binswanger, Bour Guignon, Brink, Rogier Vanden, *Agricultural Land Redistribution Latin, Towards Greater Consensus: The World Bank,* Washington DC, p. 9, 2009.

4. Janvry Alain de, Gordillo, Gustavo, Platteau, Jean, Phillippe, Sadoulet Elisabeth, *Access to Land Rural Poverty and Public Action*, Oxford University Press, p. 17, 2001.
5. Based on Article 39 (b) and (c) of the Constitution of India.

8

Recording of Sharecroppers on Land

Security of tenure is the cornerstone of the land reform in addition to the transfer of ownership of land. The state may not have sufficient land for redistribution among the poor but the state can certainly recognise and respect all legitimate tenure rights and the people who hold them, safeguard legitimate tenure rights against threats or evictions, promote and facilitate the enjoyment of legitimate tenure rights, provide access to justice when tenure rights are infringed upon, prevent tenure disputes, violent conflicts and opportunities for corruption.

According to the generally accepted principle, the land should belong to the one who tills the land. As a corollary, it is presumed that every owner must cultivate land by his own labour or by the labour of any member of his family. Cultivation should be his main source of income and he or member of his family should reside for the greater part of the year in the locality where the land is located. But it has been the long practice world over that there are majority of non-cultivating landowner. As there is less circulation of currency in rural areas, the landowners use the sharecropping as a means of accessing cheap labour which has ignited several agrarian movements. The sharecroppers generally had little bargaining power. The landlords therefore, were able to increase their own share by manipulating loans, giving threats, harassing the sharecroppers physically, misusing their wives and children including for their personal comforts and domestic chores and even evicting them from the lands so dear to them which they have been cultivating for long as the only source for their livelihood. The relationship between sharecroppers and landlords was no better than between a servant and a master. Even the employees in factories and offices have security of jobs after they are declared permanent. In Japan, there is lifetime employment. Even the eligible heir of the ex-employee has a guaranteed job in his father's organisation. Therefore, the employees work wholeheartedly. As a result, Japan has made an unprecedented progress in the world. An employee either in white or blue collar job doesn't give his hundred per cent until he has the security of his job. How can one expect that without any security of tenure, a sharecropper will give his best on the farm in the interest of productivity which is the ultimate goal of farming or cultivation or the society? Secured and satisfied employees are the best guarantors of the well-being of an organisation as per modern management principle. Cultivation everywhere has at least thirty per cent input of human labour either directly or indirectly. If this human resource (HR) is not operating in its full capacity, the resultant production will be less than the expected level. This is a clear loss to the society irrespective of the fact whether the landowner gains or the sharecropper loses.

The field data have shown time and again that there are large number of sharecroppper tenants, who have been working with the same landowner for a number of years and are entitled to be conferred the status of occupancy tenant/owner within their respective earmarked lands. To give them security of cultivation, all such tenants should be conferred with the status of occupancy tenants with retrospective effect. All such tenants should be identified, their rights should be recorded and permanent heritable rights should be conferred on them.

Take the example of India. After independence in 1947, many states incorporated tenancy reform laws in their comprehensive land reforms Acts; some states enacted separate laws in the interest of tenants. As a result, "about 30 million tenants got free-hold rights on tenure hold land and in most of the cases this has been free of cost. According to the Report of the UP Zamindari Abolition Committee, 14 million tenants got these benefits and according to the Report of the Revenue Commission in Bengal, over six million tenants were declared as *raiyats*, i.e., freehold owners. Later on, 1.5 million tenants were added up to 2010 in West Bengal alone.

In Kerala, as a result of the movements of the Tenants Association, as many as 2.4 million tenants applications for conferment of ownership were accepted. In Maharashtra, 1.492 million tenants were declared owners of land on 2.512 million hectares. Here, of course, the tenants had had to pay for ownership rights which was between 20 to 200 times the annual land tax. The tenants were given the option to pay in lump sum or in 12 annual instalments at an interest of 4.5 per cent per annum. The actual purchase prices paid by the 2.512 million tenants was Rupees 558.1 million i.e., $ 11 million. Purchasing of ownership rights by tenants in Goa, Tamil Nadu and many other states, under the governmental intervention continued till recently which secured freehold rights for not less than 30 million tenants in India. About 66 per cent of these tenants received freehold ownership without any payment of costs or compensation, an event which probably didn't take place in any other country after World War II."[1]

"A large number of tenants still remain outside the protection of the law as they are not recorded as tenants in the present land records. A study conducted by the National Academy of Administration, Mussoorie, India, in September 1990 shows that 57.7 per cent of tenants in the sample villages are unrecorded tenants."[2]

"As per field study, there are approximately 16 per cent unrecorded sharecroppers in Uttar Pradesh. Thus, there are about three million unrecorded tenants."[3]

Different Types of Tenure Systems: There are following types apart from above:

1. Freehold is the ownership in perpetuity.
2. Registered Leasehold is ownership for a specified period from a few months to 999 years.
3. Leased public land like *patta* land which is on a nominal rent but has high degree of security, providing terms and conditions of occupation specially restriction in its disposal to others.
4. Private land is taken on rent on the basis of written or oral agreement. This will include the sharecroppers.
5. Combination of ownership and rental for example big landowners take the land of small and marginal farmers on lease along with their own lands and indulge into mechanised farming. This is called reverse leasing out, i.e., sharecropping by the landowner.
6. Co-operative tenure is one in which ownership is vested in the co-operative or informal group of which small landowners are

co-owners. The co-operative farms or State farms of the socialist blocs will fall in this category.

7. *Customary tenure:* Ownership is vested in the tribe, group, community or family. Land is allocated by customary authorities such as Chiefs. These are vulnerable to capitalistic and market forces. These tenures are in practice in Africa and Latin American countries.
8. *Religious tenure system*: This is under a religious trust or a deity. Deity is the legal personality owning land and the cultivators give a share to her as per system like Lord Jagannath Trust in Orissa, India or trusts owning large chunks of land under various Christian religious groups or sects. These trusts do charity at the cost of exploitation of labour of the cultivators or sharecroppers of land. Islamic tenure has four main categories. '*Waqf*' is religious trust land to address landlessness; '*malk*' is full individual ownership; '*miri*' is stated owned/ controlled land which carries usufruct rights whereas '*musha/mushatarak*' is collective/tribal ownership.
9. Contract farming is promoted by entrepreneurs, MNCs and TNCs for market demand-oriented crops by pooling lands of small and marginal farmers, but legal validity is not there. The small landowners should be protected by giving them legal sanctum covering their risk also.
10. Tenure on the basis of temporary occupation or licenses widely practised in urban areas. Houses or lands taken on rental come within this category.
11. Non-formal tenure systems including regularised and un-regularised squatting, unauthorised occupation, possession or encroachments. In urban areas, these types of tenures are in vogue in majority of cities.
12. Manorial Systems for large parcels of lands which is known as *zamindari* system in India started with collection of taxes by the landlords as agents of state. Ultimately, they couldn't hold on their exploitative method of managing or owning lands and had to give way to the greater rights to the cultivators. Similarly, the Junker estates with large ownership continued for long with hired labourers and even with bonded labourers residing on their lands

but they also had to convert either into large mechanised commercial farms or into collective and state farms. State was compelled to support with passage of time the justified rights of cultivators. These large farms or landlords couldn't manage large investments required for cultivation and the cultivation without self or personal labour was gradually becoming non-profit venture. Forced labour became the practice of past due to long and continuous struggle by the peasants' or farm workers' organisations.

In 1919, a sharecroppers' union had been created by a communist leader, Jacinto Manahen which became known in 1924 as the National Union of Peasants in the Philippines. The peasant organisation, generally used non-violent methods such as demonstrations and sit down strikes. In 1948, President Roxes passed laws establishing fair sharing of the crop by landlords and tenants.

After the revolutionary regime came to power in Cuba, a land reform was promulgated on 17th May, 1959. More than 100,000 tenants, sharecroppers and other precarious cultivators became proprietors of their plots without any obligation to pay for the land. The large estates (many of which were foreign owned) were expropriated and transformed into co-operatives or state farms.

In August, 1964 President Sukarno endorsed the right of sharecroppers and took drastic steps to implement his policy, 'live together, eat together and work together.'

Prime Minister Robert Mugabe, in 1980 recognised the rights of tenants on lands in Zimbabwe and the foreigners had to return much of the lands, to its original African inhabitants.

In Pakistan, community-based organisations backed by NGO-run rural support programmes which go beyond credit and service provision for the rural poor. They lease out large areas from landlords at favourable rates, offering guaranteed rent to incomes over a number of years and sub-leasing to community groups.

In India, the Deccan Development Society has been leasing out underused private land in Andhra Pradesh for use by Dalit (Lower caste) women on a tenancy basis. The scheme has improved food security and has been replicated under the country's Scheduled Caste's Development Corporation programme. This was in the face of Andhra Pradesh State restrictions like many other states in India on land lease which is not a practical proposition. It has caused more evictions of sharecroppers than has triggered off people to cultivate their lands personally. In Bihar, NGOs have acted as guarantors for collective sharecropping for women's groups, on assurance of training as well as production and marketing support.

Case Study of Success of Barga Operation in West Bengal, India

In 1978, the Communist government in West Bengal initiated 'Operation Baga' a comprehensive programme designed to record the sharecroppers, who were cultivating lands of others under the sharecropping system known as adhi, barga or *batai*.

In terms of area, West Bengal is not that big a state but it is one of the most densely-populated state with about 80 million people. By 1978, sharecropping was widespread in the state about 20-25 per cent of all farms. The institution was, in most cases, highly exploitative of the poor labourers, since 1978 to 2008, about 1.5 million sharecroppers were registered in the land records of the state (LAS). It controlled extortion of rent or share from them and controlled rents or shares given to them and conferred heredictory rights to tenants.

Modus Operandi

The Left Front allies had come in power with a specific mandate to implement land reforms. After the Left Front came into power, they reorganised the state apparatus for this purpose and gave it first priority in their governance. They were lucky that their predecessor government had passed requisite pro-land reform legislations. The only need was to implement in the field. The predecessor government had made about seven ha as maximum permissible land to be held by any *raiyat*/person. In addition, they had provided under Section 16 of the WBLR Act,1955 that anybody cultivating land of another person on condition to deliver a share will get 75 per cent share of produce if the person, who cultivates the land, known as *bargadar* provides plough, seeds, cattle, fertilisers, irrigation and other inputs.

Without waiting for administrative arrangements for implementation of the above provisions, relating to the tenancy cultivation/*barga* cultivation, the *Krishak Sabha*, peasants' wing of CPI(M) started harvesting crops of landowners in an organised manner and removal of the produce to their place (*khamar*) for separation of grains. Earlier these harvested crops used to be taken to the central place controlled by the landlord or the landowner where he used to control the process of separation of produce and then he used to distribute to the *bargadars* at his sweet discretion. The landowners in such cases, never allowed more than 50 per cent of produce after harvesting to the sharecroppers or *bargadars*. The sharecroppers started claiming 75 per cent of produce where there were dispute with the landowners or the relations between the landowners and the sharecroppers were strained.

In few cases, so far exploited sharecroppers or local peasants' organisations also wanted to score with the landowners, who used to enjoy uninhibited power in the village so far. The administration stood by the side of the sharecroppers as per the changed political scenario. As a result, the landowners approached the local administration like Block Development Officer (BDO), and the Junior Land Reforms Officer (JLRO) known as Block Land and Land Reforms Officer (BLLRO). The BDO was authorised to mediate between the two but in the presence of the local peasants' organisation on behalf of the sharecropper. As the peasants' organisations were tough and uncompromising in most of the cases as they had earlier experience of rough behaviour of landowners with them. Now, law and administration both were on their side. Earlier, landowners could do this only by keeping administration specially police administration on their side. Thus, the administration slowly veered around the sharecroppers and poor cultivators in the villages and all demanded to get the sharecroppers/*bargadars* recorded. In the melee, many unscrupulous *bargadars* under the umbrella of the peasants' organisations also took undue advantage and started cultivating land and harvesting crops which they had no right. It was essential to show the cultivation through sharecropper only and the landowners did not cultivate land personally. He cultivated through him and there was an agreement to allow him to cultivate his land. This agreement in the village is to be inferred through conduct because village economy runs almost paperless and cashless. Therefore, if the alleged *bargadars* had been cultivating land of the landowners peacefully for the past two/three years, he was presumed to be *bargadars* unless otherwise it was contradicted. Or the landowner could show that he cultivated through daily labourers and that he maintained lists of those daily labourers and the proof of payment of their due daily wages. The landowners in rural West Bengal never gave receipt of produce from the *bargadars* nor maintained a register for cultivation through daily labourers. The peasants' organisations took advantages of this legal lacuna and slowly they controlled the cultivation scene in rural Bengal. Seeing one-sided swing in the rural area, creation of law and order and legal problems, the local administration approached the policy-makers unanimously to get *bargadars* recorded. This is what the political elite at the state level wanted. Without creation of demand for amendment of rule on law, the rule or law is not implemented in spirit and with speed. The top bureaucrats headed by D. Bandyopadhyay, IAS with the requisite political will draft a programme for *barga* recording throughout the State. Operation *Barga* accordingly as a programme was launched in West Bengal on 5th July 1978. As per report before 1977, the total number of *bargadars* recorded were 185,497.

The legal provisions were strengthened by amending Rule 21, and Schedule A of the West Bengal Land Reforms Rules, 1955. The Schedule A was amended by amending the second proviso by providing that "the Settlement Officer could direct that names of *bargadars* shall be incorporated in the record-of-rights by the Revenue Officer subordinate to him after holding such enquiry and after giving the persons claiming as *bargadars* and the owners of the land concerned such opportunity of being heard as the Revenue Officer may deem fit." On the question whether individual notice or general notice should be given for the purpose of giving opportunity of being heard, the relevant rule was amended in 1981 [Proviso 2 was added to Clause 1 of Schedule A appended to WBLR Rules, 1965]. It was now laid down that opportunity of being heard would be deemed to have been given if within one week before the enquiry, the Revenue Officer publishes a notice of his intention of enquiry by fixing a notice at conspicuous place in the office of the Gram Panchayat concerned. Two "Explanations" were further added, thereby legalising the issue of *bargadars*' certificates. The second amendment closely followed and the Revenue Officer was authorised to incorporate in the record-of-rights changes on account of *barga* cultivation by making necessary enquiries. These amendments accorded the required legal sanction to the methodology of Operation Barga. The immediate impact of Operation Barga was encouraging.

As Operation Barga gained momentum a counter-propaganda by the land owners and sometimes their counter-move, was discernible in the publicity media and in the law courts. This was not unexpected, as there must be some reaction to attempts at structural changes. One of the criticisms was that adequate notice was not being given to the land owners through the existing system of giving notice was legalised by an amendment of the West Bengal Land Reforms Rules, 1965. According to this amendment, parties interested would be deemed to have been given an opportunity of being heard if the Revenue Officer published a notice of his intention to make an enquiry for recording names of *bargadars* by affixing the notice to a conspicuous place or by beat of drums. This amendment was followed by another amendment by which granting of a barga certificate under Section 50 of the West Bengal Land Reforms Act, 1955 was legalised.

The programme of Operation Barga was further extended first by two months to 31st August, 1980 and then again by three months, to 30th November, 1980. Total number of *bargadars* recorded by August, 1980 was about 9.5 lakhs (about one million). Thus, in two years' time names of about 4.5 lakhs about (1/2 million) *bargadars* was recorded under the crash programme of the Operation Barga continued and up to September, 1987, 13,75,284 *bargadars* were recorded. Later on, the addition per year was gradually declining. As on date, i.e., up to October, 2007, 15,10,173 number of *bargadars* have been recorded covering an area of 1,11,12,71 acres.

Further assuming that in the present set up and legal framework, 25 per cent of the *bargadars* will remain outside the records. Thus, we may reasonably conclude that the total number of *bargadars* in West Bengal will be around 20 lakhs.

Salient Features of the 'Operation Barga'

The entire State of West Bengal (except areas of Purulia district and Islampur Sub-division which were ceded from Bihar), was for the purpose of scheme, divided into two areas; (i) Area 'A' consisting of about 24,000 mouzas/villages already covered by Khanapuri Bujharat and (ii) Area 'B' comprising the remaining 18,000 mouzas/villages not covered by K.B. For the purpose of hastening the process of recording the names of *bargadars*, it was decided that in Area 'B', a crash programme called 'Operation Barga' was to be undertaken so as to cover the entire area within one year, i.e., 30th June, 1979. Priority pockets with large concentration of *bargadars* would have to be selected in consultation with peasants' organisations and composite squads of officers consisting of Junior Land Reforms Officers and Kanungos would have to cover the specified priority pockets within a very short time. In respect of Area 'A', 'Operation Barga' would be taken up on a selective basis on information received on joint or individual petitions or from other sources.

The methodology was: A squad will, after giving due notice, hold an evening meeting on the first (D-1) day at a venue which is a place of habitual congregation of *bargadars* and agricultural labourers. A group of mouzas / villages may be taken at a time and a general public notice will be given. Care will be taken that these four points are clearly discussed in the meeting: (i) legal and economic benefits that will accrue to recorded *bargadars*, (ii) security of the right of cultivation, (iii) pooling of funds flowing of employment programmes like FFW, ITDP, NREP, IRDP, etc. The similar programmes are still there with changed nomenclatures, and (iv) need for a supportive organisation of their own for the enduring benefits of land reforms. During and after the meeting, names of *bargadars* will be tenatively enlisted. On the next (D-2) day, field enquiry and verification will be made and the verified list will be hung up at a public place so that objections if any could be raised. On the third (D-3) day after hearing objections, if any, names of *bargadars* will be recorded and bargadar's certificates will be distributed. In this way, names of *bargadars* were speedily recorded within the four walls of West Bengal Land Reforms Act, 1955 and the Rules framed thereunder. This is the success story of 'Operation Barga'.

Outcome

"Prior to the implementation of OB, it was observed that 49 per cent of the sharecroppers in West Bengal received less than the legally stipulated 50 per cent of production. Since the OB was implemented, the percentage of production going to the sharecroppers has increased from 50 per cent to approximately 75 per cent. Out of seventy one sharecroppers (90 per cent of whom were recorded and 10 per cent unrecorded), 94 per cent received a crops share that was 50 per cent or more of total production. It is significant to note that all the recorded sharecroppers received shares of 50 per cent or more and 69 per cent of them received the legally stipulated share of 75 per cent of the produce. This signifies a substantial improvement after OB when compared with the 49.4 per cent of sharecroppers who received a crop share ranging from 20 to 40 per cent only prior to implementation of OB."[4]

Following the implementation of OB, a spectacular increase in agricultural production was experienced in the State of West Bengal. The production in West Bengal grew at a rate of 6.30 per cent which was the highest growth rate experienced in any of the seventeenth major states in India and against 3.1 per cent of the average national growth during the same period. As a result, the chronic deficient in food grains and the densely populated major state in India became self-sufficient in food grains production, and it allowed the Communist government to rule over the State for long thirty years in spite of non-communist environment elsewhere.

The reforms of the sharecropping system were effective because the programme received long-term government support in variety of ways such as safeguarding the sharecroppers' interest, promoting participation at the grassroots level, creating incentives for production activities, developing new credit facilities, mitigating eviction threats and above all, changing the general attitude of the administration. Therefore, less participation by landlords did not affect the agricultural productivity.

"The programme has been successful also because of the decentralised governance through the three-tier Panchayati System. Therefore, it seems evident that a programmes of this nature can only be effectively implemented in other parts of India and in other countries, if it is accompanied by a similar state-sponsored approach to the implementation of a comprehensive and integrated programme of rural development, with grassroots level involvement, legislative mechanism that are enforced, conditions which may be different, but not impossible to replicate".[5]

The sharecropping thus provided another recognised form of access to land specially in countries where there is no excess or government surplus land to be distributed among the landless persons or agricultural workers.

Decollectivisation of Land

Collectivisation failed in agriculture in socialist countries like Russia, Eastern Europe and some Latin American countries because there was no incentive for individual entrepreneurship.

Following the military coup in Chile (1973), and the implementation of adjustment policies introduced in response to the debt crisis (starting in 1982) throughout Latin America, policy emphasis turned to the promotion of market forces and reduction of the role of the state (Williamson 1990). Lands that were held in collectives were parcelised into individual tenures, some were restituted to former owners and many public lands were auctioned. In countries where the land reform was still ongoing, it was officially brought to an end (Peru 1991, Mexico, 1992; Honduras, 1992). Decollectivisation improved resource management by eliminating incentives to free ride on labour effort and removed inefficient controls of centralised management over individual decision-making.

"In El Salvador, co-operatives created under Phase-I of the reform were given the option of parcelisation in 1991. In Nicaragua, the process of tenure individualisation started in the 1990 elections that removed the Sardinistas from power. The new government proceeded to restitute lands that had been illegally expropriated, to give individual titles to members of production co-operatives and to privatise state farms. By 1994, 90 per cent of the land formerly in co-operatives had been parcelised and co-operatives had sold an important share of their lands in response to the profitability crisis in agriculture associated with the withdrawal of state support. About 80 per cent of the state farms had been privatised, with land generally returned to private owners or sometimes acquired by their workers."[6]

Customary Rights and Privatisation

It will not be proper to disturb customary control of lands by the community mostly in tribal areas to preserve their tradition and culture.

As recognised by anthropologists and geographers, this customary land tenure system has been the suitable socio-ecological system for land use and livestock husbandry in a semi-arid climate.

However, in spite of the World Bank support to the customary right on land, privatisation policy is pursued with vigour in most African countries.

"In Malawi between 1986 and 1990, the area of customary land that was privatised doubled, land buyers converted the production of food crops into Burley tobacco and farmer land holders became wage workers and net buyers of food. With population growing quickly, at 3.7 per cent per year, food production per person fell rapidly. In Uganda, the economic policy reform towards export-led growth has facilitated shifting land use from grazing and growing food (Cassava and Millet) to commercial ranches managed by urban land buyers who had kinship relations with influential policy makers. The buyers, erected fences around their ranches, depriving pastoral households in the surrounding areas of traditional corridors used for their own passage and the grazing of their animals.

No matter how good the economic principles of privatisation, falling food productivity associated with market-orientation should be of serious concern to governments, international organisations and development analysts. FAO data show a post 1980-downward trend in food production per person in Sub-Saharan Africa compared to other regions, the index for 1990-95 is below the average for 1979-81, and the rates of growth in average daily calorie intake per person have also declined in most countries. These trends are very worrying indeed with regard to food insecurity of rural households and their increasing dependence on the imperfect market for food procurement and the increasing incidence of chronic under nutrition, particularly among young children."[7]

However, keeping the customary right allocation intact, the beneficiaries can be allotted and earmarked minimum land in their favour so that there is security of tenure to a limited extent. These allottees will be a kin to sharecroppers on these allotted land for a term allocated to them. This will be a protection from whims and fancies of the tribal chiefs. Secondly, it will have deterrent effect on buyers, who want to purchase the lands for cash crops and not for the purpose of food production. Even if they purchase these community lands they have to purchase these lands with sharecroppers' rights to cultivate those lands either for food crops or for cash crops. Thus, sharecropping system introduces security in a tenurial system.

Fisheries

It is clear that sharecropping cannot be implemented in the fisheries; as the fish resources do not stay at one place and keep it moving from one area to the other. Therefore, it has to be a collective ownership or sharecropping having the share of each fisherman well-defined in the collective production. Responsible tenure arrangements are fundamental for securing the livelihoods of tens of millions of people, who depend on marine and inland capture fisheries. Strengthened tenure rights and tenure arrangements, when coupled with good governance and the inclusion of the fishing industry and fish workers' Organisation's help ensure that fisheries are not exploited substantially and benefits are shared equitably.

However, there may be exceptions when these lands within the large fisheries are vested with government as ceiling surplus land. In that case, the government has either to allow it to function as a fishery- co-operative or demarcate the land of each cultivator of fish, i.e., fishermen. It is experienced that like collective farms in CIS, and East European and Central European countries, the fishery co-operative suffer from mis-management and corruption. As a result, bonafide fisherman is deprived of his right even for basic minimum wages. This is high time that the fisheries are also included in the definition of land world over and fishermen are recorded thereon giving them security of tenure like a sharecropper irrespective of the change of management of fishery co-operative.

Forestry

Forests are often owned and controlled by the State. Recognising and securing tenure rights of forest dependent people, including indigenous people, is fundamental for securing livelihoods in forest communities. Improved governance, increasing association of local forest dependent people, reduced corruption and greater transparency can promote sustainable forest management and reduce unauthorised activities. It has been proved that state cannot fully protect its forest wealth unless they have willing co-operation from the local fringe people. Secondly, the regeneration of forests is possible along with their protection by incorporating the participation of local fringe forest people. Now-a-days the bigger challenge is to regenerate the equal quantum of depleted forests, if not more, than the protection of the existing forests. In India, one scheme 'social forestry' was successfully implemented which *inter alia* depended on the co-operation of grassroots population. The people who participated in social forestry were given right to uproot the trees after some years of their growth. Thus, they enthusiastically, protected the fringe forests of 'reserved', 'protected' forests or wild life sanctuaries. Proper maintenance of fringe forests is the surest way to keep the health of 'reserved' or 'protected' or 'sanctuary' in proper condition.

However, there is no denying the right of the tribal or indigenous population to collect' fire wood' or dry wood lot or dry or felled leaves or even minor produce of forests.

This right, if recorded and certificates issued to forest gatherers will ensure lot of livelihood to the poorest of the poor on this earth. At present, they are hounded by the forest officials or forest guards and have to share booty with them either in cash or in kind. The forest administration also needs clearance of forests from weeds, dry wood, felled wood or leaves so that healthy trees can grow properly. If this job can be done freely by means of recording their rights on forests, there should be 'no objection'. However, the forest management has old feudal mentality and come out with lot of arguments against any change or liberalising their landlord ship. The popular governments should address both concerns and should come out with a balance solution which will ultimately go in favour of the forest dependent people, who are the real guard and preservers of the forestry.

One such experiment is under way in India known as Joint Forest Management (JFM). In the year 2004, JFM covered 17 million hectares of forests in 27 states in India.

The major elements of the programme are:

1. A degraded forest block is normally selected in a village on forest fringe for management.
2. Officials of the forest department of government and local villagers jointly manage the selected forest.
3. A Forest Protection Committee (FPC) composed of two members (one male and one female) of all willing households of the village represent the association.
4. The Forest Department's officials and people's representatives write a micro-plan (valid for 5-10 years) for the forest. Funds for implementation is mostly provided by the Forest Department. The labour is contributed by the members of the association.
5. The villagers are mainly responsible for forest protection. In lieu of the service, the FPC members are entitled to Non-Timber Forest Produce and a share of the net income when the Forest Department sells the wood as per micro-plan. Thus, the poor villagers get felled leaves and firewood or dry wood easily from the forests which help them to sustain their livelihood.

Sharecroppers in Peri-urban or Urban Areas

In case of peri-urban lands, the sharecropping still exists but these lands are also prone to acquisition for development purpose with a view to include these areas in urban areas. The interest of such sharecroppers needs to be protected. The new Act in India entitled the Right to Fair Compensation and Transparency in Land Acquisition, Rehabilitation and Resettlement Act 2013, provides that in case the land is acquired for urbanisation purposes, twenty per cent of the developed land will be reserved and offered to land owning project affected families, in proportionate to the area of their land acquired and at a price equal to the cost of acquisition and the cost of development. However, in case of sharecroppers, if his land/residence is acquired, he will be entitled for a small amount of compensation. But these people like sharecroppers and the landless persons will not like to change their place of residence where they have been residing for long. Therefore, he should be provided hamlet in exchange of his residence acquired under the project, if he prefers to continue his stay and he doesn't accept the compensation for his house site as a special case being the poorest among the poor. However, in some countries, a provision is made to compensate the sharecropper for loss of his earnings in consequence of the acquisition of land. However, the compensation to the sharecropper may not exceed six times the net average annual income which the sharecropper derived or might have derived from the land during three years, immediately preceding the date of acquisition.

The net annual income of a sharecropper in any year may be taken to be fifty per cent, of the total produce of the land cultivated by him in that year where plough, cattle, manure and seeds necessary for cultivation are supplied by the person owning the land and seventy five per cent of the land produce of the land in all other cases.

Though peri-urban areas require to be maintained as buffer zones, to feed the giant urban areas like mega or metro cities to avoid starving due to emergencies like war, flood, natural calamity earthquake, or blockade yet practically it is not possible because land market rules the roost which is spiraling every day, more or less. Therefore, it is needed that the rights of sharecroppers or cultivators are protected at least by providing them due compensation for depriving them of their means of livelihood at least for next six years so that given a chance to live in the new environment of urban competition, they can adjust with the new found economic reality and win the race again due to their hardworking habits and way of life. Thus, they require to be given proper resettlement and rehabilitation package.

Even, in urban areas, the cultivators are there in large farm houses or ranches. They should be provided at least security of shelter so that they can earn their livelihood.

Thus, the two areas, i.e., rural and urban will have different approaches to livelihood for the poor sharecroppers whose interests are to be protected at all cost.

References

1. Das, Sukumar, *A Critical Evaluation of Land Reforms in India* (1950-1995), p. 36. *Land Reforms in India – An Unfinished Agenda* Vol. 5, ed. Sinha, B.K., and Pushpendra, Sage Publications, New Delhi, 2000.
2. *Ibid* 1, p. 40.
3. Agrawal, P.K., Land Reforms in India, M.D. Publication Pvt. Ltd., New Delhi, p. 183, 1993.
4. Saha, Uday Shankar and Saha, Mandira, *Case Study: Regulating Sharecropping System; Operation Barga, Access to Land, Rural Poverty and Public Action*, ed. Janvry, Gordillo, Plateau and Sadoulet, pp. 236-273, Oxford University Press, 2001.
5. *Ibid.,* 4, p. 242.
6. The Changing Role of the State in Latin American Land Reforms: Janvry Allain De, Sadoulet Elisabeth and Wolford Wend, *Ibid.,* 4, p. 288.
7. EL-Ghonemy, M. Riad, *The Political Economy of Market-based Land Reform, Land Reform and Peasant Livelihoods*, ed. Ghimire ITDG Publishing, UK, pp. 123, 125, 2001.

9

Role of Self-governance Units and Peasants' Organisations

Karl Marx has termed 'madness' of patience among farmers, unlike industrial labourers who are conscious of their rights and have basic infrastructure and tenacity to organise themselves against exploitation. In India, the Himalayan patience of the farmers against the exploitation negatives the thesis of agrarian revolution to a large extent. The very psyche of the cultivator is perhaps one of the subdued nature.

The massive green leaves that come out of seeds in front of the toiling labour and its turning into golden crop certainly does have magic impact on the psyche of agricultural labourer. The pleasure can be equated with the 'pleasure of a mother having a baby'. They are religious and soft. They value relationship even with the landowners who come forward to help them during adversities. They are honest and god-fearing. They want to pay off their debts and dues. They are grateful to all those who care for them. All members of the family work on the farm. Therefore, they value family ties and cohesiveness. They believe in local solutions and sometimes in superstitions. They have no time after agricultural operations. Therefore, they are not organised.

"No society, has ever substantially reformed itself by a movement from above. As a matter of fact, the agrarian labour, as pointed by the International Labour Organisation, must be treated with preference but our labour laws only, cater to the needs of the organised (except the Minimum Wages Act), and their associations are strong to deal with the State and the employers. Here employers are also easily identifiable. But in agrarian field, both are unorganised and the state remain as "onlookers."[1] The scattered nature of agricultural workers, their personal contact with and the dependence on the landlord, lack of group cohesiveness arising out of diverse culture, religions, or castes and wasn't of identical goals. Lack of any permanent work status with any particular employer, their small proportion to the number of employers, and the substitutability of hired labour by family labour are some of the constraints that come in the way of organising rural labour."[1]

Thus, the farm workers require to be organised on various levels; by governmental efforts, through local self-government bodies like panchayati raj institutions in India and Nepal, through unionisation of agricultural workers, through non-governmental voluntary organisations and movements, struggles, agitation or even blood revolutions. Let us examine each separately.

Through Government

It is a fact throughout the world that whatever has been done, it has mostly been done through government. In the government too, some conscious, committed and public-spirited officers and staff have really made niche for themselves and worked for the land poor beyond the call of their duties. They had administrative will and were not only motivated due to political will. Though political will is an important factor in implementation of the agenda for the landless, sharecroppers, *patta* holders or farm workers, yet it is not all pervading. "Hobbes famously defines "will" as a last event in a casually determined chain of events as the last 'Appetite' or 'Aversion' immediately, adhering to the action or to the omission thereof."[2]

It encompasses both the political ideals and the operating norms of a polity, concepts as political ideology, national ethos and spirit, national political psychology and the fundamental values of people.

The political will is translated through the political system which is a mechanism through which interests and demands are translated into decisions. Sometimes political system may not respond properly to the needs of the poor for reasons like the vested interests controlling the government from behind or the political party has come in power with the votes of the other side. Naturally, a political party has to fulfil the promises given to its supporter voters. On the other hand, the administrative system maintains the constancy in practice. None can deny welfare measures to the poor overtly. In this gap situation, the administration comes forward to play its role as harbinger of welfare or justice to the poor and the landless. Their administrative will come into full gloom. They have served so far for the poor and not the political parties. For this educated class, cause becomes more important than the persons. 'Administrative Will' is the aggregation of values which mature as a body or group and permeate through individuals and which derives the administrative/managerial agencies to exercise their powers and functions. They receive the ripples from the political masters and send receivable waves or signals down the ladder.

In dictatorship, the administrative will is suppressed until the next groupings re-appear. The administrative will has great significance in a developing country like India or under-developed countries. The weakness of political, commercial and industrial institutions often puts administration on the strongest position in the political process. The administration is quite firmly entrenched by virtue of their expertise. "Bureaucracy is supposed to be politically neutral but at the same time it is supposed to have commitment. Political neutrality is undoubtedly necessary for an objective, impartial and rational bureaucracy. The bureaucracy as the instrument of the state should have commitment to society and people. The will of the society is expressed through the Constitution and all organs of the state, that is, executive, legislature and the judiciary are supposed to reflect that will in their commitment and action."[3]

For any worthwhile welfare of the poor, it is necessary to take up the question of organisation of rural poor as a programme with a specific set of schemes in which all those government, political parties, voluntary agencies, academic/research institutions, social activists, trade unions, etc., who are interested in taking up this work on pool their efforts. The organisation of rural poor should be a major scheme with a direct involvement of government in it. Such a scheme *inter alia* should cover the following:

"1. Training of social animators from amongst the rural poor, at least one from each village entrusted with the task of creating awareness and helping them to receive the benefits admissible to them.

2. Conscientisation camps to be held in areas of SC/ST concentration and those vulnerable to atrocities and acute exploitation.

3. Training of rural organiser to be given the task of organising rural poor as trade unions, voluntary organisations, co-operatives, registered societies, etc., for the sole purpose of motivating them for collective action and assertion in favour of their rights.
4. Assisting voluntary organisations, activist groups for above purposes.
5. Specific steps for protecting rural organisers and social animators against retaliation of landowners and harassment by civil and police machinery.
6. Annual targets state-wise for holding of awareness camps and training of social animators and rural organisers as well as for registration of organisation may be fixed with a view to put pressure on the state governments, to take up this programme seriously."[4]

Even in state of Tamil Nadu in India, religious and social reforms are being pursued by a separate agency in government. In West Bengal, the message of Vivekanand is being spread among the youths of working among the poor as serving the God. So, also *Nehru Yuvak Kendra Organisations* are being sponsored by the Department of Youth Affairs, Ministry of HRD, Government of India. Thus, government anywhere can take up the job of motivating the people for their rights. In Cuba, President Fiedal Castro used to educate his people by working himself as cultivator in the field. In Socialist countries, there is lot of State sponsored brain-washing/propaganda schemes for people.

In the 1980s, key international agencies, notably the FAO, were mainly involved in carrying out cadastral surveys, improvements in the national land registration systems and introducing the use of computers for better land records. This work is now being done by the World Bank by assisting poor countries of Africa and Latin America and by providing a joint forum for all nations by way of organising annual conferences on land and poverty to prove a point that the poverty can be removed from this earth only by providing better access to land to the poor of the World. The World Bank has successfully brought together the latest technologies in the field of cadastral surveys and preparation of land maps through such conferences at regular intervals and by publishing the most authentic material on the subject alongwith best practices available world over.

Role of Panchayati Raj Institutions (PRIs) and Similar Rural Institutions

In India, Panchayati Raj Institutions have received constitutional status. It means that the panchayats have become integral part of the State apparatus at the local level. The constitutional scheme in Part IX of the Constitution of India provides that there will be a village committee (Gram Sabha) in a village or group of village which will function like village Parliament. There will be executive body of each Gram Sabha known as village panchayat which will send all lists of beneficiaries to higher levels for inclusion in the governmental schemes and will implement schemes assigned to them at the grassroots level. At block level, there will be panchayat samiti and at the District level, there will be Zilla Parishad (District Panchayat/Council). These local bodies are directly elected by the rural people for five years.

There is reservation of seats for the have nots known as Scheduled Castes and Scheduled Tribes in proportion to their population for membership of Panchayats and office of chairpersons in a Panchayat at each level. There is reservation of not less than one-third of the seats for women including in the category of chairpersons. Thus, the landless, government allottees of land and sharecroppers are supposed to be well-represented in these local level government or semi-government bodies and they can well-safeguard the interests of the land poor in the rural India. The faith of the weaker sections, and the electorate in Panchayat can be increased and stabilised if the landless, these local bodies and assignees of government land and sharecroppers are there as they receive proper support from these local level representatives who should stand by them at all times when there is proposal of allotment of government surplus land so that only the poorest among the poor get government land as per priority list of beneficiaries based on justice and equity. These government allottees are subsequently allowed to cultivate their land peacefully without disturbance by the erstwhile landowners of these parcels of lands. The sharecroppers are not evicted from cultivation and all of them get advantage government schemes for watershed development or employment generation schemes during lean seasons and get subsidies on seeds, manure and farm equipments.

However, if allottees of government vested land and sharecroppers get some reservation, it will further strengthen their cause, because in spite of proportionate representation to the Scheduled Castes and Scheduled Tribes, the landowner, Oligarchy still control the panchayat bodies. However, the establishment of PRIs has provided a forum to the land poor to organise under their leadership and put their voice more forcefully than before. The Parliament is known as 'Panchayat' in Nepal but there are hardly panchayats at the grassroots levels in that country.

In Colombia, the municipalities draw the whole land reform plan at their level. They first identify the demand, identify potential supply and then they implement land reform through their institutional infrastructure. Thus, selection of beneficiaries is transparent and objective. The names of rejected and accepted beneficiaries are posted publicly. The publicity of the selection process seems to have increased accountability and facilitated a better understanding of the scope and limitations of land reforms by local authorities and potential beneficiaries. The municipalities like Village Committees in India decide about the approval of specific productive projects in public sessions of the municipal council–generally with record attendance.

"In South Africa also, land reform process is being decentralised. But the lack of institutional structure has not made it effective. Progress has been made but the real involvement of local players is likely to require some devolution of decision-making authority and a shift towards the post control. Minister himself signs each land allotment parcel by his designation. These shortcomings can be addressed by empowering local governments to play a stronger role in co-ordinating the different institutions involved at the local level."[5] Department of Land Affairs (DLA) neither has expertise in development of these lands nor has the willingness to involve themselves in these meaningful post land reform measures except in regulatory jobs of recording the sharecroppers or allotment of government vested lands.

Thus, local governmental institutions or local self-governing units play a vital role in motivating people for land reform and to implement the same in just and objective manner.

Peasants' Organisations

Peasant unions allied with political parties seeking peasant support had been principal actors in bringing about land reform. The political parties if they win the election on this manifesto, they try to fulfil their promises in co-operation with the peasants' organisations. As a result, lower level government machinery is initiated to implement land reforms. They do it to avoid insult to them. Secondly, they are scared of their security in jobs, because the political high-ups are for implementation of land reforms and the higher bureaucracy caves in giving space to the political encounters to go ahead with their measures of land reforms which are constitutionally and legally valid. The only problem arises about the non-availability of skilled manpower to execute the land reform policy. This gap to a large extent is to be filled in by the political leadership, who are in touch with the ground realities which may differ from country to country and can generate their own resources to help government machinery technically.

It will not be an exaggeration to conclude that Bangladesh was separated as a country from Pakistan in 1971, because rural peasantry was not taken care of. They, therefore, rose in revolt against Pakistan government of the landlords and for the landlords gradually increasing ceiling limit for exemption to please their landed class as support base.

They were even gradually grabbing government *Khas* land, i.e., land under government jurisdiction. "Nearly half of all rural households are considered landless and out of a total 14 million agricultural households, 11 million possess no more than 0.05 acres (0.02 ha)"[6]

"In 1984, in a populist move by the Ershad regime, a new Land Reforms Ordinance was promulgated. The ordinance set a new land ceiling at 20 acres (8.1 ha) per family and stipulated that the *bargadar* (sharecropper) had the right to cultivate upto five acres of land. This was to be explicit in a legally-binding contract between the landowner and *baragadar*, thus doing away with the tradition of oral contracts, which proved to be increasingly precarious. The contract set up the terms and conditions of cultivation and was valid for five years and could be renewed if the conditions of cultivation were satisfactorily met by the sharecropper (Jannuzi and Peach, 1994; Saha, 1997). Furthermore, the ordinance included a clause giving the sharecropper the option of purchasing the land. The Bangladesh administration is slowly getting into tone of implementing the Ordinance. It is hoped that they will follow the example of their counterpart in India in the State of West Bengal. At present Ordinance of 1984 have many escape clauses which can be used by landowners to their own advantage. One of them is that the land can be repossessed, if the landowner believes that it is not being "personally cultivated" by the *bargadar*.

Secondly, the owner can simply decide to take back the land "for personal cultivation". The vagueness of the terms can lead to the eviction of sharecroppers. Land purchase by a sharecropper may also be circumvented by landowners who sell or give land to their relatives. Thus, the main reason of pulling back the sharecroppers in Bangladesh is that they are not unionised unlike in West Bengal where they get full patronage by the party in power and got patronage by the Communist government in West Bengal from year 1978 to 2012.

In the Philippines, under the banner of the League of the Poor Labourers (AMT), the peasant organisations generally used non-violent methods, such as demonstrations and sit-down strikes. If there were any arrests they went together as a group into jail. Dramatic stage presentations and similar cultural activities were used to teach the peasants about the labour struggles and to turn the strikes into public recognition. By 1938, 70,000 members participated in the AMT. Landlords organised armed groups such as 'soldiers for peace', to oppose and clash with the socialists, which led to considerable violence in the rural areas of central Luzon like the landlords organised violent attacks in Bihar, India on the poor cultivators. When the Socialists, were also prohibited from holding meetings, the organisers used all kinds of gathering, such as Protestant religious meetings, to make propaganda for the peasant cause.

Charismatic, or at least solidarity inspiring, leadership among the peasants has been highly important to the organisation of peasants sufficiently to comfort elites. When the leader of a peasants' organisation took on a paternal role because of his personal qualities, the longer it existed, the organisation control became more dependent on that specific leader. This happened to Zapata's movement after his assassination in 1919, and to the HUK Movement after Lums Taruc gave up under pressure. In the process of creating a peasants' organisation it was therefore, essential for the initial leaders to stimulate leadership qualities in potential successors.

Once a rudimentary organisation existed, sympathetic urban political leadership such as Mao in Hunan province, Lino Alvarez in Cuba and from Cico Juliao in the north-east of Brazil, could help the organisation gain regional or even national impact by assuming the world leadership. In

Japan, Indonesia and Zimbabwe, outsiders with some kind of political agenda were from the outside, the crucial mobilisers. In Zimbabwe and to some extent in Indonesia, they had to rely on close collaboration or support from local spiritual leaders.

Initially, the movements started from the tenancy improvement or higher wages. Once they had successfully brought the peasants of certain area together, they gradually transformed into demands for a drastic change of the social order at the local, regional or even national level, with stress on land distribution such as the Zapata rebellion, the Japanese movement, the HUK movement in the Philippines, the BTI in Indonesia and the Bolivian and Cuban peasant federations.

However, sometimes landowners and their local elite allies tried to prevent peasants' organisations from consolidating by making parallel unions like the Free Farmers Federation in the Philippines, and the Church sponsored Unions in Brazil in the early 1960s competed in this way with the HUK movement and the Ligas Camponesas, respectively. Similarly, many landowner formed Landowners Army in Bihar, India and massacred many supporters of the peasants' organisations and burnt their houses. This gave fillip to the growth of Naxal movement in Bihar. These obstacle movements proved counter-productive. The members of such landowners were either jailed for life or were hanged.

Secondly, the peasants with or without urban political support struck back more drastically with cohesiveness out of self-defence. Thus, Zapata movement and the cases in Russia, China and Cuba illustrate how elite intransigence caused revolutionary movements to grow.

One of the most spectacular peasants' mobility turns in Asia was the Indonesia Peasant Front (Barisan Tani Indonesia, BTI)—created and directed by the Indonesian Communist Party (PKI) after Aidit became its Secretary. General in 1953. The need to organise peasants emphasised, taking as a point of departure from their most strongly felt demands and grievances. It was suggested that local organisations be created around such demands. Party cadres were instructed to identify the most acute problems in each particular area or community. Activists had to 'live together, eat together and work together' with the peasants. They also helped solve all kinds of practical day-to-day problems, such as rent payment, legalisation of titles etc. Such 'small but successful' actions were seen by the PKI and BTI cadres as the best way to be accepted by and to mobilise the peasantry (Hindley, 1964, p.16).

At the end of 1953, BTI counted several hundred thousand members and claimed 8.5 million members in September, 1964. The growing strength of the Communist and Communist-oriented mass organisations provoked a strong response from the armed forces. A PKI Party Congress planned for 1959 was initially forbidden by the army but was later allowed, thanks to support from President Sukarno. However, the scheduled elections of 1959, which could have given the Communist Party a majority in Parliament or made it the most influential party, were not held. Instead, presidential rule or 'guided democracy' was initiated and President Sukarno tried to keep a balance between the army, the Communist Party and other forces, checkmating one force with the other.

The bargaining position of the BTI as a mass organisation was, however, strong enough to take up the land reform issue successfully at the national level and to obtain the promulgation of a land reform law in 1960. According to this law, landowners who had more than the official ceiling of five ha of irrigated paddy land, had to make the surplus available for redistribution to the landless. Implementation of the law was, however, very slow.

In order to speed up the reform programme, in 1963 Aidit endorsed a 'unilateral action movement' (Gerakan Aksi Sefihak) of the peasants. The tactic most frequently used was occupation of the lands to which landless peasants were entitled under the law."[7]

Peasants collective action in the fight for land was more significant in Latin America's earlier reforms for example those of Mexico, Bolivia and Venezuela. However, there were certainly active peasant organisation that made a different in the Hindu-run reforms and, to a lesser extent, in the Dominican Republic and El Salvador. In general, the efforts of peasant organisations in Latin America were primarily to gain political power and/or to convince those in power to meet their demands for land.

Peasant unions allied with political parties seeking peasant support had been principal actors in bringing about the land reform like in states of West Bengal and Kerala in India. Electoral politics was an important mechanism pushing land reforms in Chile from a timid beginning to a radical climax, implying profound modifications in agrarian structure.

The Nicaraguan rural workers' federation and the small farmers' organisation created in 1981, played active roles in pushing the land reform. The land reform process in Nicaragua was necessarily, subordinated to the 'SANDINISTAS' struggle for political survival in the face of increasingly aggressive hostility. The USA organised and financed invading insurgent forces (Contras). It also imposed a strict economic embargo. Both sides competed for support by discontented peasants. This often accelerated land reform initiative by the government, but the war usually undermined any economic benefits that might have ensued from reform for peasants.

In 1979 the World conference on Agrarian Reform and Rural Development came out with a recommendations to promote people's organisations, including rural workers associations and co-operatives, to strengthen the participation of the rural poor in decision-making, implementation and evaluation of agrarian reform and rural development programmes. The role of peasants' organisations, the nature of their struggle for agrarian reform, depends on the objective conditions prevailing in society at a given time. Where the state is closely aligned with the landowning class, the struggle by the grassroots organisations may be more radical and revolutionary. Where a government is strong in implementing social reforms, the peasants' organisations may be more open to participating actively in implementing the programme.

Thus, unionisation of agricultural workers is an agent of socio-economic change.

Role of Non-governmental Organisations (NGOs)

NGOs are playing important role in some of the small size countries to organise the peasants for land reforms. In Bangladesh, NGOs have led the land reforms movement. *Nijera Kori*, Bangladesh Legal Aid and Service Trust (BLAST), Gonossha Hajjo Sangshta (GSS), and the Association for Land Reform and Development (ALRD) also provide valuable legal assistance to rural populations. *Nijera Kori* is one of many non-governmental development organisations in Bangladesh, but its strong participatory approach and activism have given it increasing prominence in recent years. It believes that the 'cause of poverty in Bangladesh is not paucity of resources or over population, rather unequal distribution of wealth. It views population mobilisation and consciousness raising as essential to changing the situation in favour of the rural poor and deprived social groups, including women.

"In Bengali, '*Nijera Kori*' means we do it ourselves. As such, the organisation encourages self-help, autonomy and awareness building activities and motivates the rural poor to form collective groups to resist social injustice, as well as seek to improve their livelihood."[8]

Nijera Kori considers title to *khas* land by the landless an integral part of poverty alleviation in rural areas. Firstly, it is difficult to establish whether land is *Khas* land or not. Secondly, the powerful individuals try to grab government *khas* land. The land grabbers bring false charges (such as theft) against the landless. This makes it difficult for the landless to have access to *khas* land, especially when they are not sufficiently organised and lack wider support. *Nijera Kori* has thus sought to organise the landless and to influence public opinion and government departments, as well as providing legal support to its group members. In 1996-97, it provided legal support to approximately 100 cases, a number of which involved defending its own employees, who were considered the main foe by landlords and elites. Cases involved access to and formal titling of *khas* land, land dispossession for shrimp cultivation, oppression of women and sometimes even deaths related to these issues.

Nijera Kori was very successful in restoring land which had surfaced after receeding the sea back water in two villages Char Bajja and Char Majid at Sundaram Police Station in Noakhali District of Bay of Bengal. There was lot of conflicts between the landlords and the settlers. These about 200 settlers were allotted each with one acre of land to cultivate. Subsequently, these lands became very fertile and good for shrimp cultivation and attracted landowners, politicians and local influential persons to usurp the land by hooks or crooks. Local administrators were called upon to undertake police assaults, peasants' huts were burnt and crops were destroyed.

At the same time, law suits were brought against the peasants in the local and high counts. In 1997, three peasants were in jail serving life sentence, convicted in a bogus rape case. Without timely legal aid from *Nijera Kori*, the peasants would probably have been evicted from their land.

Thus, NGOs have become very active throughout the world. It is high time that their potential is to be realised and released serving the public interest. There is no dearth of registration of NGOs but there are few NGOs which will like to serve in rural areas specially in a hostile environment created by the local landowners and their supporters in police and revenue administration. But pending creation of large peasants organisations or eruption of violent revolts or revaluations, the poor cannot wait for long. He has to live. The NGOs can help and have helped and are helping them by providing modest help specially in the form of legal and to them to fight for their right of land and right to cultivate land as sharecropper.

"Market-assisted land reform programmes are heavily criticised by Southern NGOs. In the Philippines and Indonesia, where market-driven agrarian reforms have recently been attempted, virulent criticisms have been made by local NGOs focussing attention on the negative impacts of the programmes. In the Philippines, market-assisted land reform programmes were launched by the Central government under the auspices of the Comprehensive Agrarian Reform Programme (CARP) and in Indonesia they have been implemented by the national government in collaboration with the World Bank and Aus-Aid. In both cases, evidence suggests how, instead of benefitting small producers, market-assisted land reform has generally served to tighten the hold of powerful landowners and commercial enterprises backed by the government and ironically has helped them gain access to even more land through market mechanisms (SENTRA, 1997; Anon., 1997c). In Brazil, the landless labourers' organisation *Movimentodos Trabalhadores Rurais Sem Terra (MST)* has strongly opposed the government's recent market-led land reform programmes, which are financed mainly by the World Bank. MST considers these programmes simply to be a vindictive manoeuvre by the government, landed interests and financial institutions to weaken the organised popular demands for radical land reform in the country.

As far as NGOs (both international and national) are concerned, the land reform agenda was pursued only timidly throughout the 1980s. Many of them stressed the importance of local populations' access to common property resources, of sustainable farming methods, of the need to recognise the customary rights of indigenous peoples, women's land rights and so forth, frequently in line with the international debate on the environmental and social crises in developing countries. This gave them international credibility. At the same time, the absence of a strong call for land redistribution helped many NGOs not to come into direct conflict with national and local power structures, including those dominated by large landowners and agro-industrial enterprises.

This seems to have somewhat changed in the 1990s. The establishment of a worldwide network on land reform was mentioned above. The Via Campesina, since its establishment in 1993, has brought together organisations of peasants and small farmers from eight major regions to call for rapid agrarian reforms for food security (Via Campesina, 1998, p. 2). Food First Information and Action Network (FIAN), which asserts the fundamental importance of the human right to food, has sought to mobilise its country and regional members to demand for agrarian reforms (see e.g. Anon., 1997e). The International Union of Food, Agricultural, Hotel Restaurant, Catering, Tobacco and Allied Workers' Associations, with representation from over 30 small farmers and rural workers' organisations, has sought to promote land reform as one of its main political agendas for its upcoming activities (IUF, 1998). Church based organisations have also become vocal for agrarian reforms. An example of this is the Food, Land and Hunger Working Group of the Office of the Co-ordinator for Justice Peace and the Integrity of Creation for the Society of the Divine World, which interacts with over 100 Catholic orders and is seeking to collect and disseminate information on the transnational ownership of land Saeigel, 1997). Similarly, regional groups such as the *Asociacion de Organizciones Campesinas Centroamericanas para la Cooperacion y el Desarrollo (ASOCODE)* and the Asian NGO Coalition for Agrarian Reform and Rural Development (ANGOC) have been active in policy advocacy and grassroots actions relating to agrarian reforms. In Africa, too, several of the major agrarian NGOs are active in advocating for land and tenurial reforms. These include the African Organisations Coalition for Food Security and Sustainable Development (AOCFSD), the Agriculture Peasants and Modernisation Network (APM) and the National Land Committee (NLC).

Recent examples of national and grassroots organisations involved in land and tenurial reforms are also not lacking. MST in Brazil is currently a prominent case which has been able to mobilise a large number for small farmers and agricultural labourers inside the country and generate a great deal of international support for a radical change in land ownership. In the Philippines, the People's Campaign for Agrarian Reform (AR Now!) brings together 13 major NGOs active in agrarian reform advocacy, networking and farmers' assistance programmes. In Bangladesh, the Association for Land Reform and Development (ALRD) has established an extensive network with 108 NGOs and public interest groups to play a more active role in pushing for agrarian reform. In South Africa, the National Land Committee (a major NGO focussing on land reform and rural reconstruction) brings together 12 associations, rural development committees, rural workers' unions, etc. Similarly, *Venezuela Accion Campesina* is linking with some 166 organisations to make networking more effective. In Guatemala, a country marked by extreme land inequality and rural violence, the *Co-ordinacion de ONG Co-operativas* (CONGCOOP) has since 1992 congregated 27 national NGOs and co-operatives to press for radical land reform measures and improved agrarian support services.

The ability of 'civil society' organisations, such as those mentioned above, in ultimately producing desirable changes in tenure relations and the improved livelihoods of peasants, is generally more complicated than it might appear on the surface. Their actual strength, weaknesses, internal dynamics and contradictions with external forces need to be assessed more realistically. Indeed, it makes little sense to romanticise the role of civil society organisations when neither the trends nor the outcomes favourable to poor peasants and rural workers are clear. Nevertheless, this may help in the long run to make poorer rural producers aware of their land rights and bring them into wider social movements. Socially, just and economically opportune changes in property relations are difficult to come by and even if they are produced, protecting their gains is frequently difficult.[9]

The Voluntary Guidelines on the governance of tenure issued by FAO in 2012, contain that civil society organisations can work to raise awareness and assist people to enjoy and protect their tenure rights. They can promote the participation of the public in decision-making processes. In India, the number of NGOs active in the field of land reform as much less as compared to the total number of NGOs in India. However, same NGOs have gone farther than to simply raise awareness and assist people to enjoy and protect their tenure rights in forests. As per estimate by the Ekta Parishad, an NGO, about 1.5 lakh people have been driven away from their lands and forests.

The greatest work done in the field of land reform was by Vinoba Bhave through Bhoodan movement to realise the revolutionary dream of Mahatma Gandhi. Problem of securing land for India's landless peasants was looming large in the minds of Gandhiji and other leaders. But Vinoba

Bhave took on himself as a mission and toured throughout the country. About 93 million hectare land was donated in the country voluntary purely through non-violent approach for distribution among the landless farmers which is all time record in the world. A committee consisting of a chairman and members not exceeding nine administered the land. The Bhoodan Yagna Committee is a corporate body vested with power to distribute the land among the landless specially Scheduled Tribes and the Scheduled Castes. The Chairman was nominated by the state government. Thus, it was a really NGO while government reserving overall control on its functioning. Secondly, the movement leaders distanced themselves after their mission was completed while the present day NGOs do not leave their control over the good work done by them.

"Unfortunately, even after fifty years, 0.67 million hectares land could be distributed and 0.25 million hectare as on September, 2013 land is still to be distributed."[10]

A parcel of land doesn't become unfit for distribution among the landless person unless it is offered to him, and he has declined to receive the same.

Similarly, a good idea of land army was floated by the Chief Minister Mulayam Singh Yadav in 1991. The main purpose of land army was to bring 65,000 ha of *banjar* (unfit for cultivation) land under cultivation with an intention to distribute among the landless in the state of Uttar Pradesh. Such landless agricultural labourers were to be included in the land army, who were willing to do afforestation on such land after distribution or who were allottees of uncultivable Gram Sabha lands or common village land.

Thus, NGOs can work in various ways to help the land poor in the rural areas. There is no dearth of NGOs, which have been working for the urban poor to ensure them shelter or houses in the urban or peri-urban areas. But the land right along with the house or flat to the homeless in urban areas is a distant reality firstly because required excess land is not available in urban area and secondly, because the land if allotted, will be easily disposed of by such allottees. Therefore, their cases have not be dealt within this discussion. However, there is well accepted fact that the NGOs have to play positive role to assist the governments to improve the living conditions of the poor persons in rural areas in the World.

Movements and Struggles

Though Karl Marx saw the beginning of 'stagnant and vegetative life', specially through community ownership and despotism of the state, yet violent agitations and revolts have been taking place around the world beginning from the French Revolution, the Chinese Revolution and the present day Naxalites Violent Movement in India.

Indonesia

In Indonesia, there was a spectacular peasants' mobilisation in Asia created by the name of BTI and directed by the Indonesia Communist Party (PKI) after Aidit became its Secretary-General in 1953. In order to speed up the land reform programme in 1963, Aidit endorsed a 'unilateral action movement of the peasants. The tactic most frequently used was occupation of the lands to which landless peasants were entitled under the law. In August 1964, President Sukarno more or less endorsed the movement and during the second half of 1964, drastic steps were taken to accelerate the stagnant land reform programme.

A ferociously violent reaction came in October 1965. After an abortive coup, allegedly by leftist officer, a military regime came to power. Section of the army, together with the youth of mainly Islamic rural elites, assassinated more than half a million peasants and peasant leaders as well as other Communists or alleged Communists. After this massacre, the BTI became virtually non-existent and land reform stagnated.

Russia

In 1905, there was emergence of the Peasants' Union. Peasants demanded that they had a natural right to the land. The movement was crushed in 1906. But poor peasants could not support their livelihood as most of the lands were with Kulak, rich farmers. Four million people left their villages to look elsewhere for work. In 1917, Tsar regime ended. Local committees took over local power and seized of estate land by violent means, private property of estates was abolished.

In November 1917, Lenin proposed the Land Decree and obtained the massive support for his government. Land was distributed according to local needs among those who desired to work with their own hands. This legislation rallied the peasantry behind the Communist government during the crucial years of the Civil War (1917-21), and foreign intervention. Later on the Land Decree of November 1917, formed the base of the agrarian policy of the USSR regarding collectivisation of farming.

Success in China

During the 1920s, about half of the Chinese peasants were landless or semi-landless. After the success in long march in 1934-35, Mao ensured concrete benefits to the peasants and abandonment of unjust practices. After killing of 20 million people of the opposition, Mao Tse Tung did land distribution giving all tillers access to land and then gradual formation of co-operative and collectives in rural areas to support rapid industrialisation.

Japan

The Supreme Commander for the Allied Power pressurised the post-war Japanese government to abolish feudal type relations in the country-wise and avoided the risk of peasant rebellion. Between 1946 and 1949 almost all landed property in excess of one ha of irrigated paddy was distributed among the tillers, mainly through purchase and resale. Organised peasants played a crucial role in this process, together with the rich farmers and landlords, whose tight grip on rural social life, however, was broken.

Eastern Europe

The experiment of collective farming failed after the collapse of communism in Russia and Eastern Europe, the immediate problem was faced how to manage the large state farms or to disintegrate them by giving individual ownership to farmers whose lands were earlier acquired voluntarily or involuntarily, and who have been dependent on these farms for their livelihood. It is still debated whether the collective farms in principle is bad or whether the management of these farms was not up to the mark, and the farm managers became neo-landlords exploiting the farmers working in these farms as the erstwhile landlords used to exploit the workers or sharecroppers on their farms. "Still in Estonia, about 75 per cent of land remains under state ownership and is being used on the basis of short-term leases, which is inimical to the required structural transformation. In the Czech Republic, 800,000 hectares remain state-owned and privatisation is proceeding slowly. In the Slovak Republic, most of the co-operatives continue to operate as before and average almost 20,000 hectares. State ownership of the land of farmer in state farms is still an issue in Poland, where less than 10 per cent of land is private and 70 per cent of land under the holding company APA is leased out, with 1.1 million hectares remaining fallow. In Romania about 1.7 million hectares of high quality arable land continue to be administered under State farms. A 1999 law has removed the uncertainty about land ownership that had blocked progress, but remains to be fully implemented.

In Croatia the privatisation of the remaining collective structures is slow because of their size and the complexity of privatisation procedures. "Thus, due to administrative in decision and laxity, further agitations or violent protests are brewing up in the Eastern Europe.[11]

While the incidence of inefficiently managed state land is particularly large in Eastern European transition economies, it is by no means confined to these. While less prominent, state farms also remain a large part of the landscape in West Africa (*Gueye, Ouedraogo and Toulmin,* 2002) and northern Africa (Gharbi 2002).

Latin America

Latin America represents the continuing civil conflicts centering around land issues. "In Guatemala, communal lands were in effect expropriated in 1879 by a law giving proprietors three months to register land titles, after which the land would be declared abandoned. Most of the 'abandoned' land was then allocated to large coffee growers. Redistribution attempts in 1951-54 were reversed following a military coup in 1954, when virtually all the land that had been subject to land reform was returned to its previous owners and farms expropriated from foreigners were allocated in parcels averaging more than 3,000 hectares (Brockett 1984). Since then Guatemala has seen a repeated pattern of suppression and radicalisation of resistance. The peace accords require land distribution as a critical element of the post-conflict strategy, but progress thus far has been limited and has not always led to the expected improvements in productivity.

Small land holding was similarly appropriated in El Salvador. A 1856 decree stated that all communal land not at least two-thirds planted with coffee would be considered underutilised or idle and would revert to the state. Communal land tenure was abolished in 1888. Sporadic revolts and counter-measures followed. Areas with severe land pressure emerged as centers of the revolt of 1932, during which thousands of peasants were killed (Mason 1986). Guerillas promising land and other agricultural reform gained considerable support in rural areas and violence continued to escalate until 1979, when reform-minded officers engineered a coup and introduced land reform. Narrow eligibility rules sharply limited the number of beneficiaries of land reforms and more than a decade of civil war ensured. The 1992 peace accord mandates additional land reforms.

Colombia also demonstrates the perils of land-related tensions. Conflicts over land between tenants and large-scale farmers at the frontier escalated from isolated local attacks in the early 1920s to more co-ordinated tenant actions by the late 1920s. While the government considered various kinds of reform legislation during the 1930s, the law finally passed in 1936, vested rights in previously public lands with large landlords rather than with the tenants cultivating the land (Grusczynski and Jaramillo 2002). A series of tenant evictions followed, leading to a quarter of a century of violence (1940-65). Land reform legislation in 1961 and 1968 regularised previous land invasions, but did nothing to improve the operational distribution of landholdings and far fewer peasants benefitted from the reforms than had previously been evicted (*de Janvry and Saoulet* 1989; Zamosc 1989). Peasant land invasions intensified during the early 1970s, leading to the declaration of a state of emergency after 1974. The conflict has not yet been resolved."[12]

Africa

In many African countries, the stories of rebellions against occupation of the lands of the African especially indigeneous people by the foreigners, specially the whites is one of the struggle of the oppressed against the oppressor. In Zimbabwe, there was Shona uprising in 1896-97, against occupation of the ancestral lands by the British South Africa company. The European goods were looted and delivered to the spiritual leaders. If took control of two armed columns approaching to control the rebels. In the rebellion, about 400 whites, i.e., 10 per cent of the settler population were killed. After the 1996-97 rebellion as putdown, relative peace seems to have prevented between the white minority and the grab majority of black people, though more and more land was occupied by the whites.

After the Second World War, the white population doubled to about 1,50,000 and more Africans were expelled from their lands. There was rising discontent among the Africans, as many had served in the war yet on their return, they were again treated as second-class citizens. In 1951, there was a general strike for the first time against the whites. In 1960, many African countries gained independence following the example of the Mozambican liberation movement, the Zimbabwe African Nationalist Liberation Army (ZANLA) began a guerrilla war in Zimbabwe in 1972. "The Zimbabwe African National Union (ZANU) force used the Maoist model of a liberation war, in which combatants sought the support for the local population through political education, as well as mobilising and defending them, extending the 'liberated zones' (Lan, 1983, p. 11), but avoiding possible confrontation with the technically superior military forces of the state. In order to gain real acceptance among the peasants, the guerrillas could not rely on – and in fact had to replace – the traditional chiefs. The latter had lost much of their authority because they had been integrated into the colonialist system of indirect rule. Here, the spirited mediums were to play an important role, their influence being so important that it was officially recognised and honoured by the newly-elected Prime Minister, Robert Mugabe, at the independence celebrations in 1980."[13]

Recovery of much of the ancestral land by the peasantry, however, was postponed by the Lancaster House Agreement, which was signed by the liberation forces and the colonial government before independence became official. Although land reform was recognised as a key reason for social mobilisation, the agreement stipulated (under international pressure) that a radical redistribution would not take place during the decade following 1980. Recently, within the ruling party, Zimbabwe African National Union/Popular Front (ZANUPF), pressure has been building up to finally return much of the land to its original African inhabitants. After years of waiting, a first spectacular return of peasants to 'the land of their grand parents', organised by ex-guerrillas on white farms in the fertile Marondera area, was reported in The Economist (Anon., 1998 d) as a sign of growing 'peasants' revolt.

"Ghana's Cocoa Sector can illustrate how markets and the contracts used in them evolve dynamically in response to increasing land scarcity. In the early 19th century, a share contract (the abusa) emerged as a way to attract migrants who were interested in establishing plantations, but did not have enough capital to buy land. Migrants received land on which they established a Cocoa farm and gave one-third of the developed area or one-third of the yield back to the original owners of the land. By the 1960s, more than 95 per cent of the land was cultivated by migrants, who had acquired land in this way. With increasing land scarcity, the practice became less common, the terms of the contract shifted in favour of landowners to a 50 per cent share contract (*the abunu*) and the increasing formalisation of contracts ensued. Contracts are not signed in front of witnesses, who receive a fee and are perceived as more secure than within-family access to land, where elders can behave opportunistically or even disinherit their family members. Agro-industry has also developed similarly structured outgrower arrangements with share tenants."[14]

Thus, recognition of sharecropping by government will help to reduce conflicts. Instead of forcing the landowners and tenants or sharecroppers into informality, something that will both increase the likelihood of them being disputed in the future and reduce the price that the sellers will be able to obtain, government should take appropriate steps to recognise informal transactions.

Struggle in India

The struggle for land reform in India started with the advent of the British rule. They introduced various middlemen to collect land revenue from the tenants like permanent settlement, Malguzari settlement, Jagirdari system, Ryotwari system, and Mahalwari system for assessing and collecting land revenues making them authority over land. The middlemen known as *zamindars* realised as much as four times the amount they paid to the Government as land revenue. Earlier, in fourty years (1842-1882), one quarter of land had changed hands due to default in payment of revenue. Approximately, 41 per cent of lands auctioned and transferred to families whose principal occupation was money-lending, service and law. In addition, residence of majority of the buyers was urban. Thus, the land to the tiller was gradually lost and land became a commodity. Cultivators had to pay as much as 25 per cent towards government demand, cesses and *malikana* of the *taluqdar* or *zamindar* and the village expenses. This included rupee one out of Rs 25 a year as payment to meet the *zamindar*. Such types of exploitative additions were many. They kept the recalcitrant tenants, the *zamindar* confined and tortured in dreaded dark room (*andheria kotha*). As a result, cultivation was abandoned being unprofitable and the peasants chose to starvation.

There were following famous rebellions in India but could not live long or bear fruits for long;

"*Chuar* armed Uprising in 1799

In 1799, famine and enhanced land revenue forced the Chuar aboriginal tribesmen of Midnapur to rise in arms against the British. The British insultingly called the tribal and oppressed people of Midnapur, Bankura and Jangal Mahal as Chuars, a very derogatory term which in fact had been taken from Cho-Chuhar, meaning thieves and nasty persons who eat mice.

The Kol Uprising (1831-1832)

The Kols of Singhbhum in the Chhotanagpur area enjoyed autonomy under their chiefs. They resented the transfer of land from Kol headmen (Mundas) to outsiders.

The Santhal Rebellion (1855-57)

The Santhal rebellion started in 1855 under the leadership of Sidhu and Kanhu against the oppression of police, atrocities of landlords and moneylenders, ill-treatment of small farmers by land revenue officials in the area of Rajmahal hills. Though, they gave a heroic fight to the British government, the rebellion was crushed in an unequal battle.

Pagal Panthi Movement (1825-1833)

Pagal Panthis, is semi-religiious sect formed by Karam Shah. In 1833, in region of Northern Mymensingh,Tipu, the son of Kwam Shah took up peasants cause against the oppression of *zamindars*, who realised illegal cesses from the peasants. After Tipu Shah, Janku Pathor and Dobraj Pathor took the leadership of the Pagals and organised another resistance movement against *zamindari* oppression.

Rising of the Ramosis

The Ramosis of Maharashtra were the lower ranks of police in Maratha administration. After the fall of the Maratha kingdom, as a result of Anglo-Maratha war, they were forced to go back to their agricultural land in former territories of the Peshwa for their livelihood. But they had to pay heavy land assessment and revenue putting them to great distress. Chittur Singh revolted in Satara in 1822 to protest against atrocities over the cultivators. Ramosis under this banner played a prominent part in creating disturbance and destroying forts. In 1825, chronic scarcity in

Deccan further encouraged them to break out into a revolt under the leadership of Umaji Naik and his associate, Bapu Trimbakji Sawant, in 1826. Ultimately, the Colonial government condoned their crimes, gave them land grants and recruited them as hill police.

The Poligars Uprising

The Poligars of Dindigul and Malabar took up arms against the British land revenue system during 1801 to 1805. The Poligars of the Ceded districts and North Arcot revolted against the policy of company. These sporadic risings continued in Madras Presidency up to 1856."[15]

Tebhaga Movement: This movement demanded two-third of share of crop in North Bengal in West Bengal before independence. As a result, the sharecroppers as *bargadars* received more shares of crops later on.

There was non-violent movement (*Satyagrah*) at Champaran in Bihar, where the cultivators were compelled to cultivate indigo at the cost of their fertile agricultural land and livelihood. This followed many more non-violent movements like Khera and Bardoli *Satyagrah*. Gandhiji adivsed to boycott land of *zamindars* for cultivation, who need excess land. However, working from the Behta Ashram of Gandhiji, Swami Sahajananda Saraswati took a leading role in the creation of a central organisation, the All India Kisan Sabha (AIKS) in 1936. One of its demands was the abolition of the *zamindari* system of feudal landownership. The movement slowed down but again re-appeared as a reaction to the 1943 famine in Bengal. The movement demanded that two-thirds of the crops be remitted to the cultivator, as recommended but not implemented by the 1940 Land Revenue Commission. Though, the movement was suppressed but it laid the foundation of the Communists in Bengal and gave rise to the violent Naxalite movement in the same area Naxalbari North Bengal of West Bengal in the year 1967. A comprehensive land policy has evolved around following five points:

(a) Abolition of intermediaries and bring tenants in direct contact with the government;

(b) Tenancy reforms with a view to providing security to actual tillers of land against eviction;

(c) Redistribution of land by imposition of ceiling on agricultural holdings;

(d) Updation of land records.

Unfortunately, after two decades of independence, the enthusiasm has gone down everyone in bureaucracy and politics has been singing chorus that land reforms, have been completed. However, because of growing tensions, contradiction and violent conflicts by Naxalites, the future state and Union governments will have to deal with the issue of land reforms with more vigour and enthusiasm to keep India stable.

Conclusion

"Marxists have a tendency to equate sharecropping tenancy with a particular (feudal) mode of production, thus ignoring how in the real world, the same institution adapts itself to the development of the forces of production. All this suggests that, while institutions, property structure and production relations seriously circumscribe the development of technology, one must not forget that overtime the farmer get shaped in important ways by the material base itself. That some Marxists need to be reminded of this is somewhat ironic, since it is usually a part of Marxist orthodoxy to assign "primacy" to the material base. Of course, in my judgment, the "primacy thesis" is much too narrow and it overlooks the two-way feedback process between "forces of production" and "relations of productions" in the laws of motion of history."[16]

Whatever the Marxian economists say, the fact is that without the involvement of peasants in revolutions, no revolution can be worthwhile except in the most developed countries which are in minority in number and in population. Following Marx, there were successful peasants' revolutions in China, Cuba and Russia with little variation as per place and time which keeps the system revitalised. Even the manufacturing processes in this globalisation era and information technology environment have shifted in underdeveloped and develpoing countries away from the headquarters of the multinationals and transnational corporations, and are run by the invisible owners or employers. It will be difficult to catch them and punish them. They have placed their manufacturing units in such a fashion that closing their factories on one or two countries will not materially affect them, and they will be able to absorb the shock of the revolutions. Therefore, it will be futile to wait for the ideal conditions to be created for blood revolution within the parameters laid down by the great Karl Marx. By that time, millions of poor farmers will die due to starvation and deprivation. The peasants in fact have been accepting compromise formulae during their agitations, protests or revolts. They have always been willing to give them fair chance. Elites generally didn't act in an open manner. Elite intransigence, more than anything else, was the reason that peasants' organisations finally took a revolutionary stand, demanding the radical overthrow of the system as a whole. In the process, millions of people were killed on both sides. It is a fact that right is realised only through struggle. None offers right as a platter. Therefore, peasants should not lose their revolutionary spirit. The fear of revolution or violent conflict only keeps the modern systems of governance in proper action. The government employees including police are concerned with their security of job keeping the law and order of the society in balance. Once law and order is destabilised, everyone in the government becomes conscious and active. Small and prolonged conflicts in the field of land reform will always pay provided they keep their focus intact. The peasants organisations should not indulge in headless violence just to revenge the violence inflicted on them by the security forces as that will detract them from their aim and mission which is the criticism against Naxalite violence in India and many civil wars in Africa and in Latin American countries.

Now-a-days, state has so much of sophisticated power of killing that the agitations and revolts will not be able to stand against their might. The political executives use the inherent hatred or jealousy in one group of persons in security forces against the common people of different regions. Therefore, the best way is to attempt to acquire political power through violent or non-violent means and then implement land reforms in all their forms and aspects to reach their benefits to the grassroots mass of the peasants whether they participated in the protests/conflicts or not. After assuming presidency of South Africa, Nelson Mandela, the greatest leader of 21st century recognised that the country could not prosper without ensuring that land rights were broadly distributed.

In the present day set-up of democratic governments, there is ample scope to overthrow the elected government by the peasants, who generally constitute the majority. But the political parties or vested interest groups divide them on the basis of caste, creed, colour, religion etc. As a result, they are not able even to put their voice eloquently before their own government. Even their own peasants' leaders dance on the old tune after being inducted in government. Secondly, neither the political executives nor the civil servants want to disturb the status quo though the apparent peace is the peace of the burial ground and is just waiting for an ignition to take the five-star creation of globalisation into its flames. For example, after the abolition of slavery in Africa, Latin America, UK and USA, it was promised even by the then USA President that land relations between the slaves and landowners will be redefined but it was not done. The peasants slaves in countrics like Mauritius, Caribbean Islands, etc., slowly and gradually won over their just rights on land through hard and protracted struggles over long period which is still continuing.

It is always been a great stimulus for the common peasant when any official working against their interest and in connivance with the landowners was punished by the peasants singularly so as to make an example for other officers to deter them from such blatant illegal acts. Similarly, the gherao or mild beating and even seizure of properties of the corrupt officials by the women group has demonstrated a deterrent action against the corrupt officials, who have gone all the way to work against the interests of the poor and landless.

The peace and prosperity-based on equity and justice can only sustain for long time. In substance, the peasants should be well-united for their cause and should indulge in sustained struggle to realise their rights and further their interests. However, they should be open for any good gesture or action from any corner whatsoever including from government's end to promote their right and welfare.

It is sometimes experienced that low scale conflict situation keeping the mission in front always pays as it keeps the land reform machinery on toes and their persons-in-authority are scared to take decisions against the interests of the poor peasants.

However, in the process the innocent personnel of security forces and civilians are killed in exchange of fire from both sides.

References

1. Myrdel, G., "*Rich and the Poor*", Harper and Brothers Publishers, New York-16, 1966, p. 71.
2. Hobbes, *Leviathen*, p. 127.
3. Agrawal, P.K., *Motivation and Indian Bureaucracy*, M.D. Publication Pvt. Ltd., New Delhi, p. 75, 1995.

4. Saxena, K.B., *Land Reforms in India* by Dr P.K. Agrawal, M.D. Publications Pvt. Ltd., New Delhi, p. 218.
5. Deininger, Klaus, *Negotiated Land Reform as one way of Land Access: Experiences from Colombia, Brazil and South Africa, in Access to Land, Rural Poverty and Public Action*, Janvry, Gordillo, Platteau and Sadoulet, p. 341, Oxford University Press 2001.
6. Ghimire, Krishna B., *Land Reform and Peasant Livelihood*, ITDG Publishing London, p. 143, 2001.
7. *Ibid.,* 6, p. 182.
8. *Ibid.,* 6, pp. 150-151.
9. *Ibid.,* 6, pp. 5-7.
10. *Source: Department of Land Resources, Ministry of Rural Development*, Government of India, Nirman Bhawan Annexe, New Delhi.
11. Deininger, Klaus, *Land Policies for Growth and Poverty Reduction.* The World Bank and Oxford University Press, p. 172, 2003.
12. *Ibid.,* 11, p. 158.
13. Huizer, Geril, *Peasant Mobilisation for Land Reforms*, published in Land Reform and Peasant Livelihoods, Ghimiri Krishna, B. 184.
14. *Ibid.,* 11: p. 105.
15. Internet: Google, *Land Reforms in India – struggles –* dated 18.01.2014.
16. Bardhan, Pranab K., *Land, Labours and Rural Poverty*, Oxford University Press, New Delhi, p. 2, 1984.

10

Legal Empowerment and Legal Aid

"Democracy and rule of law are the first means invented by man for correcting government, for securing that it subserved the interests of the individual. Despite what the Marxists continue to claim, the state will never wither away as long as the human race subsists".[1]

When one dives into the intricacies of land reform, one wonders whether land reform is a field exclusively earmarked for a real estate lawyer or for a peasant revolutionary.

It is presumed that law of the land is known by each and every citizen of a country. But the fact revealed is otherwise. Even the trained revolutionary is not aware of the niceties of land laws applicable to his area of action. Even the constitutional provisions are not well-known by citizens. Every constitution guarantees equitable distribution of resources among its citizens. The jurists like Roscoe Pound also talks of social engineering as end of law. Article 55(a) of the Charter for the United Nations, which binds most of the nations of the world as member countries exhorts "higher standards of living, full employment and conditions of social progress and development."

Guiding Principles of Responsible Tenure Governance under Article 3A (3.4) provides that "states should provide access to justice to deal with infringements of legitimate tenure rights. They should provide effective and accessible means to everyone, through judicial authorities or other approaches, to resolve disputes over tenure rights and to provide affordable and prompt enforcement of outcomes. States should provide prompt, just compensation where tenure rights are taken for public purpose."

Let us examine how the constitutions being ground norms of countries have addressed the international mandates for ensuring livelihood and development of the people through their respective judicial or legal systems.

Article 39(b) and (c) of Constitution of India leads the wandwagon by containing in Article 39(c) that the operation of the economic system does not result in the concentration of wealth and means of production to the common good; Even many communist countries are not having such an egalitarian provisions in their constitutions. Right to property has been removed as a fundamental right having no protection of High Courts or the Supreme Court of India. Article 21 of the Constitution of India contains the provisions or protection for livelihood and is now a well-established principle in India. There is a step forward. All the land reform related statutes have the protection or shelter or umbrella of the Schedule IX of the Constitution of India and cannot be challenged on the ground that any of it violates the fundamental right of a citizen of India.

"In China, Article 19 of the Constitution of People's Republic of China declares that all citizens have the right to work. Thus, state accepts its responsibility for providing work and for improving conditions of work. Article 100 says that citizens of China must uphold discipline at work. As per Constitution of China, the aim of the judiciary in China is to give to the citizens of China, speedy and cheaper justice.

The Constitution of Japan guarantees the fundamental human rights to the people, which shall be eternal and inviolate rights. The enjoyment of the freedoms and rights guaranteed to the people by the Constitution shall be maintained by the eternal vigilance of the people and the people shall refrain from any abuse of these freedoms and rights and shall always be responsible for utilising them for public welfare. Social equality is guaranteed by the abolition of special privileges. A large measure of local autonomy is given so that by way of decentralisation, democratic institutors may take roots in the country.

The Constitution of erstwhile Burma, which came into force in 1948, was abrogated in 1962, and at present the country is being governed by decrees issued by the government. In such a situation, it depends on the good sense of the dictator. However, the state is to direct its policy towards exploitation of all natural resources by itself or local bodies or by people's co-operative organisations.

In Sri Lanka, Parliament has power to make laws for the peace, order and good government of erstwhile Ceylon. There is no prohibition or restriction on free exercise of any religion. Local governments up to the village level are autonomous under the Central government. However, sovereignty of the people is inalienable.

The Constitution of Pakistan (1956), guaranteed certain fundamental rights to the people of Pakistan like right to equality, protection against retrospective offences etc. The Constitution of 1962, and of 1973 provided principle of law making. The policy of law making in Pakistan, apart confirming to Islamic principles, is based on good principles of polity like the fundament rights in India. It even provides right to work and employment. The Constitution of Bangladesh is based on high ideals of nationalism, socialism and democracy. It has fundamental rights and basic principles like the Indian Constitution."[2]

The erstwhile Russian Constitution 1977 also ensures that enjoyment by citizens of their rights and freedoms shall not be to the detriment of the interests of society and state or infringe the rights of other citizens. Thus, the purpose of almost every constitution of the country provides for common good and thus ensures social justice. Economic growth without social justice is inhuman. Marx has challenged that political equality can co-exist with socio-economic inequality.

Thus, the poor people are quite empowered but they are firstly not aware of their basic and constitutional rights and secondly, they don't have due legal resources to safeguard their rights. Thirdly, judiciary is an apparatus to strike a balance between individual freedoms with community interest, but the judiciary is inclined to listen to the chorus of high profile lawyers, who are controlled by people with heavy purse. However, legal education and assistance have been very helpful to offer practical solutions for resolving land problems and securing land right for rural poor across the world. The legal education and legal assistance through para legal has changed the whole gamut of land reforms. Further, they can be provided little help from filling up complaints to the arguments on their behalf before the appropriate revenue court. It has done wonders in the states of Andhra Pradesh and Odisha in India specially solutions to people's land problems through mass media like television.

NGOs and grassroots organisations working to fight rural poverty commonly encounter the power of landlords and in some cases they help peasants and other marginalised rural groups to file suits against landlords. But due to lack of effective, low-cost rural legal services, the costs of taking landowners to court are enormous for NGOs, even if the ruling were in favour of the rural poor. The legal system may also be prone to corruption. Even though the law states, that tenants and sharecroppers can appeal in writing in cases where wrong-doing has occurred, this is an extremely weak form of legal resources and the probability of waiting months before any action is taken. Even where recourse is possible, most peasants refrain from using it, given the traditional social authority of landowner and fear of apprisal. It was observed in state of West Bengal in India that hardly two or three landowner had given written receipts for having received their share of produce from the sharecroppers, in spite of clear provision in the West Bengal Land Reforms Act, 1955 (India), that the landowner will give receipt for share of produce of crops from the sharecropper even during thirty years of poor sharecropper's regime of Left Front Government in West Bengal. In the same way, hardly few courts in very few cases have held that the sharecropper has the possession of the land and has been cultivating the land in dispute and therefore, he will be declared as sharecroppers. On the other hand, the Courts take proactive action against the poor sharecroppers and the *pattadars* (Government lessees) and evict them from the possession when the government declares them sharecroppers or *pattadars* pending the decision of appropriate court or quasi-judicial authority whether the land has vested to the government or not.

The Courts always take technical stand-based on records of rights without going through the status of possession in the field which is very difficult to prove by the sharecropper or *pattadar* in front of battery of high profile lawyers on the side of the wealthy landowner, who can well-afford their fees.

"The cases from Bangladesh and the Philippines show that legal aid has been critical to the struggle of landless peasants for land. In these two countries, even though legal assistance did not enable the peasants to break the power of landowners, it did help to restraint the latter in some cases. Despite the fact that landowning classes were able to pay top price for legal advice, they could not completely ignore the interests of their tenants, the local landless peasants or public opinion. Legal proceedings often went together with complex negotiations with the landless, their representatives or opposing lawyers."[3]

Bangladesh is leader in the field of NGOs providing legal aid to the land poor and spearheading movement to legally empower the landless, government lease or *patta* holders and the sharecroppers. They have even led the land reform movement in Bangladesh and compelled the government to implement the land reforms. BLAST, one of Bangladesh's largest voluntary legal aid organisations, provides legal assistance for the marginalised population. It employed 390 lawyers and handled 1037 cases. The GSS provides legal assistance in disputes arising from violence against women, the rights of peasants to *khas* land. It covers 25 per cent of legal costs, administrative and financial services for members and non-member. GSS also provides legal education *inter alia* in respect of land dispute.

The ALRD, an organisation concerned with the co-ordination of NGO activities on land reform, also includes a legal aid programme as part of its activities. The organisation recognises the importance of legal awareness raising and services in a context where over 80 per cent of rural litigation has to do with land disputes, especially false title. Thus, some legal aid is available to peasants and other marginalised rural groups seeking access to land or better livelihood possibilities.

In the Philippines, peasants, NGOs and legal aid groups have denounced the continuous harassment of beneficiaries by landowners, who have used legal loopholes and resorted to outright violence, often with the aid of paramilitary forces, to evict tenants. Other miscarriages of justice have involved the issuing of false claims, showing down or cancelling the issuance of legal land titles, multiple titling of the same plot and the rapid and sometimes illegal conversion of agricultural lands to industrial or commercial plots. Over the years, a number of NGOs, farmers' groups and legal organisations have provided legal assistance to peasants and rural workers during various conflicts with landowners and employers. SALAG, has provided not only legal assistance, but also initiated long-term awareness-building and training programmes on land questions.

Similar work is undertaken by the KAISAHAN and the Legal Resources Centre. Local and provincial groups also provide legal assistance to peasants; one such group is Center for Alternate Rural Technology (CART).

Availability of Legal Services

During the late 1980s, the International Commission of Jurists (ICJ), an international association of independent lawyers, held a series of seminars in South Asia, South East Asia and Latin America, focussing on the role of lawyers and legal services for the poor in rural areas. The term 'legal services' was preferred to legal aid, as it encompasses training of para legal, the production of simplified legal materials and information dissemination, counselling, mediation and negotiation.

"All seminars pointed to the poor provision of legal services in rural areas. In Peru and Colombia, for example, government legal services are concentrated in urban areas, making it difficult for the rural poor to access them. A second problem, confronted by indigenous peoples (often a significant proportion of rural populations), who have lost customary lands, was a feeling of alienation as a result of linguistic and cultural differences. This often leads to their marginalisation in the few legal aid programmes that do exist (Garcia-Sayan, 1987). The South and South-East Asian seminars brought out the social and geographical distance separating most lawyers from peasant issues, which may lead them to be viewed with suspicion rather than as potential allies in defending local interests. In all regions, however, the importance of having peasant organisations, NGOs, church groups and other local organisations incorporate legal services into their agenda was highlighted.

Cameroon discusses women's land rights on both radio and television. The Youth Association of the Ziquinchor Region in Senegal translates laws and relevant documents from French into local languages and disseminates this information via seminars and workshops. The Society for Participatory Research in Asia (based in India) transcribes relevant land laws into accessible languages for rural legal activists and leaders. Casa Campesina in Peru holds radio and television discussions on legal aspects of agrarian questions."[3]

"Given the high cost of professional legal services, the training and use of paralegals has grown in recent years. For many NGOs, this has been a way to avoid costly outside professional help, yet still provide marginalised rural groups with some legal assistance. Paralegals are generally local actors (community leaders, social workers, teachers, law students, development workers, etc.) who receive training and education on legal question and act as assistants to lawyers in locating evidence and other information that might be necessary to defend their case. They may also conduct research on certain cases and provide referrals to lawyers where necessary. Furthermore, they often play a wider social role, mediating situations of conflict, mobilising communities and assisting in the establishment of people's organisations (Ravindran, 1988. p. 7). Their role in society can potentially encompass far more than a lawyer's and because they come from local areas they are often deemed more credible than outsiders. Because they may be more aware of customary law and can thus use it where applicable, their approach may be more flexible.

Lawyers may play a central role in training paralegals, however, as many social workers, academics (sociologists, psychologists, etc.) and others (ICJ, 1997). Paralegals are often hired by local organisations or are requested to assist on a voluntary basis, although the latter appears to be rare.

The fact that the pay is less and rewards in terms of other material and social gains fewer, may dissuade lawyers from providing legal services to the rural poor. Dias, in his discussion of obstacles facing 'law as a resource for the poor' in South-East Asia, points to the desire of lawyers to monopolise information and knowledge on legal matters (Dias, 1987, pp. 27-42). In other words, they may fear losing their professional hegemony of knowledge about land legislation. According to this specialist, rural communities and individuals require lawyers to impart a degree of information and skills.

However, lawyers do sometimes get involved in local legal service programmes. A noteworthy case is the Legal Resource Foundation (LRF) in Zimbabwe, a non-profit organisation whose board of trustees includes a former Chief Justice, a Supreme Court Judge, as well as other prominent lawyers (Coltart, 1993). The foundation's lawyers actively train paralegals, provide legal advice, carry out research and litigate in public interest cases through Legal Project Centre set up in rural areas. In order to overcome resistance by lawyers, who might perceive the group's activities as potential competition, the LRF formulates and implements its programmes in close collaboration with the Law Society of Zimbabwe (Coltart, 1993).

Similarly, the Legal Resources Centre (LRC) is one of eight legal institutions in South Africa helping the urban and rural poor in land restitution cases. It represents poor black communities in land conflicts, contending land claims in protected areas and the provision of formal titles. It also provides legal education and training on subjects including acquisition of land, subsidies for land purchase and loan repayment (LRC, 1995). But demands for legal services are much greater than LRC, and other organisations are able to offer (personal communication with a lawyer working for LRC, October 1997); significant conflicts over land-related issues and land reform persists in the country."[4]

Legal Aid: Case Study of India

The Supreme Court of India in an epoch making judgement[5] in 1978, held that it is the duty of the State to provide legal aid to the poor. In similar vein, the Supreme Court of India has been protecting the rights of the landless, government lessees, poor sharecroppers and other beneficiaries of land reform measures as custodian of the Constitution and the protector of interests of the poorest in India. The Supreme Court has hardly held any ceiling law as *ultravires* of the Constitution. It has consistently upheld that the umbrella of the Schedule IX to many of the land reform legislations promulgated by States is effective, non-penetrating and sacred to the basic spirit of the Constitution.

But the Courts below are not working with that jealous and missionary spirit having eye on the last man in the society. The high volatile and eloquent lawyers confuse them with the traditional concept of private property being there for centuries in statute books of every country. To guard against such moves to the poor and illiterate cultivators, India has the Legal Services Authorities Act, 1987 in place to provide free and competent legal services to the weaker sections of the society to ensure that opportunities for securing justice are not denied to any citizen by reason of economic or other disparities and to organise *Lok Adalat* to secure that the operation of the legal system promotes justice on the basis of equal opportunity. The Lok Adalat will be guided by the legal principles and the principles of justice, equity and fair play.

The Act has a provision to constitute a National Legal Services Authorities to guide the States' Legal Service Authorities. The State government in turn has to constitute the District Authority with District Judge as its Chairman. The State and District Authorities will organise Lok Adalats. The Lok Adalats so organised will have judicial officers and other members possessing such qualifications and experience as may be prescribed by State government. They have jurisdiction to determine and arrive at a compromise or settlement between the parties to a dispute in respect of any matter falling within the jurisdiction of any Civil Court or revenue Court or any tribunal constituted under any law for the time being in force in the area for which the Lok Adalat is organised.

The Lok Adalat has brought legal consciousness among the rural poor. The legal methods of alternative dispute settlement like mediation, reconciliation and arbitration have gone down on the doorstep of the litigant which is the ultimate aim of any ideal judicial system in the world. These courts have overcome that procedural dilemma and delays which mar modern judicial courts specially pressure of reputed lawyers. These courts settle larger number of cases in one day than are disposed in all courts taken together in the District Court in a month. These are called open Courts or public Courts. There is no appeal against the orders of Lok Adalats.

Further, there is a provision of institution of *Nyaya Panchayat* (Judicial Panchayat) at the block or police station level in few states or provinces in India which entertain and dispose of petty nature like demarcation of lands, settlement of disputes regarding possession, etc., apart from petty civil and criminal matters. In these bodies, local elected or nominated people conversant with basic legal provisions sit who also have local knowledge of every local incident or offence or dispute either indirectly or directly. Therefore, they cannot be misguided by the flavouring arguments couched in legal language though based on false facts and thereby justice is likely to flow from their delivery in the form of orders or judgements of Courts or authorities. The poor marginal farmers or sharecropper cannot afford any lawyer to defend his just cause or right nor is he able to put across his own fact of possession over the parcel of land. Sometimes, he even doesn't have the proper certified copy of his record-of-rights of land possessed. As a result, either *ex-parte* order is passed against him or case is decreed against him.

The landowner goes to the local police to evict the poor sharecropper from the land and police is too happy to oblige him in lieu of bribery. In large cases, the landowners similarly get favourable orders from High Court and then go for contempt against the District Police Chief or District Collector head of revenue department, who ultimately help the landowner due to fear of losing their job or being punished for contempt by the superior court. The political executives despite their good intention cannot deter the revenue or police officer from helping the landowner.

The only way is that the farmers' organisation stages a violent clash with the police force which they will not be able to sustain for a long time nor police force will be able to put the landowner in possession time and again. Thus, possession is a riddle in law which is more solved by force than by dry provisions of law. But before getting protection of law for possession, the poor cultivator atleast should know the basic dimensions of his possession for cultivation.

Luckily in few states like West Bengal, Lawyers are debarred from appearing before the revenue courts but it cannot be sustained for long because lawyer's lobby is very strong everywhere.

The campaign of legal education in the field of land laws requires lot of fillip in India. As per an estimate, "Land related conflicts account for two-thirds of all pending court cases, while part of these are related to land ceiling legislation. Nearly 20 lakhs acres land is tied up in disputes, especially at the local level which are more mundane but never get resolved because the courts are over loaded. Options to settle out of are either not known or not available, or where court orders are not being implemented because those affected, often tribals, are ignorant about the enforcement mechanism available. A number of states, including Gujarat, Karnataka and Andhra Pradesh have embarked on programmes to make legal assistance available on a number of fronts such as:

1. Systematic identification and pursuit of pending land cases through law students.
2. Courses to familiarise members of self-help or other community groups with key land related legislation, and
3. Conduct of a systematic inventory of pending land issues to identify and subsequently resolve all land related problems in a locality.

"In tribal areas, the latter will include not only conflicts between individuals but also those relating to lack of regularisation and alienation of tribal lands, forest boundary issues and scrutiny of cases under land transfer regulations that have not been enforced. These efforts have elicited a very positive response."[6] Similar facility is also available for urban land disputes as all these organisations run for rural as well as urban areas. In fact, people in peri-urban areas and urban areas avail the legal services and legal aid more easily and more frequently because of all these offices have their main offices in urban areas, and prefer to hold Lok Adalat in urban areas and secondly because urban people take more fancy to work for the land poor of rural areas rather than the elite of rural areas because poverty has become the part of their life and they have developed inertia and even indifference towards it. But the strong, new, local leadership can change the situation as people rally behind it as opposed to the traditional elites.

Tribunalisation of Land Related Cases

To tackle laws' delay and to provide export input into the decision-making delays one of the alternatives is to establish land tribunals to settle land disputes. There is a tremendous growth of tribunals and quasi-judicial bodies in view of increasing span of administration and its complexities all over the world including India, USA and UK. For land matters to be correctly and expeditiously disposed of, it is essential that the courts or tribunals should engage themselves in field enquiries for fact finding and should adopt summary trials without giving more than three adjournments even without representation by a lawyer. It is expected that the few non-official members on the bench of tribunal will have practical experience of field situation like the jury system in USA. Thus, the system of tribunal combines the east and west system of judicial process. It will also do away with the hegemony of revenue department or land department and bureaucracy, who help the land owning classes and capitalists except few glaring exceptions.

"The main arguments in favour of this system are that:

(a) The ordinary courts are already overburdened with work;

(b) Their procedure is technical and costs are prohibitive;

(c) Questions arising out of a social land reform or industrial legislation are better decided by persons, who have an intimate and specialised knowledge of the working of land reform statutes."[7]

A body which decides on controversies or the rights of parties is called 'a tribunal' when it possesses some but not all the trappings of a court. The word tribunal is wider than Court. All courts are tribunal but all tribunals are not courts. Tribunals have been set up in many countries.

The tribunals consists of members three or more than three. Chairman is generally a knowledgeable person in law but he needs not be necessarily a man from judiciary. A man from judiciary generally puts his previous practice of long procedure of courts which is being dispensed with. This has been experienced as the main problem of functioning of consumer courts throughout the world especially in India. Therefore, the tribunals should have majority of non-official members, and cases should be decided with majority but Chairman has to be necessarily there unless he nominates to some other member or some other member is appointed as officiating Chairman by the concerned department of the government. This may not be supported by the highest court, yet it should be there in the interest of expeditious justice. There may be mistakes of law but there will not be blunders with regard to facts of the case or matter. Appreciation of facts or ground position is more important than delving into law.

The land tribunals may have following main characteristics:

(i) The land tribunals may be constituted at the district level or even at lower level. The appeal may be to the High Court just below the apex court of the country.

(ii) The land tribunals may consist of one chairman, one judicial officer and two or more non-official members.
One of the members should be from the indigenous community or backward caste or class, an allottee of government vested land, agricultural landless labourers or sharecroppers.

(iii) The pleaders may be debarred from appearing in the tribunal. However, if the poor party like the allottee of vested land or sharecroppers has a lawyer on his side, other party should have option to have a lawyer on his side to represent his case.

(iv) The selection should be transparent and on objective considerations.

(v) The tribunals should be empowered to take evidence in the field and get the same signed and authenticated by them there only.

The procedure to be adopted by these Tribunals should be simple. Individual notices are first to be served to the landowner and other persons interested. A public notice has also to be issued. Then the applicant and other claimants and opposite parties are called upon to appear before the tribunal. Simultaneously, secretary of the tribunal collects the official records and record-of-rights of the disputed property. The statements are briefly noted. The parties can submit written arguments on affidavits even without appearing before the tribunal. Then the tribunal deliberates the matter. If the tribunal fees it necessary, they may visit the site in the village or in urban areas and then a judgment be delivered after completion of enquiries.

In case of *benami* transaction, tribunal has to be more arduous. However, there is now the reality that in land matters, tribunals should invariably have specialist and should expeditiously dispose of land related disputes.

Conclusion

It is criminal that in a change of title and its registration, one has to pass through 60 to 70 procedures in few African and Latin American countries. It is high time that the land recording and correcting system is simplified and expedited. In Mexico, new 42 land courts and one appeal court were created to clear the huge backlog of cases. In dealing with conflicts in a systematic manner, these courts were explicitly instructed to seek settlement out of court and special mechanisms were put in place to ensure accessibility by the poor. Since, small farmers who had been under the tutelage of local authorities for a long period of time would still find it difficult to ascertain their rights especially to correct past irregularities—a special institution, the **Procuraduria Agraria**, was created to provide legal assistance to land holders and represent them in court dealings, perform an Ombudsman function and supervise the implementation of the regularisation pnrogramme.

To avoid the land matters away from the rigmarole of regular civil courts, many statutes bar the jurisdiction of civil courts in land matters. As these are the special statutes, these will prevail over the general law that civil court will have jurisdiction regarding matters of possession and title etc. These basic law provisions are essential to be included in land reforms laws or regulations before these can be effective for the poor man. If the foregoing precautions are not taken in the very text of the statutes, these will be hijacked by the resourceful and powerful land owners and their associates in legal fraternity, bureaucracy and in police. As it is very difficult to change the present law and its implementation-oriented towards private property, it is essential that landless groups and peasant organisations should have their own band of lawyers devoted to the cause of the land poor. For that purpose, a legal curriculum more sensitive to agrarian problems, land laws and rural poverty could help increase future lawyers' awareness of land disputes and perhaps increase their support of land reform measures. Otherwise, lawyers will take a brief from a peasant and will meekly surrender before the judge in favour of elite lawyers from the side of the landlord. The poor farmer will come to know when the damage will become irreparable.

Raising the awareness of school teachers, agricultural extension workers, NGO activists and so forth about land laws and reform initiatives could produce a valuable local pool of paralegals, as these actors constantly interact with the landless and marginalised rural population.

Efforts to raise rural people's consciousness through literacy classes, community training programmes and legal education could also yield results. Last but not the least, if the lawyers on behalf of the poor work against their clients, they should be hauled up by their professional bodies like Bar Council. The apex courts should not be class consciousness while deciding matters coming in appeal before them on some technical ground or the other to make them ineffective. If the land poor do not get due justice from the courts, their next stage of revolution will be directed towards them. The courts should see that justice is not only done, but it should also be seen to be done to the majority of people in a democracy.

References

1. Agrawal, P.K., *Land Reforms in India*, M.D. Publication, New Delhi, p. 232.
2. Agrawal, P.K., *Legal Reforms for Sustainable Development*' in 'Eye on Development' ed. Das, Chandreyee and Ghosh Dipankar, Sampark, p. 34, Kalindi Housing Scheme, Kolkata-89, pp. 58-59, 2006.
3. Ghimire, Krishna B., *Peasants' Pursuit of Outside Alliances and Legal Support in the Process of Land Reforms in Land Reform and Peasant Livelihoods* ed. Krishna B. Ghimiri, ITDC Publishing London, 2001, pp. 161-162.
4. *Ibid.,* 3, pp. 140-142.

5. *Madhav H. Rao Hoskt* vs. *State of Maharashtra*, AIR 1978, Supreme Court, p. 1548.
6. World Bank: Report No. 38298-IN-India: *Land Policies for Growth and Poverty Reduction*, pp. 43-44, 2007.
7. Kesari, U.P.D., *Lectures on Administrative Law*, Central Law Agency, University Road, Allahabad, p. 70, 1975 (first edition).

11

Developmental Support to the Implementation of Land Reforms

Many people confuse land reform with land improvement. In fact, land reform is an institutional measure of improvement of the land sector whereas the development sector of land is altogether is related to developmental aspects of land like improvement in production, fertility of land, water-shed development, arrangement of irrigational facilities, soil conservation, cutting and bunding in land etc. Achievement of optimum productivity of land is the goal of every society from the time immemorial. It is also well-established fact that without proper institutional framework and without continuous reforms, the land cannot achieve optimum production nor the cultivators will get the satisfaction in return of his hard labour.

Therefore, it is equally well-established fact that alongwith institutional measures of land redistribution and providing stability to the tenurial security including recognising sharecropper tenants, development measures by the government or otherwise should be taken. The developmental measures can be divided in three categories:

(i) Agricultural workers are provided work during lean season or during under employment of the agricultural work-force. Such employment generating schemes, play a role of double-pronged strategy. They provide work to the otherwise laid-off work force of agriculture during lean season. Secondly, through these employment generating schemes, the fields are developed and the condition of village or their habitat is improved.

(ii) The cultivator and sharecropper are provided crop finance through government, banks or credit co-operative societies. This delinks them from the exploitation of the local money lenders. Crop credit is available on concessional rates of interest. Even government provides them subsidy to avail such credit facility so that they may not land up again in the clutches of local moneylenders at an exorbitant rates of interest either two or three times of the rate at which bank provides them crop finance. The crop credit finance is generally available to purchase plough, cattle, manures, small and mechanised equipments for ploughing or thrashing, insecticides and seeds etc.

(iii) Third type of development may be the provision of house sites for the poor cultivators near their farms and to the erstwhile cultivators in peri-urban areas and housing for economically weaker sections of the society in urban areas. If they have permanent houses, landowner cannot dare evict them from cultivation. They, in return will be in a position to dictate terms of their work or employment because their shelter is not dependent on the mercy or whims of the landlord. On the other hand, they will be provided due compensation and alternative rehabilitation and resettlement if their land or house sites are acquired by the government for development purpose in the public interest exercising the power of eminent domain by the government as the government in place of the king, has taken the role of moulding their destiny as per law of the land. Lastly, they will be provided with means to increase production like during green revolution in nineteen seventies.

The Voluntary Guidelines (15.8) by FAO also *inter alia* enjoins upon the states or Nations that "States should ensure that redistributive land reform programmes provide the full measure of support required by beneficiaries, such as access to credit, crop insurance, inputs, markets, technical assistance in rural extension farm development and housing." The provision of support services should be provided wherever beneficiary of land reform moves.

(i) Employment Generating Schemes

A cultivator is not employed for the whole year. Once the seed is sown, he has to wait for some time for the seed to germinate. Then after the harvesting, there has to be a gap between two crops to conserve the soil-productivity. Thirdly, many areas are on rain-fed agriculture. In these parts of the world, the cultivator and his family remain unemployed for major period of the year. It is essential that during this gap period, he is fruitfully employed elsewhere specially in schemes which are labour intensive. Then only he and his family can be saved from starvation. He has the economy-based on daily wages except for the crop period when he can support for 4-5 months. Otherwise, he is habituated to run his household on the proverb; 'dig the well daily and drink the water'. They have subsistence economy and not the surplus one. To support this poor section of society, many countries have such employment generating schemes. You eat white you work. In India, one very ambitious scheme is in operation known as Mahatma Gandhi National Rural Employment Guarantee Programme in which Government is bound by the Mahatma Gandhi Employment Guarantee Act 2005, to provide 100 days of work to each and every household depending on actual demand. Thus, a legal obligation is cast upon the government to provide upto 15 days, employment in a month to a person asking for the work and is desirous to work on the schemes which are generally rural areas development schemes.

Under the scheme, labour intensive works are executed with 60:40 wage and material cost. At least 50 per cent of the works will be executed by the Gram Panchayats. At least one-third of beneficiaries are women. This is a seven (7) billion dollar scheme during the financial year 2013-14. Priority of works is to be decided by Gram Panchayat in general meetings of Gram Sabha and the ward Sabha in urban areas. The drawback of the scheme is that only three billion dollar reaches out of $ 7 billion at the grassroots level and out of $ three billion only assets worth $ one billion will be created during 2013-14. Though, Ombudsmen have been posted in many districts in some states in India, yet the corrupt panchayat pradhan (chief) have their way out. It is good that now onwards from January, 2014, the scheme is targetting to make the land unfit for agriculture as fit for agricultural directly on the basis of group formation of government allottees of vested land, and also the gorup of sharecroppers apart from beneficiaries or allottees of forest fringe land. The scheme also permits watershed related works such as contour trenches and bunds, boulder checks, farm bunding, gabion structure, underground dykes, earthen dams, dugout farm ponds, stop dams, fish drying yards, belt vegetation, construction of storm water drains for coastal protection, deepening and repair of flood channels, rehabilitation of field channels or irrigation canals etc.

Besides there is a programme called Integrated Watershed Management Programme which covers Drought Prone Areas Programme (DPAP) for frequently severe drought affected areas. There is also a Desert development programme the waste land is also developed under IWDP. "A total number of 1,433 projects covering an area of 7.8 million hectare were completed upto 31.12.2012 out of which 130 projects were completed during 2012-13."[1]

Similarly, under the Indira Awaas Yojna (IAY), Ministry of Rural Development, Government of India provides houses to families below poverty line (BPL) in rural areas. Housing schemes are there in urban areas for the squatters or slum-dwellers landless families.

Even the persons who do not have house sites, can avail this benefit and construct house up to total cost of Rs. 70,000 in the plain area and Rs. 75,000 for hilly/difficult areas.

Under the MNREGA, the village roads have been improved, ponds have been renovated and one finds far better infrastructure now in rural India which gives impetus for the cultivators to work more in their farms with a view to add to the granary of the country.

Case Study of Good Practice-1 (India): Reviving Springs to Mitigate the Impact of Climate Change

"Springs are the main lifeline of people of Sikkim. Sikkim is a small state situated in the Eastern India in the Himalayas. Around 80 per cent of the State's rural households depend on springs form hills for drinking water and irrigation. Many of the springs have dried up or are having declining natural recharge. Using scientific and people-centric approaches, under MNREGA through various line departments and NGOs, ground water recharge activities were undertaken to improve the eco-system services of the State's mountain forests. In the last four years, i.e., (2009-2013), the project has improved ground water table, ensured irrigation for cash crops like bananas, oranges, guavas throughout the year. Overall, 40 srpings and four lakes have been resurrected covering an area of 400 hectares of land and more than 15 hectares of horticulture plantations, with around 20,000 saplings, have been developed."[2]

Case Study 2: Restoring 45 Hectares of Barren Lands Belonging to Poor Families (*Pattadars*)

Based on demand of the villagers through Kuraparthi Varipalle Gram Panchayat in Erragutta Block, District Chittor, various activities under fallow land development, i.e., jungle/bush clearance, stone bunding, silt application, trench cutting etc., were designed and executed along with rock filling dam works. As a result, the entire 45 hectares of barren land has turned into a well-developed mango-orchard. Each of the beneficiary derived income of about $200 in the first year. Inter crops like groundnut, millets, watermelons, tomatoes etc., have also been taken up. These provided an additional income $1500 to each beneficiary. The scheme under MGNREGA has transformed lives of the poorest of the poor Scheduled Castes, Scheduled Tribes and marginal farmers by changing their status from agricultural labour to proud owners of orchards. This has also exploded the myth that so-called waste or barren lands cannot be distributed among the landless families as these lands are unfit of agriculture."[3]

Case Study 3: Development of Pastureland Near Sea Belt

The district administration of North and Middle Andaman surrounded by sea has developed 60 hectares of settlers' or indigenous people's land for horticulture and 90 hectares of grazing land for fodder and mixed plantation and minor forest produce through convergence of the MGNREGA with other schemes.

The water conservation projects such as farm ponds were taken up. Then technical support for cutting terraces and digging trenches based on slope of land was given. Vermi-compost manure was supplied. As a result, unused land was converted into productive land increasing income of the collective group of poor farmers through Gram Panchayat substantially."[4]

(ii) Credit Availability

In West Bengal, India, by arranging crop finance from banks to sharecroppers (*bargadars*) and allottees of government surplus land, the state got phenomenal 70 per cent increase of foodgrains. Even the government of West Bengal provided 25 per cent subsidy to the landless belonging to the Scheduled Caste and Scheduled Tribes. This has freed cultivators from the clutches of moneylenders. As per an estimate, about three million farmers had committed suicide for not being able to pay off their dues towards their moneylenders so far. This shows how sincere and honest are farmers in paying off loans. At the same time, it exposed unholy alliance of moneylenders with the police, politicians and media. The moneylenders in the worst affected region of Vidarbh (Maharashtra-Nagpur) was led by the ruling party Member of Legislative Assembly who also owned the most popular local daily newspaper and had an army of muscle men and goons to realise dues from the farmers at compounded exorbitant rates of interests. Money Lending Act is there but it cannot be enforced against the moneylenders by government.

On the other hand, banks only charged about four per cent or less interest on the crop loan before two major seasons, i.e., Khariff and Rabi in India. These cultivators have their identity reflected in their citizen identity card known as Aadhar Card and they can obtain latest record of rights.

On the other hand, if bankers find that the allotted land is developed, they will be too glad to finance the loan. Thus, the scheme with the Banks was quite a success in India.

In Brazil, in November, 2003, the National Programme of Land Credit was launched. It supported the established family farmers. Its aim was to benefit 50,000 families. It was first implemented from July 2002 to the end of 2004. The beneficiaries could apply directly for credit which has no grant component. He can purchase the land and the purchase price is paid directly to the selling landowner. In December 2008, the credit was allowed alongwith grant by the government. Thus, linkage of credit was also appreciated as part of land reform in many Latin American countries.

(iii) Provision of Homestead

When the quantum of land available with public authority is inadequate as compared to the demand for cultivation, the landless person can be allotted atleast homestead land proportionately as per availability of total surplus land to the beneficiaries subject to the minimum 100 square meters in rural areas or 50 square meters in peri-urban or semi-urban or urban area or maximum 16 decimal of lands. As the quantum of land increases, it can be used for allied activities like for goatery, piggery, poultry or cow rearing. The life of villages is integrated with animals. If they can rear one cow, they will be free from diseases and environment will improve and they will sustain their basic livelihood during the milking period of a cow. However, two cows alternatively, can support one small family. If the land is available upto 10 decimal he can have vegetable cultivation. A 16 decimal plot provides them basic livelihood because they can have three layers of cultivation. On the ground, he can have cash crops like gram, pea, pulses, mustard, sunflower crops, or high price vegetables. In second layer, he can go for horticulture crops like papaya, guava, banana, lemon, etc., and at higher heights, he can have fast growing high trees as per the climate and soil condition which can be sold in nearby markets easily like eucalyptus or popular trees. Additionally, he may have flower cultivation if market is available in addition to livestock invariably. These allied sector of agriculture like dairy is a better safeguard to their livelihood.

In Bangladesh, land per capita is only 6/7 decimal per person (perhaps lowest in the world). In Bangladesh three-layer cultivation has started on small plots, i.e., on ground cash crops, above horticulture crop and top layer of timber tree. Nobel prize has been won for linking agriculture with micro-financing. "If land is not available, government in many countries provide grant to purchase homestead unit. Even the small landholding given by government about 1700 square feet or 170 square metres or less is creating confidence in rural masses and make a good sense."

Under the 'Homestead Scheme' in India "funds amounting to Rs. 347.47 crore have been released to states, namely, Bihar, Andhra Pradesh, Karnataka, Kerala, Rajasthan, Sikkim, Uttar Pradesh and Maharashtra for purchase of land."[5]

"During four years, i.e., from 2005-06 to 2008-09, 71.76 lakhs were constructed in India with an expenditure of 3.5 billion dollar, approximately."[6]

In urban areas, there is similar Rajiv Gandhi Housing Scheme known as RAY for the squatters or slum-dwellers landless families. There is reservation of 20-25 per cent of developed land for Economically Weaker Section/Low Income Group housing in every new public or private residential development and for a non-lapsable earmarking of 25 per cent of the budget of all municipalities/other bodies providing municipal basic services to meet the revenue and capital expenditure of urban poor calories and slums. However, there is a minimum beneficiary share of 12 per cent and 10 per cent for weaker sections.

A good work has been done by the Scheduled Caste-friendly Mayawati government in the most populous state (150 million population approximately) in India by making colonies for scheduled caste poor beneficiaries and for slum dwellers in Mumbai by government of Maharashtra. But there should be restriction on further transfer of house or homestead by them so that they do not join the army of homeless persons again. Their homestead or house if sold informally, should vest in state government, so that the state can reallocate the same to the deserving person. This will be a disincentive for the unscrupulous persons to play with the distressed condition of the urban poor in a situation where social securities are almost non-existent.

A revolution is underway in India, sponsored by the government. Lakhs of social-mobilisation institutions or formal and informal groups known as Self-help Group (SHG) have grown up. A SHG is an informal voluntary association of poor people preferably from the same socio-economic background. The group enables its members to gain their identity as individuals and their combined capacity to arrange raw material for rural handicrafts and inputs for cultivation and their joint efforts for marketing of their produce. It provides them with a platform from where they can access banks and public services and spearhead changes that affect them as poor people. There are SHGs of 10-20 poor women in general (5-20 poor women in hilly or difficult areas) belonging to the same village and sharing a common socio-economic background.

These SHGs have brought many social changes like opposing drinking by their male counter parts and infusing for reprisals among corrupt officials in some parts of India. Support from NGOs has also been solicited through government channel in increasing public co-operation, organisation of beneficiaries, advancement of rural technology, arranging for buyer-sellers meets in big cities successfully through an open organisation called Council for Advancement of People's Action and Rural Technology (CAPART).

Further, with the growth of joint management, the Gram Panchayats can co-ordinate all these efforts by individuals and will prepare its own plan of development. It is quite likely that the village shopkeepers will give place to co-operative shops in which perhaps they will themselves be absorbed as employees with a share in profit. Similarly, organisation of villages will control the selling of their agricultural products or foodgrains, in government or semi-government markets or *mandi* which are now not very effective and a conduit for remunerative prices to the farmers for their products due to their corrupt alliance with private traders. The village SHGs will also implement to utilise the surplus manpower in the village ranging between one-third and one-fourth. If the marketing of village industry product is not feasible, the market forces will compel the village artisans to become wage-earner again. The same market forces compel the farmers to move to the urban areas as share of agriculture in GDP in India is gradually declining as a part of globalisation process. When they don't find any job in urban areas, they move back to the villages.

Thus, a sizeable disgruntled and discontented population is growing or shivering with discontent due to non-lucrative prices of agricultural products. "Thus, through SHGs, India requires most favourable setting for such rural, urban and industrial integration with agriculture and the household sector in rural India into production and service units of adequate size, which will have the ability to grow from their own strength, generate resources for investment from their current operations, readily assimilate new technology and, in turn, stimulate a growing demand for new forms of work and service requiring higher levels of skill and education."[7] The same was sought to be done earlier but as it happens, the old institutions like co-operative societies, co-operative credit society's and community or co-operative agriculture farms or fishery farms wherever, are not functioning properly can give way to the new groups SHGs which are more democratic, small and have real participation of grassroots level persons and are free from possibility of corruption because of their transparency and small size.

As the urban poverty is increasing gradually which increased to 24.9 per cent in 2003 as per a United Nations report, the urban community organisations have to be strengthened and NGOs are to be actively associated with the cause of the poor. "Between 2001 and 2004, three serious fires broke out in the informal settlement in the Philippines. The fires occurred in March, 2001, March, 2002 and January 2004. (There was a fourth fire in January 2010).

Some residents suspected they were deliberately set to remove some families from the list of qualified beneficiaries of the (costly) land proclamation. However, there were no formal complaints or investigations. After each fire, community members had to fight the authorities to be allowed to return to their former homes. Fortunately, Kabalikat's 2001 community survey could be used to determine which families should be allowed to return. People had to constantly assert their right to return to their former home sites and their eligibility for lot (lottery) awards. As a result of Kabalikat's efforts, some 700 homeowners were first to be awarded lots and renters and shares were eventually given lots in nine new sites within the area."[8]

In India, the initiative to settle or to provide housing to the slum dwellers started at the intervention of the apex court of India i.e., Supreme Court in the Public Interest Litigation case *Olga Tellis* vs. *Bombay Municipal Corporation*[9] which is popularly known as Pavement Dwellers case, directed the state to provide the evictees having identity cards from footpaths, pavements or any other public place, the alternative sites for their resettlement and to earn livelihood. The Court equated the right to livelihood with right to life which is enshrined in every Constitution broadly as follows:

"The right to life includes the right to livelihood. If the right to livelihood is not treated as a part life, the easiest way of depriving a person of his right to life would be to deprive him of his means of livelihood to the point of abrogation. Deprive a person of his right to livelihood and you shall have deprived him of his life."

Restoration of Alienated Land due to Distress

A poor has always a deficit economy. However, he cannot withstand pressure of one of his closest relatives like son, daughter, wife being terminally ill. To save life of his dearest ones, he sells off his only asset, i.e., land or house site. Such cases are to be seen in the light of human misery and failure and not in strict sense of law. As per strict principle of law, he will have no claim on the land or property already sold off.

To restore him the parcel of land or property and to discourage such sales, popular governments around the world have come up with suitable legislations or statutes. In such cases, the state pays compensation to the buyer if the seller cannot pay, at the rate the land or property was sold off alongwith reasonable rate of interest from the date of sale. Such provisions can be discovered in many existing statutes. In the erstwhile state of Bihar, India, Jharkhand Mukti Morcha had forcibly occupied those lands which had passed on to the non-tribals or non-indigenous people after lot of violence and bloodshed. These lands later on again went back with the transferees, i.e., non-tribals as per law and thereby police was with them. But the Collectors of various districts passed orders to transfer back the land parcels to the original tribal landowners discovering a loophole in law. These parcels of land are still with those indigenous persons. Thus, result of land related violence or mobilisation can be permanent if it follows lawful route. Despite Jharkhand Mukti Morcha (JMM) came into power in Jharkhand after its separation from Bihar, subsequently, the JMM didn't pursue those promises which it had given to the people when it had raised the revolt against the existing system and government. A great job has been done in India by restoring lands to the tribals in 2,05,645 cases involving 4,01,816 acres of land. But still 30,615 cases are pending for disposal involving 54,906 acres of land which is due to unusual delay in disposal of cases by the revenue courts or higher courts.

However, indigenous people in USA and Australia still are waiting for justice for restoring back their lands. In Africa and Latin America, this is the main issue and requires top attention of the policy makers, law makers and administrators.

Social and Religious Reforms

Land Reform without social and religious reforms will be ineffective and the poor man will go to its original level of poverty. Only a well-conscientious person can keep the asset acquired with the help of a movement or through government. Poor people are very religious and emotional. Poor people spend a lot of money on festivals and ceremonies and do not go to work on a number of days to celebrate many unknown local festivals or rituals due to superstitions or orthodoxy. They also indulge in indebtedness and drinking. Habitual drinking among the poor has caused lot of drainage of their petty income whatsoever comes out of his labour or from the labour of his wife. The women are better keeper or protector of interests of the family specially the children universally. Thus, women have to play vital part to organise themselves and stop their men from indulging into drinking and thereby ruining themselves and their families.

The education and health of the family become two casualties apart from running of hearth at his home. All social and religious reformers have preached against the vice of drinking but the modern media is more indulging into highlighting the same to earn from advertisements and to support their patrons of globalisation, i.e., MNCs and TMNCs. Taking loan or giving loan is prohibited under the Islam, yet many of the Muslims indulge into indebtedness throughout the world. As a result of consumption of tobacco through *biri* (handmade cigarette), cigarette or other products of tobacco, the poor people are afflicted with lot of fatal diseases like cancer, etc., and they have to sell their land being the only source of livelihood for them and their families. Thus, they leave behind a legacy for their family to live in perpetual poverty.

It is seen that the poor spends disproportionate percentage of their income or asset on ceremonies like marriages, birth and death ceremonies of their dear ones. It is well-known fact that after a bummer crop in India, lot of religious congregations take place. As a result, surplus earned is lost without waste of time. The economy of the poor is always in deficit. Awareness campaign should run in their villages or slum colonies to convince them to have saving habits to meet unforeseen expenses. However, it is well-established fact that such a sustained campaign will be more effective among women.

And secondly, if the land allotted by government or in land records, their names are recorded first as owners or allottees so that their husbands will not be able to part with the land without their concurrence and except for the benefit of the estate or family or in case of emergencies with the permission of the social activists or government authority.

It is accepted that it is very difficult to undertake such initiatives by government. Firstly, because such an issue is not within the realm of secular government, and secondly, because government officials don't have training or patience for such motivational jobs. However, few governments like Union government in India and state governments of West Bengal and Tamil Nadu have created such outfits with public-private partnerships or through NGOs to motivate youths through *Nehru Yuvak Kendra* and spreading tenets of prohibition among public. In Gujarat, being the land of Mahatma Gandhi, prohibition has been implemented for last 65 years successfully. The revenue lost due to restriction on sale of liquor, has been many times more earned through development of Gujarat society. And Gujarat is now leading in India in many fields including industries and is one of the richest states of India at present.

In African countries, the Church groups have played an important role in motivating and securing tenurial rights to the poor and also guiding them for religious and social reforms. These were religions of Islam and Hindus which allowed the occupation of vacant land by those who can cultivate them. Thus, religions cannot be termed as enemies of struggle of peasants who are by and large religious.

Consolidation of Land

Voluntary Guidelines on the Responsible Governance of Tenure in its Guideline No. 13.1 provides—

> "Where appropriate, states may consider land consolidation, exchanges or other voluntary approaches for the readjustment of parcels or holdings to assist owners and users to improve the layout and use of their parcels or holdings, including for the promotion of food security and rural development in a sustainable manner. States should ensure that all actions are consistent with their obligations under national and international law and with due regard to voluntary commitment under applicable regional and international instruments and ensure that participants are atleast as well off after the schemes compared with before. These approaches should be used to co-ordinate the preferences of multiple owners and users in a single legitimate readjustments."

The phrase used is that consolidation should add to the total productivity of land alongwith the satisfaction of its participants or stakeholders. But the experience of consolidation has been mixed in India. Whereas it had been successful in increasing production and prosperity in Punjab and Haryana, it has not paid dividends in Uttar Pradesh. In Uttar Pradesh, it is not the institution of consolidation of land holding but the corruption among the consolidation officers is responsible for a dismal performance of consolidation in Uttar Pradesh.

However, the co-operative farms or state farms have been very successful in socialist countries led by the erstwhile Russia and Eastern Europe until they also sank under their weight of heavy dependence on government subsidies and grant and due to their mismanagement.

"Egyptian co-operative system is worth emulating which combines co-operative farming while keeping the individual ownership of the farm land intact so that the basic instinct of the ownership of land of man is also served which also motivates him to work harder even on co-operative or joint or state farms. Designating the Egyptian co-operative system as an "individualistic" model, as distinct from a strictly collective co-operative, one co-operative movement expert contends that Egyptian system may suit the agricultural needs of a developing country such as India. In the opinion of another specialist, the Egyptian co-operative system has basically similar features to the highly successful Israeli co-operative farms. In fact, one can argue that Israel's co-operative farm system is better organised but less applicable to other developing countries than the Egyptian. Israeli co-operatives are socially and economically integrated institutions organised largely on a voluntary basis. They enjoy almost complete independence from the government. But they were created under rather unique conditions. First, Israeli farmers were immigrants, who obtained and operated their land in a hostile environment. They had to maintain a high degree of internal cohesion in order to survive. Second, Jewish culture may be said to exhibit a strong trait of communal solidarity, thus favouring group activity. Finally, many Israeli immigrants are ideologically attuned to the socialist way of production. These conditions generally do not exist in the developing countries; hence the applicability of the Israeli co-operative experiences to these countries is much limited. Among the three models of co-operative farming, the Indian system appears to be merely an aspiration that has vapourised; the Mexican system is an institution large in size but weak in structure; the Egyptian system appears to be the only one that deserves imitation by other countries."[10]

This system will ensure proper inputs in agriculture and will provide wide scope of remunerative marketing of agriculture produce resulting in high production and high return from cultivation.

Acquisition of Land for Development *vis-à-vis* Peasants' Interest

None denies predominant prerogative of the state under the power of eminent domain to acquire land for industrial purposes to give fillip to the economy of a country. It is a fact of the modern day world of globalisation that agriculture sector is gradually losing its edge as its share in GDP of a country is being continuously reduced. But one shouldn't overlook the fact that ultimately people will have to fall upon the agriculture sector to feed themselves. When globalisation or industrialisation doesn't perform, the agriculture sector being evergreen sector, saves the humanity from famine irrespective of the economic cycle and its complicated calculations.

In developing and less developed countries (LDCs), inspite of reduction of share of agricultural sector in GDP, the percentage of population on agriculture is not being reduced in the same portion though urbanisation is the first brother of globalisation. Therefore, a balance is to be struck between the requirement of development of industries and services and basic needs of agriculture sector so that it always can cater to food, needs of the growing population of every country without considering the interstate movements of food grains which might be adversely affected during war, hostilities or civil strife.

It is therefore, essential that most productive agricultural land giving three crops in a year are spared from acquisition for industries and the persons dependent on agriculture are also protected so that this sector is always ready to fulfil the basic need of food of the population without which man cannot survive. The Voluntary Guidelines of FAO suggests that land banks should be set up to facilitate the acquisition of private land for such public projects and to provide affected owners, farmers and small scale food producers with land in compensation that will allow them to continue and even increase production. Thus, land, unfit for agriculture or low-productivity lands either of public or private persons will be kept in each land banks and industrialists will be given choice only to choose among those parcels of land insptie of increase of overhead expenditure to them. Similarly, lands for environment protection or involving forests and fisheries will be tactfully spared from the acquisition of land by the state except for emergencies like the defence of the country, natural calamities or for making basic amenities available to public like drinking water or water supply. But for these purposes too, only minimum feasible land should be made available to the public authorities.

In the present day scenario, the acquisition of land by the most powerful Communist Government of West Bengal ruling the state for last thirty years was dethroned by the public. The land acquisition is the good trigger for public mobilisation as it is very obvious and the people have immediate fear of losing their livelihood. People have lost faith in industrialists as they feel that they are part of capitalist system which lives to serve itself more and more. The dichotomy between industrial development and agricultural development is best illustrated by following two cases of land acquisition in West Bengal, India.

(A) Setting up of Manufacturing Unit: A Case of Small Car Project of M/s Tata Motors in Singur, West Bengal

About 1000 acres of land was acquired by the West Bengal Industrial Development Corporation for the Small Car Project of M/s Tata Motors Pvt. Ltd., in 2006. Tata is the most reputed industrial house in India. It was a privilege for West Bengal Government to host the plant of Tata Small Car Project to manufacture Rs 1 lakh dream car for the Indians. This was expected that with the arrival of Tata, other big industrial houses and companies will follow suit in the industrial starved state of West Bengal, which had otherwise earned an ill-reputation of labour problems and lack of work culture.

Government of West Bengal decided to acquire land in record time for the Tatas on their conditions and provided them many concessions in land acquisitions costs, sales tax etc. The land was acquired without studying the pulse of local people and without the knowledge that it was the multiple cropping land and was one of the best for agricultural purposes in the State.

While the land was acquired, the opposition in West Bengal opposed it tooth and nail saying that the farmers would not give away their lands as these lands were only sources of their livelihood. As a result, farmers of 234 acres of land out of 1000 acres (approx) did not accept the compensation amount. This became the cause of ever-simmering discontentment. They formed an organisation under the banner 'Save Farm Land'. The supporters often disturbed the ongoing construction work and demolished the boundary wall many times. But the strong political will of the Government of West Bengal duly supported by M/s Tata Motors, did not surrender to the demands of the local people to return back their fertile lands and instead using the land in front of the proposed unit which was less fertile.

The battle for the political supremacy had the following unwanted consequences:

(a) One emerging young woman supporter of 'Save Farm Land' was raped and murdered and this offence was committed at the instance of the local ruling CPI(M) elite.

(b) There were cracks among the partners of the Left Front government, which had been well-cemented so far and has been ruling in West Bengal for more than thirty years.

(c) There was a protracted court battle in the High Court of Calcutta through the Public Interest Litigation.

The problem of Singur attracted the World attention to the complex debate of land acquisition *vis-à-vis* development. If the local populace doesn't desire development, then why the development work is thrust on them. This also brought out the lax attitude of the West Bengal bureaucracy and the political elite who had been vouching as the only spokesman of the poor in the state. The development work was undertaken even without providing for a well laid down rehabilitation and resettlement policy even in the Communist regime of the Left Front government. Ultimately, Tatas withdrew from the project and are in the process of vacating the site. Government of West Bengal has been left with no alternative.

The agitation against the setting up of the car manufacturing plant has cautioned the administrators and the policy makers that they should not take for granted the support of the poor. They are not only the deciders of their destiny. Their fate or progress has to be well chalked out in consultation with the local people at the grassroots level. Even elected panchayats or local bodies cannot take for granted their support. The support is only issue-based and election mandate does not give sole right to the elected representatives to speak or do everything on behalf of their electorates.

The common people have no faith that they will be employed. They cannot support jobless growth. The land evictees should be trained in skills whereas they can get a job of their liking. The industrial house or management should provide jobs for the land-losers and should make provisions for due compensation considering development in the area as a result setting up of the industrial unit. The manufacturing unit should plan for people's needs and aspirations, to run the plant successfully in future. An unit cannot run smoothly without the support of the local people. These are the important lessons from the Singur land debacle.

(B) Agitation Against Proposed Industrial Hub: A Case of Nandigram, West Bengal, India

Nandigram is a very interesting case study which brings out the fact that apprehensions can also cause large scale public agitations and violence.

The chronology of the events run as follows:

Pursuing the declared policy of promotion of industries, government of West Bengal had declared unofficially that there will be a chemical hub and other housing projects near Haldia Industrial Centre under Haldia Development Authority. For that purpose, land will be acquired to the tune of more than 5000 acres. Rumours were having their sweep. In the meantime, the local political MP (Member of Parliament) being the most influential person, got published a pamphlet through a semi-government organisation Haldia Development Authority that they would acquire land in 10-12 villages near Nandigram. This created panic among the villagers and they grouped under a non-political organisation known as 'Save Land Eviction Committee' irrespective of party affiliation.

They even restricted entry of government officials to those 10-12 villages where the land was supposed to be acquired. They cut roads and put up barricades. Once, they were cutting government *pucca* road, the police intervened. They stoned police force and in the melee, one police sub-inspector was killed and was thrown in the nearby Haldi river. The police force was sore about the incident and wanted to take revenge. Arrests on large scale were not possible because of resistance by about ten thousand people of the villages. Their anger was severe on CPI(M) supporters. As a result, the CPI(M) supporters were compelled to leave their houses. They took shelter in their nearby party bastion village Khajuri. All ten villages covering a population of about thirty thousand were united for one cause that the takeover of their land should be opposed at all costs even at the cost of their lives.

When a large police contingent under a senior officer of DIG rank went to arrest the culprits in earlier cases filed, the villagers started pelting stones and put up obstacles on the roads leading to their villages. As a result, police resorted to bursting of tear gas shells and then firing as the crowd became uncontrollable and became very violent using bombs, grenades and arms against the police force. The ruling party supporters joined hands with police force and used brickbats, arms and bombs against members of 'Save Farmland Committee' which was locally known as 'Resistance Group against land eviction' (Bhumi Uchhed Pratirodh Committee). In the melee, 16 people died including women who were opposing the land acquisition. Many policemen also got injured and were admitted in various hospitals.

This became a major issue at the State and the National level. The 'Left Front government' in the state went on the back foot. The Chief Minister declared that the so-called notice/pamphlet issued by the HDA for the proposed industrialisation stands cancelled and withdrawn. Henceforth, land acquisition will be done only on approval of state government through one agency, i.e., the Land and Land Reforms Department of the state government and Collector, Purba Medinipur. The mass killing was criticised even by all national leaders. Government of India declared that no fertile land will be acquired for Special Economic Zones and this will be left on sponsors to mostly purchase land for SEZs. However, after getting power, the protestants' party didn't do much for the public.

The conclusions of the Nandigram fiasco were the following:

(i) Cases of land acquisitions should be scrutinised closely by the higher echelon of administration and only minimum land required for the project should be allowed to be acquired.

(ii) As far as possible, fertile agriculture land should not be acquired. If the industry or unit cannot be placed elsewhere, then alternative land should be arranged or offered for the cultivators to cultivate in nearby area out of the compensation paid to the land evictees.

(iii) The people of the area should be heard properly before land acquisition plans are finalised.

(iv) Land acquisition evictees should be given proper compensation even considering future increased value of the land due to industrialisation or development.

(v) Land-losers should be given jobs in the new unit as far as possible through a well-represented body set up for the purpose.

(vi) No land acquisition proposal should be cleared by the authorities unless it has proper rehabilitation and resettlement plan.

Conclusions

Thus, we should have a society with large sector of agricultural production that work in tandem with a certain kind of industry, rather than are dominated by an abstract thing called industry—irrespective of whether it produces poison, nuclear hazards or automobiles. It is a misconception that in developing countries, private sector can replace the public sector in one go. It is to be softly done because the populace is not ready to absorb the reform, culture and are doubtful of the private sector due to their past history and practices. The South–East Asian countries had gone fast on private sector involvement and their economies were at the brink of collapse in nineties. On the other hand, China and India have been involving the private sector cautiously. Any reform without people's involvement will be lopsided. It is bound to fail ultimately. For example, uncontrolled land acquisition for industries is being opposed violently in India by masses especially for setting up of Special Economic Zones, because large manufacturing units are on fertile lands. The multinationals should not also be allowed to exploit raw materials of developing countries like India without ensuring improvement of quality of life of people. This type of development has become development terrorism. One cannot afford to have oasis in the poor neighbourhood. Equitable distribution is the only way out.

References

1. Ministry of Rural Development: Annual Report 2012-13, Government of India, New Delhi (www.rural.nic.in) p. 162, Krishi Bhawan, New Delhi.
2. Government of India, Ministry of Rural Development: *Enhancing Sustainable Livelihoods of the Poor through Convergence of MNREGA with Various Scheme*, pp. 1-2, 2014.
3. *Ibid.,* 2, pp. 112-113, www.mgnrega.nic.in
4. *Ibid.,* 3, pp. 128-129.
5. Homestaad, Tim and Lokesh, S.B., *Allocating Homesstead Plots as Land Reforms: Analysis from West Bengal*, India published by Rural Development Institute, New York, USA, 2002.
6. *Ibid.,* 1: p. 72.
7. Singh, Tarlok, *Poverty and Social Change,* Orient Longmans, New Delhi, p. 342, 1969.
8. UN Habitat: Report 5/2012, Innovative Urban Tenure in the Philippines, Nairobi, Kenya, 2012, p. 22. www.unhabitat.org.

9. *All India Reporter*, 1986, *Supreme Court of India*, p. 180.
10. Wariner, Dorren, *Land Reform in Principle and Practice*, Oxford 1969, pp. 174-175 in *Land Reforms in India* by P.K. Agrawal, M.D. Publications, New Delhi, pp. 231-232.

12

Strengthening Land Administration System

The real test of the success of any system is how much it has added to the welfare of the people. The best policy, if implemented badly by an incompetent set-up will be a fiasco whereas a defective policy, if implemented properly, can prove to be a boom. For this purpose, instrument or organisation implementing is equally important. Land Administrative Systems around the World have been there for centuries. People have developed emotional attachment with the system and a vested interest has also simultaneously grown up which wants to continue with the system.

The system or institutions which cannot keep pace with the changing world lose their importance and gradually go into oblivion. The present Information Technology age is moving very fast which was not come across by the human race. It demands continuous change and continuous improvements at whatever costs.

If a bureaucratic procedure inhibits land development, it will be taken over by IT. Professionals and will be replaced by a new and quick procedure based on transparency, accuracy and objectivity.

"In many countries, administrative procedures for registering a land parcel, obtaining planning and building approvals, or effecting property transfers are so cumbersome, expensive and confusing that they actually encourage the very unauthorised development they seek to prevent. Addressing this important issue will require political and administrative leadership.

In Egypt, acquiring and legally registering a plot on a state-owned vacant land involves atleast 77 bureaucratic procedures at 31 public and private agencies. In Peru, building a home on state-owned land requires 207 procedural steps at 52 government offices. In the Philippines, establishing a legal ownership takes 168 steps and between 13 and 25 years. In Haiti, obtaining a lease on government land–a pre-requisite for buying–takes 65 steps."[1]

Such procedural rigmarole calls for immediate corrections. To achieve this goal, if the LAS of a country is to be changed. It should be changed on both counts, i.e., system/procedures and personnel. The procedures adopted have some or the other way co-relation with the relevant statute. Therefore, if it is required, the relevant provisions of the statute or Act or Law should be amended to take the actual benefit of LAS set-up design and functioning to the last man in the society.

Land has long been known to be one of the sectors most affected by bad governance–something that is not difficult to understand in light of the fact that not only is land a major asset, but also its value is likely to rise rapidly in many content of urbanisation and economic development. The most authoritative survey of global corruption finds that, after the police and the courts, land services are the most corrupt sector, ahead of other registry and permit services, education, health, tax authorities, or public utilities (Transparency International 2009).

"Although individual amounts may be small, such petty corruption can add upto large sums. In India, the total amount of bribes paid annually by users of land administration services is estimated at US$ 700 million (Transparency International India 2005), equivalent to three-quarters of India's total public spending on science, technology and environment. Large-scale corruption associated with acquisition and disposal of public lands is more notorious in some contexts. For example, in Kenya, land-related fraud by public officials reached systemic proportions since the 1980s and was identified as "one of the most pronounced manifestations of corruption and moral decadence in our society" (Government of Kenya 2004, 192). For private land, bad governance manifests itself in the difficulty of accessing land administration institutions to obtain land ownership information or to transfer property to another party. Together, large and small scale corruption will reduce the perceived integrity and, because of high transaction costs, the completeness of land registries, thereby undermining the very essence of land administration systems.

In addition to reducing opportunity for corruption and bribery, good land governance is also critical as precondition for sustainable economic development and social justice in a number of respects (Deininger 2003)."[2]

"The rising recognition of the importance of good land governance at the political level is noticeable. For example, the African Union, whose heads of states agreed in 2009 to the framework and Guidelines for land Policy in Africa, has called for the development of benchmarks against which to measure country performance in terms of land governance (African Union 2009)"[3]

"The International Bank for Reconstruction and Development (Bank) has granted to the Republic of Croatia (RoC) a Project Loan. The Ministry of Justice (MoJ) and State Geodetic Administration (SGA) are the Project stakeholders and fund beneficiaries. The Project was initiated with the main objective of building an efficient land initiated with the main objective of building an efficient land administration system aimed at contributing to the development of the efficient real property markets. The reform of the land administration system is today half way through, preconditions have been created for the implementation of an efficient real property registration system. The Joint Information System of Real Property Registration and Cadastre (JIS) has been developed completed, i.e., a unique database and application for keeping and maintaining the land registry and cadastre data has been established. In the next phase, it is necessary to implement the JIS throughout the Republic of Croatia which will streamline both systems and simplify the business processes. Among other numerous functionalities, such system will have the official extracts issued electronically which will save time and money for the citizens."[4]

Computerisation of Land Records as a Solution in India

"The manual system of land records management came under huge pressure due to increase of population and division of land parcels, inefficiency and corruption in Land Administration System in India. Many initiatives have been taken to computerise the land records management system. The National Land Records Modernisation Programme is one of such efforts, which strives to put in place an effective Land Information system which is real-time and easily accessible by the citizens. There are about 103.5 million e-transactions in India every month. To strengthen the infrastructure for such huge transactions, the National e-Governance Plan has been launched. Its main components are, Common Service Centres, State Wide Area Net Work, State Data Centres and State Portals along with State Service Delivery Gateway. Further, to secure the land rights, the laws related to land are proposed to be amended, so that frauds are reduced and economic growth is unleased through the development of an efficient property market."[5]

The new computerised system of land records is more explicit and transparent. The village level officials have no chance to manipulate the land records. Any representative of the land owners can obtain land records under the new, computerised system of land records. Obtaining RORs under the new computerised system is more time-effective and can be easily procured on payment of requisite fee Rs 15 per plot (1/4th dollar) from the computer. A land record document (ROR) has valuable information which includes ownership, tenancy, cultivation, irrigation, trees tax liabilities, crop and soil details including government details. After the integration of registration department, with the land department (LAS), the registration is done after verifying the ownership from the copy of the land record produced by the seller and there is automatic mutation of change of ownership after the registration. This is a great achievement as mutation of land is one process which is hardly accessible by public easily in all systems.

The computerisation of land records has enhanced transparency and there is avoidance of malpractice and manipulations. At the same time, collection of revenue increases.

However, the old land or revenue machinery faces a great challenge to transform themselves to the new technology which they had not habituated so far. It is really troublesome for them. Secondly, there is frequent breakdown of computer and power back-up machines causing dislocation and breakdown in service to the waiting public. Thirdly, for small correction and thumb print, they have to travel to *Tehsildar* wasting lot of time to provide an authenticated copy of RORs.

Let us summarise the lessons from the successful implementation of '*Bhoomi*' as a module of computerisation of land records and improvement in functioning of LAS/revenue department in state of Karnataka in India.

- Farmers often have to travel long distances to obtain RORs resulting in delays and greater cost. Therefore, additional computer kiosks must be established to reduce the distance and travel time for farmers. It will be better to find out the location, which will be within a radius of 20-km from the village instead of setting up the kiosk at *taluk*, sub-divisional or district headquarter.

- The *taluk* centre is plagued by regular, almost daily, power outages, since the computer kiosk does not have a generator back-up for uninterrupted power supply, the process of obtaining RORs often involve long delays. UPS generally cannot work for more than two hours. It is therefore, necessary that 5-KVA generators should be provided in every *taluk*.
- Depending on the workload, the number of computer kiosk operators can be increased so that ROR seekers do not have to wait while the operator is taking a break or is on leave.
- The ROR copies should be issued on per landholder basis rather than on per land plot basis.
- Establish a ticket number queuing system to establish efficiency and equity in the queuing process at the computer kiosk.
- Extra printer should be provided to overcome the problem of any fault in the existing printer.
- Farmers need up-to-date ROR in terms of crop details. At present the updating takes some time and there are also some errors in updated crop details. The system needs to be further streamlined.
- Whenever any problems related to software as well as hardware occurred in the computer system, no expert was available at *taluk* office, an expert had to come from district headquarters to tackle the problem. Due to this, inconvenience was caused to the users. Therefore, a trained person should be available at *taluk* level to sort out these problems or the government should tie-up with computer agencies at *taluk* level to provide solutions.
- There should be a mechanism to upgrade the hardware in view of technological advancements and also to take care of new and unavoidable requirements, for example, higher capacity hard disks, new OS, RAID controllers, etc.
- To empower farmers, touch screen kiosks should be installed in all *taluks* as has been done in Bangalore, South *Taluk*.
- After the implementation of the programme in *taluks*, it would be

necessary that computers be maintained all the time. The downtime should certainly not be more than 24 hours. Annual maintenance contract has to be entered into with competent parties which should be stationed at *taluk*-level so as to rectify computers and peripherals in less than 24 hours. Ten per cent of the machine's cost should be provided for the maintenance of the hardware every year. This maintenance cost should be payable every second year onwards for at least five years.

- There is a need to integrate departments dealing with lands, such as survey and land records, registration department at village, *taluk*, district and state levels which could facilitate simultaneous updating of land records caused by mutation, sale of property, conveyance, partitions, exchange, gifts, settlements, release deeds etc. This may also help in the faster updating of land records, which may be useful to landholders.
- There is a need to train land survey and revenue officials including village-level functionaries for upgrading their skills in computerisation of land records.
- The computerisation process should integrate registration of land titles. Land laws/mutation process should be simplified for easy and fast implementation of computerisation.
- The land information data should be web enabled. This will provide easy access via Internet."[6]

It is therefore essential that popular governments must provide well-defined titles to their citizens through government records. It is the irony of the situation that information about land in the government by using records is not available properly though it is also a major asset of the government. Many countries, including Indonesia, Malaysia, Laos and China regard maps and plans as quasi-military information and impose substantial restrictions on their availability. Another group, including the United States and New Zealand, make land and spatial information, including digital maps, generally available at little or no cost to stimulate the economy. And still another group, including Australia and European countries, generally adopt cost recovery path and relies on the primary audience for land information to pay an estimated price reflecting the cost of maintenance and sometimes cost of data collection. In African countries, the land records either are non-existent or they are in a preliminary stage. In countries like India, Bangladesh, Pakistan and Middle East countries, the land records are not updated and the major portion of the land is with resourceful landowners. We cannot see rural areas in isolation as there is constant growth of urban areas and they might overtake the rural areas as regards the percentage and total population of the poor in urban areas.

Property Records in Urban India

The position of land or property records in India are worse than in rural areas. Ultimately, all urban areas once were rural areas and some of the land records and maps are still available for these areas like Smart maps for Kolkata. Secondly, the ownership of flat holders should be invariably recorded along with their proportionate share of land whatever little it may be, in the housing complex because land is the only permanent existing entity in this World.

(i) Preparation of Records of Properties in Urban Areas in India

Lot of efforts have been made by the Urban Development Department, Government of India and by the State Governments, but the records in urban areas, i.e., Municipalities/Town Areas/Municipal Corporations are not yet available. Many efforts were also made outsourcing mapping and preparation of property records by the urban local bodies (ULBs). But there is hardly any success. Therefore, it is high time that the land record machinery of the rural area is also entrusted with this job in urban area because they have been doing this job for centuries. As it is gigantic work, it is possible only when on dedicated wing for land records is created in each district exclusively which will not be involved in day to day revenue administration under the Collector. It will take care of recording and updation of records of property in rural areas as well as urban areas.

Ministry of Housing and Urban Poverty Alleviation, Government of India, has been insisting on use of Remote sensing and Geographical Information System (GIS) in implementation of the projects under them. But Urban Local Bodies (ULBs) are not equipped with such in-house capacity. They can take help of maps from their State's land records and survey organisation, Survey of India, State Remote Sensing Application Centres but they are not doing the job at present. The process is simple—scan the map available from the land records and survey organisation, do geo-referencing and then do digitisation. Ultimately, a digitised map of the area or town will be prepared on a scale say 1:2000 which can be modified from time to time as changes take place. But these will not be prepared until this is incoporated in the Model Urban Code by the Ministry of Urban Development, Government of India and the Acts and Rules governing large municipal corporations and urban local bodies throughout the country. They should then be authorised to issue record of rights of a property in the concerned metro, mega city or municipality or town, At present a register for property tax, called Municipal Assessment Book is maintained in each urban local body which has the legal authenticity as far as only tax payment right is concerned.

Relevant provision under Section 2(34) in the Delhi Municipal Corporation Act, 1957 says that occupier includes an owner in occupation of, or otherwise using his land or building Section 2 (37) defines which "owner" includes a person entitled to receive the rent. According to Section 2 (38) premises means any land or building and includes garden, ground or out houses. Nowhere the Act defines the ownership on the basis of records maintained by the Delhi Municipal Corporation.

Similarly, in WB Municipal Act, 1993, the main attribute of a town are the existence of houses in close proximity, concentration of large number of people in a comparatively small area etc. Nowhere it contains that there will be definite map or record of properties. Section 2(24) of the Act defines holding very close to title which means land held under one title or agreement and surrounded by one set of boundaries. The building rules provide only obligation on the part of the owner to submit details but there is no in-house check by the municipal bodies against the authenticated records maintained by it. This should be invariably provided in statute so that ULBs start the process of preparation of land records and maps for urban areas.

(ii) Integration of Land Records Department (LAS), with the Registration Department

This has been more or less achieved in the developed countries especially in European Union. However, African countries are struggling and are facing lot of resistance. The Asian countries have still to achieve positive results of this process.

The experiment of Integration of land records department with registration department in government has proved as a boon for the public in Karnataka and Andhra Pradesh in India for two reasons:

(a) The registration is being done after 'no objection' or after seeing update record of rights maintained by the land record department, or local revenue authority (LAS) by the sub-Registrar's office on line. As a result, lot of requirement of paper is reduced and corruption is almost eliminated.

(b) After Integration, the mutation by the land record department of the government (LAS) done automatically after transfer deed is registered. Thus, record of rights is updated automatically and lot of paper work is reduced. However, the mutation is carried on cautiously as per rules in complicated cases. This experiment is successfully going on in Andhra Pradesh and Karnataka. In Andhra Pradesh, the integration of registration department with the land administration has been done on the basis of data transfer. The sub-registrar verifies data of land revenue department before allowing registration. On the other hand, *Tehsildar* immediately starts the process of mutation after the information is received from the office of the sub-Registrar that a particular land or property has been transferred on his computer through their server. Then the mutation is completed within 30 days after the date of transfer of land or property. Thus, there is a integration of two department, in a broader meaning. However, in Karnataka, there is no line integration of authorities of two departments. In State of Assam also, integration of both wings has facilitated mutation on registration of transfer deeds. It has resulted in reduction and simplification of work in both wings of the government.

It was very heartening to note that the Karnataka High Court even consults the latest records of rights on line if a case comes up before it involving a property or land. The system is working successfully in State of Karnataka.

(iii) Simplification of Mutation and Conversion of Land

State of Madhya Pradesh in India is the best example for simplified procedure for 'conversion of land'.

In M.P. legal provisions exist for the conversion of land. Section 172 of the M.P. Land Revenue Code, 1959 provides that if a *bhumiswami* (landowner) of land held for any purpose wishes to divert his holding or any part thereof to any other purpose except agriculture, he shall apply for permission to the Sub-divisional Officer who may, subject to the provisions of this section and to rules made under this Code, refuse permission or grant it on such conditions as he may think fit;

Provided that should the Sub-divisional Officer neglect or omit for three months after the receipt of an application under sub-section (1) to make and deliver to the applicant an order or permission or refusal in respect thereof and the applicant has by written communication called the attention of the Sub-divisional Officer to the omission or neglect and such omission or neglect continues for a further period of (one month), the Sub-Divisional Officer shall be deemed to have granted the permission without any condition:

Provided also that if a *bhumiswami* (land owner) of a land wishes to divert his land or any part thereof which is assessed for agriculture purpose and situated in any area other than an area covered by development plan to the purpose of industry, a written information of his intention given by *bhumiswami* to the Sub-Divisional Officer shall be sufficient and no permission is required for such diversion.

Such a provision can be inserted in the relevant statues applicable to the Mega towns, municipalities and in peri-urban areas or urban agglomerations, if they have already been included by government notification within the jurisdiction of the municipality or municipal council.

In State of West Bengal, a government order has been issued for effecting mutation within a month, if there is no need of enquiry. The mutation will be deemed to have been done if there is no need of enquiry and mutation certification will be given after lapse of one month by the authority concerned. Similarly, for conversion in W.B., three months' time is prescribed for the completion of the process for cases which need no enquiry. However, a provision should be added that if an authority or officer is not observing these stipulations or schedules laid down by the government, they should be personally accountable and liable to pay compensation to the affected citizen. Such types of provision should be introduced in the Land Reforms Acts in other States in India and in other countries too. Many African countries are adopting these fast track processes but are faced with various challenges to change the old system of land records. Yet, they are on the job because it is very much beneficial for the public. The corresponding amendments in the Indian Stamp Act, 1899 is yet to be made containing that the sub-Registrar will verify the land records on line or from the data before the registration and send information on line to the respective land records authority or wing after registration. It is not possible to amend the Act, the rules and executive instructions should so provide urgently. The state governments have also power to amend the Indian Stamp Act as applicable to them. Therefore, the state governments in India can also take initiative on their own. They need not wait for the initiative from the federal or Union government.

It is well-known that Department of Revenue, Ministry of Finance in Government of India and Finance Department in States are not very keen to make changes in the Stamps Act due to fear of fall in revenue. Levy of Stamp Duty is an important source of revenue for running the government. However, if they institute a study, they will find that more *bonafide* transfers will come for registration which will act as balancing factor and secondly additional economic development will earn much more revenue for the urban bodies and the government.

However, rampant corruption prevalent in the registration offices will have initial jolt. Therefore, this initiative in the public interest should not be overlooked at the behest of the vested interests in government and even outside the government.

(iv) Expeditious Conversion of Land for Public Purposes

Many of the State Governments have allowed deemed conversion for industrial purpose or other public purposes if the land revenue authority does not pass such a order within 90 days. This is good approach because delay is causing more harm than the risk involved. However, it should be seen that before diverting such land, it is to be scrutinised thoroughly whether the minimum land is the requirement and the department or the agency concerned has adequate fund or resources to execute the public purpose proposed. It is a crime to allow land to lie fallow after acquisition in the public interest under the State power of *eminent domain*. Land is a precious asset and is meant for production of food grains to sustain the population/livelihood. Therefore, while providing concession of in conversion of land for public purpose, its actual usage should be kept under watch by the State constantly. If the land is not used for public or industrial purpose within three years, it should be reconverted into public land and landless or homeless persons should be allotted this land, if the State cannot use, it otherwise more fruitfully, who will invest their labour to increase production of the country and contribute to foodgrain reserve stock of the country during lean seasons. Three years are sufficient to a person or company at least to start the process of implementation of public purpose or industrial purpose to give fillip to the economy of the country.

Suggestions

We can summarise our findings as follows:

1. There should be amendment in the Indian Stamps Act, 1899 so as to register the agriculture land or property after prior reference of record of rights or record of property in Land Administration System or in the record of urban local body as the case may be and automatic mutation procedure should be started by the Land Administration System as regards agricultural property and by urban local bodies as regards urban property.
2. In case of urban properties, the mandatory requirement should be incorporated in all statutes governing the functioning of the Urban Local Bodies that they will maintain and update the records of properties within their jurisdiction.
3. There should be simplified procedure of conversion of classification of land by the Land Administration System and Urban Local Bodies even providing for deemed mutation or conversion within a prescribed time limit after submission of application, if no objection is received by the Land Administration System within the prescribed time.
4. As urban local bodies are not conversant at present to survey and prepare the records of properties, existing machinery of LAS may do the job for them until they acquire the due skill and competence.

Statutory initiatives will trigger proper recording of urban properties in most of the countries like India. Once statutory provisions are amended or newly added, these give rights to the public to clamour for the same. Legal empowerment is always a proper device to initiative reform or change. It is likelihood that some conscious leaders heading the urban bodies or councils will find funds and will implement the same without the government's help. But without the inclusion of statutory provisions are amended or newly added, these give rights to the public to clamour for the same. Legal empowerment is always a proper device to initiate reform or change. It is likelihood that some conscious leaders heading the urban bodies or councils will find funds and will implement the same without the government's help. But without the inclusion of statutory provisions by the government, they will face resistance by the vested interests to bring about reforms. As such legal reforms have not created revolutions or upheavals. The legal reforms demonstrate the *bonafide* of the persons in power.

The above suggestions will promote investment in land and the agricultural landholders and property holders in urban areas will get better prices for their land. Ultimately, people in urban areas will be able to live peacefully without any disturbance to their house flat or property.

Capacity Building

One of the important reasons for under performance by the LAS and by urban local bodies is that the work load is heavier than the staff present for disposal of applications for updating records of rights and distributing among the landowners or persons entitled termed as *raiyats* in some systems. For example, state of Bihar in India has about one third of staff in its LAS than state of West Bengal though Bihar is bigger in size and is having more acute land related problems. However, the old LAS machinery is said to be very powerful which is heavily entrenched in the system and is the kingpin of the administration. None can afford to overlook them.

Howsoever bad is the LAS, the public has century old loyalty towards it as this is the government machinery which has stood test of time to help public during many emergencies like flood, drought, earthquake or other natural calamities and has its wings up to the last man in the village and the highest man in the government. This machinery is technically sound and given due opportunity and scope, through training and continuous training can learn latest methods of IT as made applicable in LAS through more investment of funds. These funds in underdeveloped countries should come from the World Bank or other international institutions, bodies or donors. It is also a fact that none can finance the permanent bureaucracy of LAS or revenue department. However, they can always assist in doing survey work including boundary demarcation through modern technologies and can help in computerisation the land records of property. Details can be worked out recorded by the staff and officers of land department and urban local bodies. However, it is not an easy task. Even after involvement of Ministers in training in African countries by UN Bodies, things didn't change much. However, political will is a must for implementation of land with a view to alleviate poverty from the globe. There were occasional good performances by the public spirited and motivated civil servants in the field of land reforms. The diagnostic or comparative or assessment tool like the Land Governance Assessment Framework (LGAF) as envisaged by FAO and UN Habitat under the leadership of World Bank can create healthy competition among the nations to march forward to wipe out poverty from the face of the mother earth. A poor wherever he is located, is to be traced and is to be brought at a stage of respectable livelihood that at least he doesn't starve or die due to hunger. Then only one can say that the system of governance or management by Land Administration System or Urban Local Bodies is people-oriented.

The personnel posted at the helm of affairs in the Land Department should be motivated and technically competent who can give leadership by example to his subordinates. Now-a-days, subordinates in office obey more by the example or conduct of his superior rather than his instruction or position. They should be led by a minister, who is well-versed in land reforms laws and practical methodologies. He should be so powerful that he can say 'no' to the Chief or Prime Minister if any proposed action goes against the interests of land poor, i.e., landless persons, *pattadars* (government lessees) or sharecroppers. He should be popular among the poor people. Most of the people and media are either against land reforms saying that land reforms have been completed and no further land is left for distribution without verifying factual position on the field. Even the normal officials of bureaucracy find the subject uninteresting. In such a situation, adequate incentive should be put in place for officials working in LAS, so that cream of officers and staff are attracted for working in this set up. They then, will make the LAS very attractive and speedy which will in turn deliver results to the poor. However, there are some motivated and patriotic officers and staff who work and will continue working for the rural and urban poor without any incentive or appreciation from their bosses because of their commitment and mental makeup. These reform personnel or change agents present in administration in a sizeable number, who also keep on suffering for their support to the poor and will continue bleeding for them. It is hoped that their lone battle will bring good sense among the rest of bureaucracy and the political elite who at least will allow them to work impartially and objectively without unnecessary and unwanted interference from the top. The blessing eyes of the dumb majority of the indigenous people and the tribals are enough sources of inspiration, which will keep them and their families happy in long run because they are serving the '*daridranarayan*', i.e., (poor-God) of Gandhiji.

In India it is widely recognised that implementation of land reforms has not been satisfactory. Lack of clear direction from the State Government has been one of the factors responsible for this situation. The task force set up by the Planning Commission in the year 1972, headed by P.S. Appu, I.A.S. examined in detail the reasons for the poor performance of the various measures including legislative in the implementation of the land reforms intended to be achieved during the period. It was realised that the enactments of progressive measures and their efficient implementation called for hard political decision and effective political support, direction and control in the context of socio-economic conditions prevailing in the rural areas of the country. No tangible progress can be expected in the field of land reform in the absence of the requisite political will.

However, it will be difficult to implement land reforms in feudal or dictatorial regimes unless they are compelled to undertake land reforms by the mass mobilisation. The case study of Peru throws light on this aspect of land administration system. Government services should be impeded by the same representative institution whose manifest purpose is to reflect constituent's interests. Therefore, to implement land reforms, a strong political-will is required.

"The land reform implemented in Peru during 1969-78 stands out as something different, if not unique, compared to both the land reforms of the Latin American countries as well as the earlier reform efforts undertaken in Peru in the early 1960s. While the radical land reforms of Mexico (1917), Bolivia (1950) and Cuba (1917) were the direct consequence of revolution, the land reforms of Venezuela (1960), Colombia (1961) and Brazil (1964) undertaken under the US sponsored "Alliance for Progress" programme, were more land colonisation than land redistribution proper. The Chilean reform (1964) that subsequently became radical under the elected Marxist president Allende (1970-73) was completely reversed after his assassination in 1973. Like other Latin American countries, Peru also implemented two make-believe reforms during 1960-68 which aimed to pacify the peasants and depoliticise the issue of land reform. But the highly organised peasant movements in Peru that resorted, at times, to *de facto* land reform. Also, the radical land reform during 1969-78 was most effectively implemented by a relatively progressively military leadership with very little political disturbance. Moreover, land reform formed an integral part of the military's comprehensive programme for the economic and political modernisation of Peru with a view to create the necessary conditions for autonomous industrial development supported by state capital. Giving the assigned role for land reforms within the military's overall programme, land reforms were implemented with the major objective of modernising the traditional agrarian structure by creating a market-oriented and technically responsive rural middle class capable of providing economic and political underpinning to indigenous industrialisation and moving land-based agrarian capital to the industrial sector."[7]

The two conclusions are drawn from land reforms in Peru. Firstly, the land reforms were due to political pressures from radical peasant movement and the economic crisis in agriculture. Secondly, the military regime could not solve the problem of the feudal set-up and problem of landlessness. "If the disintegration of Soviet Union is any example then it is clear that political dictatorship in the name of crushing fissiparous tendencies by making stronger center creates more gulf. The local police and administration continue to be seen as agents of a remote, repressive authority, at cross purposes with the needs and aspiration of all but those with close connections to the ruling elite in politics and the bureaucracy."[8]

"One of the promises of democracy is that it makes government service available to all citizens regardless of wealth or status. The failure to professionalise public administration, however, makes that promise hard to keep. It is ironic that the reforms that improve efficiency and fairness in the provision of government services should be impeded by the same representative institution whose manifest purpose is to reflect constituent interests."[9]

It is a fact that socialist bureaucracy in USSR was one of the main causes of the collapse of communism in USSR, and disintegration of USSR in number of republics. Therefore, Karl Marx advocated withering away the state and bureaucracy. That is not a near possibility as farmers and peasants and workers will not unite to put up a joint resistance or revolt against the system but it has now become a higher possibility as the poor in rural and urban areas are equally deprived of in this globalisation era. It is also proved a ploy of autocratic ruler to plead for a committed bureaucracy. The neutral and impartial professional bureaucracy or administrative set up has been proved to the people as well as to the rulers equally that they fend for themselves for their narrow interests as per Parkinson. The land bureaucracy or LAS should thus not be committed to an individual leader or to a political party. Instead, it should be committed to the Constitution of the country and to the welfare of the poor people of the country. This is their duty or '*dharma*' reflected now-a-days in their rules of service or their motto or the mission of their organisation, i.e., LAS. At present, there is general dissatisfaction that the Land Administration System is not working for their interest. For example in Tanzania, the squatters, who took possession in good faith, are protected by law. Informal rights in urban tenure, even if not recorded enjoy protection against eviction and are eligible for compensation and non-documentary evidence is accepted.

A client or citizen service charter has been established but service standards seem arbitrary and in some cases, technically impossible. Thus, many a times, the officials connive with the land sharks, real estate developers and other vested interests and help them to evict the poor persons from their precious land parcels in rural and urban areas both. For their illegal activities, they also secure support from political municipal councillors and other elected office bearers when they otherwise oblige against norms. Thus, a vicious circle runs against the urban poor specially. An officer of Ministry of Urban Development, Government of India accepts that "the ground reality reflects a situation in which cities and towns are visibly deficient in quality of services they deliver the current state of service delivery is far short of what is needed to realise their economic potential. As such, the way forward consists of creating urban infrastructure and reframing governance for service delivery, providing access to universal service standards for all including the urban poor, consciously building rural urban synergy."[10] World Bank representative reports about well-managed city of Ahmedabad "Notwithstanding a substantial increase in public housing production in recent years, providing subsidised formal homes from government or through reservations for lower income groups in private developments would take more than a generation just to handle the current slum population–representing one-third of household."[11]

Funding is generally not a problem except in Latin America and African countries and few countries of disintegrated USSR and South East Asia. "In India, all the projects have been treated as infrastructure projects and have been totally funded by the government. In the USA, it has been totally federally funded and in the UK partly by the Ordnance Survey and partly through some private participation. In other countries such as Singapore, Malaysia, New Zealand and other European countries, it has been a mixture of federal and state involvement."[12]

Thus, the strengthening of Land Administration System is a joint effort by the government having a political will and the bureaucrats having administrative will to work for the land poor.

References

1. UN-HABITAT, *Secure Land Rights for All*, GLTN and United Nations Human Settlements Programme, Nairobi p. 31-World Bank 2001 cited in the Challenges of Slums, UN-HABITAT-2003.
2. Deininger, Klaus, Selod, Harris and Burn Anthony, *The Land Governance Assessment Framework*, The World Bank, Washington DC, p. 13, 2012.
3. *Ibid.,* 2, p. 15.
4. The World Bank: Maro Lucic, *Joint Information System of Land Registry and Cadastre in the Republic of Croatia: Lessons Learned, Annual World Bank Conference on Land and Poverty*, 2013, p. 64.
5. *Ibid.,* 4, Charanjit Singh, *Improving Land Governance and Securing Land Rights in India*, p. 79.
6. Rao, A. Rama Mohan and Bhatt, P.V., Bhoomi, *A Case Study, published in Land Reforms in India, Computerisation of Land Records,* Vol. 10 ed. Wajahat Habibullah and Manoj Ahuja, Sage Publication India Pvt. Ltd., New Delhi, pp. 115-117, 2005.
7. Saleth, R. Marla, 'Land Reform under Military Agrarian Reform in Peru', 1969-78', published in *Economic and Political Weekly*, July 27, 1991. p. E 85.

8. Bhattacharjea, Ajit, 'Indian need not go the Soviet way' published in *'The Pioneer'*, Lucknow, December 27, 1991. p. 6.
9. Geddas Baralora, "A game theoretical Model of Reform in Latin American Democracies. Published in *American Political Science Review*, June 1991. Vol. 85, No. 2, pp. 372 and 387.
10. *Ibid.*, 4, Mediratta Achala, *Adjusting Laws and Institutions to address Urban Expansion and Governance*, p. 74.
11. *Ibid.*, 4, Annez, Patricia, Ahmedabad, More but Different Government for 'Slum Free' and Livable Cities, p. 81.
12. Suresh Kumar, P.S., *Do We Need a Digital Cadastre, published in Land Reforms in India*, Vol. 10, Sage Publications, New Delhi, p. 253, 2005.

13

Concrete Approach towards Land Reforms

Everybody talks about land reforms in his own way. We live in the age of science and information technology and everything is attempted to be weighed mathematically so that it is near to exactness. Only one Karl Marx could produce a theory closest to exactness based on social science and historical facts. Therefore, it is desirable to measure the status of land reforms in concrete terms so that its correlation with poverty can also be established.

Secondly, such a formula will always help the willing governments by revealing their shortcomings and suggesting them way forward.

Thirdly, it will pin down bureaucrats who always boast of their performance without concrete results because there are no concrete parameters to monitor and measure their performance in a concrete way and show them the mirror of their position of performance *vis-à-vis* others. This will also help the poor man, because out of the persons who measure their poverty, none is really poor and mostly they have not faced stark poverty or hunger. They always claim of them that the problem of poverty is not as serious or critical as projected to be. Therefore, a mathematical approach will place the status of land reforms in its most objective form and in a different manner. Of course, a formula is always a complex one taking into account some inherent digression or regression.

Therefore, we shall adopt one simple addition formula which will also cover the urban areas as per population of the poor in rural areas and urban areas respectively.

The World Bank has developed the Land Governance Assessment Framework (LGAF) together with many multi and bilateral partners (e.g., FAO, UN Habitat, etc.) "LGAF is intended as a first step to help countries deal with land governance issues. It is a diagnostic tool that is to be implemented at a local level in a collaborative fashion, that addresses the need for guidance to diagnose and benchmark land governance and that can help countries prioritise reforms and monitor progress overtime.[1]

The LGAF can have number of benefits as follows:

- Help facilitate communication and collaboration between different Government Departments as well as the private sector, civil society and academics to agree on key gaps and priority actions in the land sector as a basis for specific actions to foster change and in doing so establish a reference group of qualified and interested stakeholders with a shared understanding of the challenges of land governance and ways to address them;
- Document good practice against global standards and allow broad dissemination, evaluation and eventually upscaling of innovative approaches to improving land governance that have been taken by individual states to address common challenges to improved land governance, and
- Put in place a structure (and associated institutional arrangements) to monitor progress in states' quality of land governance and the effective service delivery that can increasingly be used to inform national policy decisions and allocation of resources.

The LGAF has number of indicators numbering about 21 which are grouped within five broad thematic areas that have been identified as major areas for policy intervention in the land sector.

Legal and Institutional Framework: Indicators related to the legal and institutional framework are designed to help policy-makers assess (a) the extent to which the range of existing land rights is legally recognised, (b) the level of documentation and enforcement, the cost of enforcing or gradually upgrading these rights, and (c) whether regulation and management of land involve institutions with clear mandates as well as policy processes that are transparent and equitable.

Land Use Planning, Management and Taxation: The intention of this category is to assess whether (a) land use restrictions are justified on the basis of the public interest, (b) necessary exemptions are granted promptly and transparently, (c) the process for land use planning is efficient, and (d) taxes on land and real estate are transparently determined and efficiently collected.

Management of Public Land: A focus on public land management aims to help assess the extent to which (a) public landholdings are justified and transparently inventoried and managed; (b) expropriation procedures are applied in the public interest through clear, transparent and fair processes involving the compensation of all those who lose rights and (c) the transfer or devolution of state land is transparent and monitored.

Public Provision of Land Information: Indicators related to this category assess (a) whether land information systems provide sufficient, relevant and up-to-date data on land ownership to the general public and (b) whether land administration services are accessible, affordable and sustained.

Dispute Resolution and Conflict Management: This fifth set of indicators can be used to assess (a) whether a country has affordable, clearly defined, transparent and unbiased mechanisms for the resolution of land disputes, and (b) whether these mechanisms function effectively in practice.

Based on foregoing broad thematic areas LGAF dimensions are worked out which will help to evaluate the implementation of land reforms or land related policies to tide over the problem of poverty at various levels like nation, state or province within a country and even at the distinct level. The LGAF factors are as follows:

Thematic Area

(I) Legal and Institutional Framework

LGI 1: Recognition of a continuum of rights. The law recognises ranges of rights held by individuals as well as groups (including secondary rights as well as rights held by minorities and women).

(i) Existing legal framework recognises rights held by most of the rural population, either through customary or statutory tenure regimes.

(ii) Existing legal framework recognises rights held by most of the urban population, either through customary or statutory tenure regimes.

(iii) The tenure of most groups in rural areas is formally recognised and clear regulations exist regarding groups internal organisation and legal representation.

(iv) The tenure in informal urban areas is formally recognised and clear regulations exist regarding groups' internal organisation and legal representation of groups.

(v) The law provides opportunities for those holding land under customary, group, or collective tenure to fully or partially individualise land ownership and use. Procedures for doing so are affordable, clearly specified, safeguarded and followed in practice.

LGI 2: Enforcement of rights. The rights recognised by law are enforced (including secondary rights as well as rights of minorities and women).

2. (i) Most communal lands have boundaries demarcated and surveyed or mapped and communal rights registered.

(ii) Most individual properties in rural areas are formally registered.

(iii) Most individual properties in urban areas are formally registered.

(iv) A high percentage of land registered to physical persons is registered in the name of women, either individually or jointly.

(v) Common property under condominiums is recognised and there are clear provisions in the law to establish arrangements for the management and maintenance of this common property.

(vi) When loss of rights occurs as a result of land use change not involving expropriation, compensation in cash or in kind is paid such that these people have comparable assets and can continue to maintain prior social and economic status.

LGI 3: Mechanisms for recognition of rights. The formal definition and assignment of rights and process of recording of rights, accords with actual practice or, where it does not, provides affordable avenues for establishing such consistency in a non-discriminatory manner.

3. (i) Non-documentary forms of evidence are used alone to obtain full recognition of claims to property when other forms of evidence are not available.

(ii) Legislation exists to formally recognise long-term, unchallenged possession and applies to both public and private land, although different rules may apply.

(iii) The costs for first time sporadic registration for a typical urban property is low compared to the property value.

(iv) There are no informal fees that need to be paid to effect first registration.

(v) The requirements for formalising housing in urban areas are clear, straightforward, affordable and implemented consistency in a transparent manner.

(vi) There is a clear, practical process for the formal recognition of possession and this process is implemented effectively, consistently and transparently.

LGI 4: Restrictions on rights. Land rights are not conditional on adherence to unrealistic standards.

4. (i) There is a series of regulations regarding urban land use, ownership and transferability that are for the most part justified on the basis of overall public interest and that are enforced.

(ii) There is a series of regulations regarding rural land use, ownership and transferability that are for the most part justified on the basis of overall interest and that are enforced.

LGI 5: Clarity of institutional mandates. Institutional mandates concerning the regulation and management of the land sector are clearly defined, duplication of responsibilities is avoided and information is shared as needed.

5. (i) There is a clear separation in the roles of policy formulation, implementation of policy through land management and administration and the arbitration of any disputes that may arise as a result of implementation of policy.

(ii) The mandated responsibilities exercised by the authorities dealing with land administration issues are clearly defined and non-overlapping with those of other land sector agencies.

(iii) Assignment of land-related responsibilities between the different levels of government is clear and non-overlapping.

(iv) Information related to rights in land is available to other institutions that need this information at reasonable cost and is readily accessible, largely because land information is maintained in a uniform way.

LGI 6: Equity and non-discrimination in the decision-making process. Policies are formulated through a legitimate decision-making process that draws on inputs from all concerned. The legal framework is non-discriminatory and institutions to enforce property rights are equally accessible to all.

6. (i) A comprehensive policy exists or can be inferred by the existing legislation. Land policy decisions that affect sections of the community are based on consultation with those affected and their feedback on the resulting policy is sought and incorporated in the resulting policy.
   (ii) Land policies incorporate equity objectives that are regularly and meaningfully monitored and their impact on equity issues is compared to that of other instruments.
   (iii) Cost of implementation of land policy is estimated, expected benefits are identified and compared to cost and there are sufficient budget, resources and institutional capacity for implementation.
   (iv) Land institutions report on land policy implementation in a regular, meaningful and comprehensive way, with reports being publicly accessible.

Thematic Area 2. Land Use Planning, Management and Taxation

LGI 7: Transparency of land use restrictions. Changes in land use and management regulations are made in a transparent fashion and provide significant benefits for society in general rather than just for specific groups.

7. (i) In urban areas, public input is sought in preparing and amending land use plans and the public responses are explicitly referenced in the report prepared by the public body responsible for preparing the new public plans. This report is publicly accessible.
   (ii) In rural areas, public input is sought in preparing and amending land use plans and the public responses are explicitly mentioned

in the report prepared by the public body responsible for preparing the new public plans. This report is publicly accessible.

(iii) Mechanisms to allow the public to capture a significant share of the gains from changing land use are regularly used and applied transparently based on clear regulation.

(iv) Most land that has had a change in land use assignment in the past three years has changed to the destined use.

LGI 8: Efficiency in the land use planning process. Land use plans and regulations are justified, are effectively implemented, do not drive large parts of the population into informality and are able to cope with population growth.

8. (i) In the largest city in the country, urban development is controlled effectively by a hierarchy of regional and detailed land use plans that are kept up to date.

(ii) In the four major cities in the country, the urban development is controlled effectively by a hierarchy of regional and detailed land use plans that are kept up-to-date.

(iii) In the largest city in the country, the urban planning process or authority is able to cope with the increasing demand for serviced units and land as evidenced by the fact that almost all new dwellings are formal.

(iv) Existing requirements for residential plot sizes are met in most plots.

(vi) The share of land set aside for specific use that is used for a non-specified purpose in contravention of existing regulations is low.

LGI 9: Speed and predictability of applications for restricted land uses. Development permits are granted promptly and predictably.

9. (i) Requirements to obtain a building permit are technically justified, affordable and clearly disseminated.

(ii) All applications for building permits receive a decision in a short period.

LGI 10: Transparency of valuation. Valuations for Tax purposes are based on clear principles, applied uniformly, updated regularly and publicly accessible.

10. (i) The assessment of land and property values for tax purposes is based on market prices with minimal differences between recorded values and market prices across different uses and types of users and valuation rolls are regularly updated.

(ii) There is a policy that valuation rolls be publicly accessible and this policy is effective for all properties that are considered for taxation.

LGI 11: Tax collection efficiency. Resources from Land and property taxes are collected and the yield from land taxes exceeds the cost of collection.

11. (i) There are limited exemptions to the payment of land and property taxes and the exemptions that exist are clearly based on equity or efficiency grounds and applied in a transparent and consistent manner.

(ii) Most property holders liable for land and property tax are listed on the tax roll.

(iii) Most assessed property taxes are collected.

(iv) The amount of property taxes collected exceeds the cost of staff in charge of collection by a factor of more than five.

Thematic Area 3. Management of Public Land

LGI 12: Identification and clear management of public land. Public land ownership is justified, inventoried and under clear management responsibilities and relevant information is publicly accessible.

12. (i) Public land ownership is justified by the provisions of public goods at the appropriate level of government and such land is managed in a transparent and effective way.

(ii) The majority of public land is clearly identified on the ground or on maps.

(iii) The management responsibility for different types of public land is unambiguously assigned.

(iv) There are adequate budgets and human resources that ensure responsible management of public lands.

(v) All the information in the public land inventory is accessible to the public.

(vi) Key information for land concessions is recorded and publicly accessible.

LGI 13: Justification and time efficiency of expropriation processes. The state expropriates land only for overall public interest and this is done efficiently.

13. (i) A minimal amount of land expropriated in the past three years is used for private purposes.

(ii) The majority of land that has been expropriated in the past three years has been transferred to its destined use.

LGI 14: Transparency and fairness of expropriation procedures. Expropriation procedures are clear and transparent and compensation in kind or at market values is paid fairly expeditiously.

14. (i) Where property is expropriated, fair compensation, in kind or in cash, is paid so that the displaced households have comparable assets and can continue to maintain prior social and economic status.

(ii) Most expropriated land owners receive compensation within one year.

(iv) Independent avenues to lodge a complaint against expropriation exist and are easily accessible.

(vii) A first instance decision has been reached for the majority of complaints about expropriation lodged during the past three years.

LGI 15: Allocation of public land is transparent, Transfer of public land to private use follows a clear, transparent and competitive process and payment are collected and audited.

15. (i) Most public land disposed of in the past three years is through sale or lease through public auction or open tender process.

(ii) A majority of the total agreed upon payments are collected from private parties for the lease of public lands.

(iii) All types of public land are generally divested at market prices in a transparent process irrespective of the investor's status (for example, domestic or foreign).

Thematic Area 4. Public Provision of Land Information

LGI 16: Completeness. The land registry provides information on different private tenure categories in a way that is geographically complete and searched by parcel as well as by right holder and can be obtained expeditiously by all interested parties.

16. (i) Most records for privately held land registered in the registry are readily identifiable in maps in the registry or cadastre.
   (ii) Relevant private encumbrances are recorded consistently, and in a reliable fashion and can be verified at low cost by any interested party.
   (iii) Relevant public restrictions or charges are recorded consistently and in a reliable fashion and can be verified at a low cost by any interested party.
   (iv) The records in the registry can be searched by both right holder name and parcel.
   (v) Copies of extracts of documents recording rights in property can be obtained by anyone who pays the necessary formal fee, if any.
   (vi) Copies or extracts of documents recording rights in property can generally be obtained within one day of request.

LGI 17: Reliability. Registry information is updated and sufficient to make meaningful inference on ownership.

17. (i) There are meaningful published service standards, and the registry actively monitors its performance against these standards.
   (ii) Most ownership information in the registry or cadastre is upto date.

LGI 18: Cost-effective, accessibility and sustainability. Land administration services are provided in a cost effective manner.

18. (i) The cost for registering a property transfer is minimal compared to the property value.
   (ii) The total fees collected by the registry exceed the total registry operating cost.
   (iii) There is significant investment in capital in the system to record rights in land that the system is sustainable but still accessible by the poor.

LGI 19: Transparency. Fees are determined and collected in a transparent manner.

19. (i) A clear schedule of fees for different services is publicly accessible and receipts are issued for all transactions.

    (ii) Mechanisms to detect and deal with illegal staff behaviour exist in all registry offices and all cases are promptly dealt with.

Thematic Area 5. Dispute Resolution and Conflict Management

LGI 20: Assignment of responsibility. Responsibility for conflict management at different levels is clearly assigned, in line with actual practice; relevant bodies are competent in applicable legal matters and decisions can be appealed.

(i) Institutions for providing a first instance of conflict resolution are accessible at the local level in the majority of communities.

(ii) There is an informal or community-based system that resolves disputes in an equitable manner and decisions made by this system have some recognition in the formal judicial or administrative dispute resolution system.

(iii) There are no parallel avenues for conflict resolution or, if parallel avenues exist, responsibilities are clearly assigned and widely known and explicit rules for shifting from one to the other are in place to minimise the scope for forum shopping.

(iv) A process and mechanism exist to appeal rulings on land cases at reasonable cost, with disputes resolved in a timely manner.

LGI 21: Low-level of pending conflict. The share of land affected by pending conflicts is low and decreasing.

(i) Land disputes in the formal court system are low compared to the total number of court cases.

(ii) A decision in a land-related conflict is reached in the first-instance court within one year in the majority of cases.

(iii) Long standing land conflicts are a small proportion of the total pending land dispute court cases.[2]

The responsibility for the conduct of the exercise lies with a country co-ordinator, who is a local expert in law or land administration. Second, dimensions to be rated are grouped into sets of about 10 topics.

Panels are then formed, with three to five members, who have experience with the relevant topic. And then all are aggregated and in the end, discussions are held to implement good practices elsewhere to fill the gap and formal decisions are taken for implementation of parameters or good practices which will help to alleviate poverty through improvement in land-related policies and their implementation on field.

As the foregoing formula is difficult to grasp and has equal weightage for land reforms in urban areas, it is suggested for the time-being, following arithmetic formula may be adopted which will be very simple and easy to implement on the field. Some factors for urban areas may accordingly be modified giving due weightage of that factor in the urban areas of a District, Province or a Country.

The following factors can be considered to arrive at a mathematical formula for quantifying land reform. The following linear equation has been suggested.

The term factor analysis "embraces a variety of techniques." Our discussion focusses on the one procedure 'principal component analysis' and the factors derived from the analysis are expressed as linear equation. These linear equations are of the form:

$$T(LR) = R_1L_1 + R_2L_2 + R_3L_3 + R_4L_4 + R_5L_5 + R_6L_6 + R_7L_7 + R_8L_8 + R_9L_9 + R_{10}L_{10} + \ldots\ldots R_nL_n$$

T(LR) is the Total/Resultant Land Reform.

R is the weightage or ranking of the factor.

T(LR) is the Total/Resultant Land Reform.

R is the Weightage or Ranking of the Factor.

L indicates factor related (to land reform on the basis of conclusions arrived at earlier. It may represent one factor or combination of factors. The factors are thus as follows:

L_1: Existence or implementing of Employment Generating Schemes like Jawahar Rojgar Yojana, N.R.E.P[3] I.T.D.P.[4] or P.M. Rojgar Yojana or Mahatma Gandhi Rural Employment Guarantee Programme (MNREGA).[5]

L_2: Whether Tenancy or sharecroppers are recorded or unrecorded and are given their rights. They should not be ejected. This also includes tenants on urban properties or persons in possession on urban lands for long as squatters.

L_3: Practice of co-operative farming or assistance by panchayats by developing local leadership and helping the cultivators locally in all matters. This will also include the ward committees or councils or Residents' Welfare Associations formed for common purposes.

L_4: Distribution of Government surplus land after vesting in State and giving possession to the *pattadars* or assignees of the vested lands after distribution of surplus lands and thereafter. This will include distribution of excess lands as homestead or providing of house sites after earmarking precious urban lands.

L_5: Position of land records, detection of *benami* lands and whether land has been equitably distributed and passbooks of land-details have been issued.

L_6: Extent of social and religious reforms.

L_7: Availability of legal aid to the landless agricultural labourers, *pattadars*, sharecroppers or poor peasants or to unauthorised occupants of government or public lands for more than 12 years or squatters.

L_8: Financial assistance or credit for supply of timely inputs and other investment support. In urban areas, this will mainly mean availability of credit for house building or even to start small business or labour co-operatives.

L_9: Success of consolidation operation, or co-operative or group housing societies including Self-help Groups in rural as well as in urban areas.

L_{10}: Allotment of house sites and restoration of alienated tribal land or lands transferred due to distress. In urban areas, the allotment of house site should be made non-transferable and restoration of the same, if transferred due to distress or under coercion or violence.

$T_{i(LR)}$: R_1L_1 and R_1 is the multiplication factor, where,

$$I = 1, 2, 3, 4, \ldots 10 \ldots n$$

The co-efficient R_1 may be determined for each factor depending on the relative importance of that factors R_1 R_2 R_3 R_4 R_5 R_6 R_7 R_8 R_9 R_{10} or any other co-efficient or factor taken later on.

The weightage *inter se* can be determined by developing closed ended response based on the concept or decision of the research. Here, one cannot avoid subjectivity. To reduce the subjectivity, even detailed discussion can be made to determine the allocation of the weightage. For this purpose, a rating scale may be fixed. Rating scales, by and large, try to secure the intensity of the respondents' feelings on a predefined set of response alternatives. Here, guidance has been taken from Likert Scale which is also called a 'summated ratings' scale. Let us construct the following six statements or decisions relating to issues under investigation, very adequate, adequate, so so, inadequate, very inadequate, nil. Let us assign the numerical values or rank ranging from 0 to 10 different categories as follows:

Very adequate	assigned	10 marks
Adequate	assigned	8 marks
So so	assigned	4 marks
Inadequate	assigned	2 marks
Very inadequate	assigned	1 mark
Nil	assigned	0 mark

Using this method of scoring, total scoring is calculated depending on the strength of the factor.

Let us, therefore, assign percentage importance to each factor taking clues from discussion as follows. Under the same factor weightage to urban and rural areas may be given as per ratio of urban and rural poor.

T(LR) is taken as 100 per cent. Therefore, each factor will be determined on the basis of 'a/100 where 'a' represents percentage weightage *inter se* of each factor.

L_1: Four per cent is given maximum value for Employment Generating Schemes during lean season of work or otherwise. This can be maximum as R_1 $L_{1,}$ = 10* .04 = .4 similarly.

L_2: 20 per cent weightage is given to recording of sharecroppers and protection to their rights of cultivation. Therefore, L_2 factor will be 20 per cent in ideal condition but on rating scale, it will vary from zero to 10* .2 = 2. In urban areas, it will mean recording and protection to tenants on urban properties or squatters on public lands.

L_3: Local Assistance, it is given 10 per cent weightage. If the Panchayats are established and are functioning well, there is semblance of co-operative farming or pisciculture and there are organisations of *pattadars*, agricultural labourers or sharecroppers, the adequate weightage will be given. In case of ideal situation of covering the entire village through co-operative farming, full weightage or very adequate category will be given. However, before the stage of co-operative farming, rural organisations are necessary to safeguard rights of cultivators. In urban areas, the houseless workers can be organised from various industries, business or service. They can be potential change agents and can help peasants in urban areas to bring change.

L_4: 40 per cent weightage is earmarked for distribution of government vested lands. This is the main target specially in the Indian context. In fact, aim of Imposition of Ceiling Acts is to take away excess lands from the big land holders and to effect redistribution. It is not sufficient that the lands have gone to government but also should be distributed. Therefore, if the lands are still with the local landlords, it will be of very inadequate category. If the lands are vested to government but possession is not taken over and *benami* lands are not unearthed, it will be within inadequate category. If the Acts have been implemented, this will be 50-50 category of case. If the lands are distributed but the possessions not given, it will be classified as adequate category. Only in case of lands are properly allotted along with possession given over, it will be classified as 'very adequate' category allocating 10 marks. In case of urban areas, distirbutioin of public land is a different proposition. Instead, houses may be built thereon and distributed among houseless urban poor.

L_5: Weightage eight per cent is given to the position of land records and existing position of landownership or landholding. If lands are more or less equitably distributed and there is no cultivation beyond ceiling limit in the village, it will get allocation of rank within 50-50 category. If land records along with village maps properly do exist, then, it will have a ranking in adequate category and if passbooks detailing individual holdings are distributed, it will be a perfect system in 'very adequate' ranking with full 10 marks. The land records for urban areas are to be started by the same machinery and may cover all urban areas gradually. If in urban areas, public lands are not taken over, it will be in inadequate category. If public lands are taken over, it will be in 50-50 category. If housing is built or house-sites are built, it will be in adequate category. If the houses are flats or house sites are distributed and records or pass books are issued to the allottees, it will be 100 per cent success category.

L_6: total weightage three per cent is given to social and religious reforms. Poor people spend a lot of money on festivals and ceremonies and do not go for work on a number of days to celebrate many unknown local festivals or rituals due to superstitions or orthodoxy. They also indulge in indebtedness and drinking. If there is lot of indebtedness, it will be 50-50 or normal category or average category. Social reforms like keeping villagers away from gambling or drinking, will earn "adequate classification". If the agriculturists are free from religious dogmas, they will be placed in the highest ranking. The same facts apply for the urban poor. However, weightage will be given as per population proportion of rural *vis-à-vis* urban poor.

L_7: Weightage three per cent is allocated for legal aid to the poor. If legal aid is available only through mutual conciliation without any statutory system, it will fall in very inadequate ranking. If conciliation or disposal of disputes is done through the aegis of *panchayat* bodies or *nyaya panchayats* or through official agencies, it will fall within inadequate category. If legal aid facilities are available up to revenue courts, it will be in 50-50 or normal category. If legal aid is available up to District Judge Court's level, it will be adequate. And if legal aid system free of cost actually is available up to High Court or Supreme Court level, it will be given the highest ranking. For urban areas, the weightage will be contributed as per percentage of urban area.

L_8: Five per cent weightage is given for financial assistance for crops through government or co-operative or Panchayat agencies including subsidies. This also reflects the credit facilities available for cultivation to delink the sharecropper or *pattadar* from the moneylender. In this category, mostly crop-credit finances are included, i.e., credit available to purchase plough, cattle, manures and seeds etc. However, if soil conservation work has been done or irrigational facilities are available, the village will be placed in very inadequate or inadequate rankings respectively. If credits from banks are available, it will be of adequate category. If government subsidies are available fully, then the situation will be of very adequate nature. In case of urban area, it will mean bank loans or government grant or subsidy for construction of houses for the landless persons.

L_9: Only one per cent weightage is given to consolidation operations. Without co-operative farming, consolidation has come under criticism due to corrupt practices. Therefore, if the consolidation operations are started, it will be of 50-50 category. If the parcels or plots are finally demarcated, it will be of adequate category. If the plots are dispute free, it will be placed in 'very adequate' ranking. It will include co-operative or group housing projects in urban areas.

L_{10}: Six per cent significance or strength is given equally to allotment of house sites to the rural poor as three per cent and three per cent for restoration of alienated land due to distress. As tribal population, is very scanty, the restoration of tribal land has also been put in the latter category. If the house sites are allotted, it will be adequate ranking. If the house sites are so made that the poor classes are free from fear of the upper classes and they are properly put in effective possession, the ranking will be very adequate. In an deal case L_{10} is ten. In urban areas allotment of housing by government will be highly appreciated even if it is for caste based urban poor as their condition is worse than the rural poor.

In case of ideal situation, all L_{is} will have 10 ranking points. Accordingly, the estimate may be made whether a village, sub-division, district or state comes within the type of category, i.e., very inadequate, adequate, 50-50, inadequate or very inadequate state of affairs of land reforms.

The co-efficients in the factor equations are called "factor loadings". They appear in each factor column, corresponding to each variable. The equation may be depicted in a random case as $L_{(LR)} = 10L_1 + 8L_2 + OL_3 + 0l_4 + 4L_5 + 0l_6 + 0l_7 + 2L_8 + 1L_9 + 1L_{10}$ where L1… to L_{10} are fixed already.

The factor loadings depict their relative importance of each variable with respect to a particular factor. In the above equation, we have got positive loading factor indicating that they are variables of importance in determining the extent of land reform in a given sample. Similarly, some factors with negative attribute may be included which pull back land reforms. But as this study is a part of legal study, there is not much scope to go into acute niceties or finer mathematical details with the help of statistical regression analysis. It is to concretise the ideas so that real focus may not be lost sight of while viewing the land reforms as an integrated whole.

It means that the important factors to contribute towards land reforms are distribution of surplus land or land for house site or house itself, recording of sharecroppers or tenants and organising the rural and urban folk for implementation of land reforms. The three factors will amount to 70 per cent of resultant land reform, i.e., $L_{(LR)}$.

In the ideal solution, the factor derived will explain 100 per cent of the variance in each of the original variable or factor.

There are two important subject issues which should be properly resolved before employing factor analysis model.

1. How best the factors should be employed in attempting to reduce the data? How best the criteria should be used in establishing that number?
2. The labelling of the factors is intuitive and subjective. The following resultant land reform (LR) is obtained for the state of Uttar Pradesh.

$T_{(LR)}$ = .068(I) + 0.23(II) + .16(III) + 2.34(IV) +.3(V) + .0085(VI) + .35(VII) + .1 (VIII) + .00(IX) + .41(X) = 3.90, i.e., about 39 per cent[6].

Applying preceding empirical formula, we find that land reform beyond over 50 per cent category should be good. Beyond 80 per cent, it should be adequate. On the basis of above formula we find extent of land reform in two provinces of India, i.e., U.P. and West Bengal, is 39 per cent and 74 per cent respectively.

Similarly, the formula can be successfully applied to assess total land reforms from macro to the micro level, i.e., from national level to province, district: sub-divisional/taluka/tehsil, block or village level and accordingly, corrective steps can be taken to improve the extent of land reform at that level.

For West Bengal, the leading province in India in land reforms, we may give following weightage:

L_1 = As landless and poor farmers get only about 50 days of work out of 150 days required. The work is allotted more or less equitable except with little party colouring which should not be there. Poor is poor irrespective of caste, creed, community, colour or political affiliation.

Therefore, weightage will be just below average, i.e., inadequate = 2.

L_2= This factor of recording of sharecroppers is very successful. Though, as per an estimate there are more sharecroppers and there can be conferment of ownership rights to them like in Maharashtra. Yet, this factor gets full marks due to very poor performance of other states in this regard. But the same security couldn't be given to tenants of properties in urban areas. Secondly, peri-urban lands couldn't be recorded in favour of sharecroppers nor public lands are being properly utilised. Therefore R = 8.

L_3= This factor also gets good marking as Panchayats and Peasants' Organisations are very strong so much so there is hardly any scope of injustice to the poor farmers. But the organisations of homeless people or economically weaker sections without shelter or homestead are not strong. Moreover, as co-operative farming is yet far off and efforts by governmental agencies are nil, this may get adequate marking, i.e., eight.

L_4= There is equitable distribution of land more or less but all lands could not be distributed as yet because about 1.70 lakh acres of land is locked in litigation. Therefore, this factor can only get at the most adequate category, i.e., eight.

L_5= Position of land records is improving day by day by means of computerisation of land records and updation of maps through digitisation. However, there is no substantial progress as regards property records in urban local bodies (ULBs). The situation is likely to improve as agitation of homeless people in urban areas is likely to flare up. Therefore, it is average R = 5.

L_6= Social and religious factors are to some extent dormant in society but are very much effective in personal lives. Therefore, farmers are occupied with the social rites and religious rites. L_6 is, therefore, very inadequate with one rating. They spend lot of money or percentage of their earning on liquor drinks and organising community worship now and then which drain out their savings even in the production year.

L_7= Therefore, R_7 = 5. The Nyaya Panchayats or rural courts are not in existence in the state. Legal Aid has not reached the village Legal Aid campaign is very active for urban poor in cities and up to the sub-divisional courts. Therefore, R7 is five ranking.

L_8= Facility of crop credit is satisfactory through Panchayats but due to poor recovery, bankers retard progress. It will be of average, category, i.e., R_8= 5 Allotment of house site, is O.K. but construction is inadequate. However, construction of houses in urban areas is picking up as lot of finances are available from so many agencies of government or private.

L_9= Neither consolidation is taken up nor is likely to be taken up. Therefore L_9=0. Though, there is a provision of co-operative farming in the statute book in the West Land Reforms Act, 1955 but no step has been taken to implement these provisions.

L_{10}= Restoration of alienation land due to distress is done but restoration of land to tribals shows lethargy as cases before Special

Officer, Scheduled Castes and Scheduled Tribes and Revenue Officer are not processed expeditiously. They follow lengthy procedure and grant frequent adjournments which mar the spirit of the statute and the poor's organisations get disheartened. The factor gets a weightage as adequate-8.

Calculating above factors, we find:

$$T(LR) = .4 \times 2(I) + 2 \times 10(II) + 1 \times 8(III) + 4 \times 8(IV) + .8x5\ (V) + .3 \times 1(VI) + .3 \times 5\ (VII) + .5 \times 5(VIII) + 0 \times .1\ (IX) + .6 \times 8(X) = .8 + 20 + 8 + 32 + 4 + .3 + 1.5 + 2.5{+}0 + 4.8$$

$$= 73.9 \text{ per cent} = 74 \text{ per cent.}$$[7]

Which is over 50 per cent category but is below adequate category (80 per cent).

(A) Assessment of Land Reforms in Peru

Based on data and information available from the World Bank in their book 'the LGAF', Peru can be assessed as per formula factorwise as follows:

(i) Implementation of Employment Generating Scheme

There are not many explicit employment generating schemes in Peru. But the community ownership system takes care of the poor persons or non-working or hungry members of the community through the principle of equitable distribution of land for work purpose. Thus, this factor can be assigned only to very inadequate category and through employment generating schemes i.e., $R_1 = 1$.

(ii) Recording of Tenants

As community ownership is mostly prevalent, there is hardly any scope of sharecropping to individual owners. However, the chiefs of such farmers' communities sometimes or at places behave like local lords. In such a case, they require recording of cropping or sharecropping by the person who has been cultivating as a member of the community. Thus, it is more a community farming or group farming without state's intervention. But there is still 3.3 million hectare area with 1 million parcels for about 1.5 million population to be recognised. As there is ample land in urban areas, there is no dearth of homestead. Thus, this factor in Peru will be termed as so-so with marking four.

(iii) Local Self-governance Units and Collective Farming

The community system is very strong in Peru. However, land rights of Andean and Amazonian Community have still to be settled. In their guise, private farms are 'planting' settlers without traditional ties with the land. The local government machinery is not adequate. Therefore, we may put this factor in 50-50 average category with marking –4.

(iv) Distribution of Government Surplus Land

There is a continuous system of distribution of surplus land by the community leadership based on the principle that the one who works or willing or capable to work on farm, will get the land. Even the most autocrat or dictatorship government carried on distribution of public land or government surplus land to keep themselves in undisturbed power. Whatsoever, may be the reason, many groups are using land under common property. Thus, the government land is being freely used but its legal recognition is still inadequate. As a result, the disputes may arise. As there are few landless persons, this factor can also be given average category with four marking. If the government or community records along with possession of parcels of land is provided, then it would have been in adequate category, i.e., eight marking.

(v) Position of Land Records

The status of land records both in rural and urban area is very much lagging behind. As a result, overlap occurs and there are conflicts sometimes violent too. Overlap is there with state property and in some cases with private properties. Even in urban areas, individual properties are not supported by property titles. Access to land records or registries is very frequent through professionals. Thus, the factor relating to land records and title is given only very inadequate marking –1. However, adequate steps are being taken to update land records by the National Public Registries System.

(vi) Social and Religious Reforms

The success of land reform will also involve that the customary leaders are not corrupt and guide the community or indigenous people more by their conduct than through exercise of their brutal power entrusted by the people themselves to them. They easily come under the influence of land speculators, private investors and colonisers or real estate dealers. They should teach the poor people to inculcate savings habit and discard lot of consumption of liquor or locally brewed wine. The women should be given due right in land ownership as they are mostly working on field and support families. Their names should be recorded in land records along with their husbands, so that lands are not alienated against family interests. Thus, it will come under very inadequate category with marking –1.

(vii) Availability of Legal Aid to Settle Disputes

Legal pluralism is enshrined in Peru's Constitution. Andean peasant and Amazonian indigenous communities (tribals) perform judicial functions following customary law within their territories. Informal but legitimate and recognised justice institutions, including community assemblies, peasants' civil squads, city civil squads and 'neighbourhood presidents' play an important role in settling disputes for the roughly 50 per cent of the population in rural areas. But after losing in these courts, the clever people go to the formal judicial system which doesn't recognise the informal system of justice dispensation and formal justice system is as biased as in other developing countries, and there is no special consideration for poor persons. As justice is available to the poor persons through informal system even without legal aid, we may categorise this factor in adequate category and fix ranking as eight.

(viii) Availability of Credit

For encouraging cultivation by the poor farmers, readymade bank credits at the lower rates should be made available under government subsidies. Similarly, in urban areas, easy credits should be made available with the government support so that shelterless persons can build their houses. This will save the poor men from the clutches of money lenders, profiteers or land-speculator or real estate mafia. As this is only available to some extent for urban housing, it may be kept in inadequate category with ranking at two.

(ix) Collectivisation and Group Housing

As the cultivation is under the community, and the poorest among the community members is assisted by others, it is good. Secondly, urban housing is also constructed by the government as well as by the private developers. It will be better if the poor people are allowed to renovate their existing dwelling units or add a storey or add rooms to their houses. If they can be provided small parcels of land as homestead they will be satisfied as regards growing vegetable, keeping their domestic animals and build their customary house on it. This factor thus can be kept only inadequate category with marking two.

(x) Allotment of House-sites and Restoration of Alienated Land due to Distress

State land is transferred by public auction. Thus, there will be no scope to distribute land for house-sites in rural and urban areas. Government should reserve a part of public land for the poor and allot among them based on well-laid down policy and principles.

However, in respect of expropriation of land for public purpose, Peruvian law is very specific that the land can be acquired for reasons of national security or public need such as to build road or bridge so as to ensure that state is the direct beneficiary. The lands are restored to the original owners or land evictees if the land is not used for its planned purpose within one year. Thus, one can give only inadequate rank to the factor as two.

Summing up the foregoing discussion, we arrive at following total land reforms.

T(LR) = .4 × 1 (i) + 2 × 4 (ii) + 1 × 3 (iii) + 4 × 4 (iv) + .8 × 1(v) +.3 × 1(vi) + .3 × 8(vii) + .5 × 2 (viii) + .1 × 2 (ix) + .6 × 2 (x) = .4 + 8 + 3 + 16 +.8 + .3 + 2.4 + 1+ .2+ 1.2 = 33.3

Thus, Peru falls within the so-so category, and inadequate category of land reform *vis-à-vis* its poor. It calls for unorthodox measures to correct and improve indices of poverty *vis-à-vis* land. Lot of good steps already taken are underway. I am sure that Peru will do considerably better and come within so-so category (average) soon.

(B) Tanzania

Let us take one country from African continent. Tanzania is forward looking country in land reforms. The government adopted ambitious 1999 Land Act, and Village Land Act but these are still to be adequately implemented.

Land in Tanzania are of three types: Village land which covers 70 per cent of mainland Tanzania, with 28-30 million people. Reserved land is 28 per cent land which comprises forest land, conservation areas, national parks and game reserves. General or Public land is rest two per cent. Let us assess the land reforms implemented in Tanzania on a foregoing formula.

(i) Employment Generating Schemes

There is a vast population of pastoralists or shifting cultivators, who are required to be given employment during lean seasons or during hostile seasons like rainy season, storms etc. However, whenever foreign or international grants are available, then some of these schemes are implemented. These schemes depend on the health of economy which is not surplus in most of the underdeveloped countries of Africa. Therefore, this factor is given 0 (zero) weightage.

(ii) Recording of Tenants or Sharecroppers

The land records and maps are almost non-existent. Therefore, there is no effective security of tenure on land less for the sharecroppers. They work as and when work on the field or farm is available. However, communal use of land is recognised under the 2007 Unit Titles Act. So also it is prevalent in urban areas. There is customary communal tenure but there are often conflicts between pastoralists and farmers. Thus, this can be given only inadequate category with marking as two.

(iii) Local Self-governance and Peasants' Organisations

Tanzania has community administration. The Tanzania farmers are not well-organised as Tanzania is a small country as compared to the sophisticated fire power with the developed state or government. There are village councils in rural areas, and ward councils in urban areas which are available to redress grievances of the rural people. Thus, this can be put in 50-50 category with rank: four.

(iv) Redistribution of Government Surplus Land

General surplus land is there but there is no regulation in place by the state. Therefore, people informally occupy these lands. Even about 3,00,000 to one million people informally occupy forest land but they are neither recorded nor they have been given formal right of cultivation. They should be given right of cultivation on fringe forest lands which they have been traditionally cultivating for generations. They are the real protectors of forests as their livelihood depends on forest produce. The land with big landowners beyond ceiling limit should be vested to the national government and then it should be distributed among wanderers and shelterless people in urban areas. About 3,00,000 to one million squatters should be given first priority in allotment of land, if they are landless also. If such land is public land, there is no problem. If the land belongs to private persons, government should pay compensation to the landowners to expropriate their land if the squatters are otherwise eligible for these lands. About 80 per cent of housing in urban cities including capital Dar es Salaam remains informal. Almost 87.5 per cent of urban residents live on plots of size 400 square metres or less.

This problem should be solved otherwise this vital factor will remain under inadequate category at two.

(v) Status of Land Records

The land records are in its initial stage. Hardly, any record-of-rights is issued because boundaries of villages are not yet demarcated. In urban areas, the encroachers can be considered as deemed licensees and they should be given such certificates known as certificate of occupancy (CRO).

Similarly, the process of issuance of the certificates of customary right of occupancy (CCRO) to individual landholders within the communal village is demand driven. However, in early 2010, more than a decade after passage of the relevant legislation only 753 of Tanzania's 10,397 registered villages (or seven per cent) had received certificates, which raises concerns mainly because of the lack of clarity about the legal status of land in unregistered villages. The status of 'squatters' on national reserved land is also unclear.

In view of foregoing, this factor can be kept in 50-50 category with four marks.

(vi) Social and Religious Reforms

About 20 per cent of land is registered in the names of women. Public education and affirmative action by public authorities is necessary to encourage more women to get land registered in their names or jointly with spouses. There is no other social and religious reform being undertaken in Tanzania.

Thus, it can be assigned only very inadequate category with one mark.

(vii) Legal Aid

There are four tiers of land courts in Tanzania starting from village Council to the High Court. However, instead of improving access to justice, the system resulted in an increased number of conflicts and accumulation of a backlog of unresolved cases. One main reason for the delays was that, instead of using informal dispute resolution to resolve issues quickly, lower level councils or courts adopted court like proceeding. Secondly, there is overlap of jurisdiction. Thirdly, there is forum shopping. But no legal aid is available. Therefore, this factor will be given zero (0) mark.

(viii) Financial Assistance for Cultivation

There are hardly anti-poverty schemes being implemented except efforts for survey and updation of land records with the help of foreign or funding by UN bodies. However, banks keep on financing agriculture sector in a routine way. Therefore, this factor may be kept in very inadequate category, and may be given one (1) mark. Similarly, in urban areas, sometimes encroachers may also arrange to build up their houses with the help of credit by the banks.

(ix) Co-operative Farming

As community institute is quite strong in many of the traditional areas, this factor may be given adequate marking, i.e., eight.

(x) Allotment of House Sites and Restoration of Alientated Land

This factor is also not very much available. The government's economy is not very surplus so as to fund taking over lands for allotment of house sites in rural areas and houses/flats in urban areas. However, restoration of land on ground of undue distressed condition is done but the compensation to the transferee becomes a problem. The house sites in urban areas in a small way are made available.

Therefore, this factor may also be kept in very inadequate category with (1) marking each.

On the basis of foregoing discussions and marking strength of each factor, the formula is concretised as follows:

$LR_{(Total)}$: .4 × 1(i) + 2 × 2(ii) + 1 × 4(iii) + 4 × 2(iv) + .8 × 4(v) + .3 × 1(vi) + .3 × 0(vii) + .5 × 1 (viii) + .1 × 8(ix) + .6 × 1(x) = .4 + 4 + 4 + 8 + 3.2 + .3 + .5 + .8 + .6 ~21.8 = 22

Thus, Tanzania in Africa falls within inadequate and 50-50 category of nations as far as land reform is concerned. However, there is lot of scope for further improvement which I gather is underway. Thus, African counties are lagging behind in implementation of land reforms also *vis-à-vis* other countries in the world which calls for radical steps by the Organisation of African Union (OAU) and by the World Bank to ameliorate the situation.

(C) Indonesia

Let us analyse the land reform implementation is one of the most populous South East Asian countries having about 230 million population.

Indonesia has lot of forest land like its neighbour country the Philippines. It has modern set-up of the state divided between provinces, districts and municipalities. Side by side, Indonesia also has traditional communal land tenure significantly unlike in India which is confined only in few pockets of North-Eastern States known as seven sisters. As it has the largest Muslim population in the world, all the laws of Indonesia including laws relating to land are influenced by the Mohamedan Law as expounded by the Shariat and other sources and the women have limited rights on lands. Let us take up the prevalence of land reform factor-wise.

(i) Employment Generating Schemes

The economy of Indonesia is not so surplus as to accommodate employment generating schemes during rainy seasons or lean season of the cultivation. Lot of employment generating schemes can be undertaken in large forests for cleaning the forests from weeds, fallen leaves and dead wood or timber.

Thus, this factor can be assigned as zero (0) weightage.

(ii) Recording of Tenants or Sharecroppers

Forest land is 70 per cent on which no right is recognised. Even on forest fringes on degraded lands, people are living there for generations, but they have no legally recognised right which they should have like India has started the process under STORFA. Rest of land is regulated by 1960 Basic Agrarian Law (BAL) that provides legal recognition of different types of tenure, including individual registrable rights of ownership (Hak Milik), plantation, building or use rights including rights of community.

Thus, lack of well-defined rights cause conflicts. Rights of cultivation on community land is just like the right of sharecroppers. Therefore, this factor can be assigned 50-50 category of strength, i.e., four.

(iii) Local Bodies and Peasants' Organisations

There are lot of communities in Indonesia who manage land locally. There are village councils and wards or communes in urban areas which help to manage land and problems of the poor locally. These were well-organised peasants' mobilisations like Indonesia Peasant Front (BTI) under the Indonesian Communist Party (PKI) beginning in 1953. Local demands were satisfied through creation of local outfits. In 1959, the Communist movement got support from the popular President Sukarno. BTI had 8.5 million members in 1964. They helped the landless to occupy those lands which they were entitled under the law. In 1965, a military regime came in power which assassinated more than half a million peasants and peasant leaders. Thus, Indonesia has the seeds well-sown for peasants' movements which are only awaiting an ignition. Thus, we may give Indonesia, category 'adequate' with marking '8' (eight).

(iv) Redistribution of Government Surplus Land

In Indonesia, rural land has been distributed like in India except in respect of forest land. In India, even title is being given to people occupying forest or forest fringe lands for generation for cultivation or residential purpose. In Indonesia, the 70 per cent land is locked in forests which is not subject to private allotment or right.

In rural areas, land controlled by the communities known as *adat taki* land is available for grant of title by the land office to the landless persons. Even the forest land can be given on the basis of community rights by the forest department. The state lands are also granted to the deserving persons for 30 year rights which is further renewable. In urban areas, Indonesia, shows the lead. Once a plot of land is government land, it should be possible for the person who has possession over it for 30 years and 20 years in case of private lands or who can prove possession or chain of possession over it, to apply for registered titles (Hak Milik). It provides the most comprehensive land right in Indonesia. It is transferable and inheritable and can be subject of security. Thus, Indonesia is given 'adequate' category under this factor with marking/ranking as eight.

(v) Status of Land Records

The position of land records in Indonesia is less than 50 per cent as less than half of the registered properties are shown on maps or in government land records. The cost of registration is very high. Therefore, poor people only depend on unregistered title and without any reflection in government land records. The forest land is largely in government or military control and remain either unrecorded or is recorded with errors.

However, in Jakarta, 80 per cent of land is titled and information is digitised. In other major cities like Java, the coverage is very low. As urban land records are good, Indonesia can be placed in adequate category above average category with ranking as eight.

(vi) Social and Religious Reforms

As women are not given due weightage in land ownership and records of title and the country is dogmatic with principles of Islam, there is hardly any perceptible social or religious movement to improve the habits of rural folk so as to safeguard their title. As there is less prevalence of money-lending in Indonesia, being a Muslim country, there is no availability of easy credit or loan to the government land guarantees or sharecroppers or tenants to indulge into vices like gambling or alcoholism. Thus, this factor can be kept only in very inadequate category with strength as one.

(vii) Legal Aid

There are administrative courts and dispute settlement for to handle disputes relating to land maladministration and errors in land registration or titling by the National Land Agency (BPN) . The BPN also administers the communal tenures. As usual, the procedure in formal courts is dilatory. No legal aid is available. As BPN is taking care of disputes on communal lands and other lands as specialised agency, this factor can be put in 'very inadequate' category as strength one.

(viii) Crop-credit for Cultivation

In Indonesia, the crop credits like things do not exist nor there are so many anti-poverty schemes to improve upon the wasteland or land unfit for agriculture. Therefore, this factor is given zero ranking.

(ix) Co-operative Farming

There was communism for some time which was crushed in Indonesia by the military junta along with Islamic movements. Therefore, this factor is also given 0 (zero) weightage.

(x) Allotment of House-sites and Restoration of Alienated Land

There are not so many schemes for construction of houses or colonies in rural and urban areas. However, there is a good system in place to regularise a person in possession in rural as well as urban areas to get title if he is in possession for long time. This is self-financed system to have homestead in rural and urban areas. As the non-documentary forms of evidence of possession are not available, few such claims get judicial or administrative approval.

Therefore, this factor is also kept in 'very inadequate' category with ranking as 1.

On the basis of foregoing analysis, we can arrive at total land reforms as follows:

$LR_{(total)}$: .4 × 0(i) + 2 × 4(ii) + 1 × 8(iii) + 4 × 8(iv) + .8 × 8(v) + .3 × 1(vi) + .3 × 1(vii) +.5 × 0(viii) + .1 × 0(ix) + .6 × 1(x) = 0 + 8 + 8 + 32 + 6.4 + .3 + .3 + .6 = 55.6 ~ 56 per cent

Thus, land reforms is above average in Indonesia like India yet there is lot of scope for improvements and should be further improved in respect of factors discussed to make a real impact on the poor population of the South Asian giant, i.e., Indonesia.

In an address at Delhi, on March 26, 2008, international expert on land reforms Roy Prosterman has put Japan, Taiwan and South Korea in top category followed by China and Vietnam and then India and Indonesia. In Japan 81 per cent landless households have received land from the government while in China more than 90 per cent have received land while in India less than 28 per cent landless household have received government surplus land in rural areas for cultivation. It shows that the redistribution of government vested land or surplus arable land distributed is directly proportional to the economic growth of a country because Japan, Taiwan, South Korea and China are economic tigers in Asia whereas other countries in Asia are lagging behind. Similar can be said about USA, Europe and Australia that their take-off stage for economic development started after they completed the implementation of land reforms to a large extent. Thus, successful implementation of land reforms provides platform for growth and economic development. Therefore, no country even the developed countries cannot overlook land reforms and should monitor their constant implementation in whatever small way, it is possible.

Though no formula for land reform will give the required accurate results, yet it gives a concrete idea. The implementation of land reforms is most required in African countries closely followed by Latin American countries and Asian countries.

References

1. Deininger, Klaus, Selod, Harris and Burns, Anthony, The Land Governance Assessment Frame Work, The World Bank, Washington DC, USA, p. 1, 2012.
2. *Ibid.*, 1, pp. 40-45.
3. NREP stands for National Rural Employment Programme.
4. IRDP means Integrated Rural Development Programme.
5. MNREGA, Mahatma Gandhi Rural Employment Guarantee Act/ Programme.
6. Agrawal, P.K., *Land Reforms in India*, p. 189, M.D. Publications, New Delhi, 1993.
7. *Ibid.,* 6, p. 191.
8. Notes:
   I. Stands for Employment Generating Schemes.
   II. Stands for Position of Sharecroppers.
   III. Stands for Local Self-goverenance and Peasants Organisation..
   IV. Stands for Distribution of Surplus Land.
   V. Stands for Status of Land Records.
   VI. Stands for Social and Religious Reforms.
   VII. Stands for Availability of Legal Aid.
   VIII. Stands for Financial Assistance for Crops.
   IX. For Consolidation of Holdings and Co-operative Farming.
   X. For Allotment of House Sites and Restoration of Alienated land.

14

Epilogue

The adoption and issuance of the Voluntary Guidelines on the Responsible Governance of Tenure by the Food and Agriculture Organisation of the United Nations (FAO) is the greatest achievement of the protagonists of land reforms. UNO and the World Bank have ultimately reached to the conclusion that without implementation of land reforms, poverty cannot be removed from the face of the mother earth. The guidelines have additionally covered fisheries and forests within the ambit of land reform because both these sectors are ultimately based on land and have also poor workers dependent like peasants on agricultural land. Though these are known as 'soft laws' yet these are not as soft as these have such a nomenclature. 'Soft Laws' have an advantage over binding international agreements because they are usually easier for countries to reach agreement on. Also, soft laws are more comprehensive and provide more details, that they are often suited for variations in technical matters and best practices as per specific circumstances. Soft law instruments have a positive impact in guiding national policies and legislation in many countries. When a country enacts all or part of an international soft law instrument, that soft law becomes 'hard law' within that country.

The governance of tenure is placed in the context of human rights. The guidelines recommend that countries should ensure that all actions regarding tenure and its governance are consistent with their obligations under national and international laws. The guidelines lay down following broad framework of land reforms.

"(i) Make access to land, fisheries and forests more equitable.

(ii) Protect people from the arbitrary loss of their tenure rights, including through forced evictions.

(iii) Help ensure no one is subject to discrimination under laws, policies and practices.

(iv) Lead to more transparent and participatory decision-making.

(v) Help ensure that all people are treated equally when laws are enforced.

(vi) Help ensure disputes are resolved before they degenerate into conflict.

(vii) Simplify the administration of tenure and make it more accessible and effective to all."[1]

Land reform measures aim at alleviating the poverty in the following manner:

1. By taking over excess land from large landholders and then to distribute surplus government land among the landless persons to provide a better equitable environment and to ensure livelihood to the landless persons and their families who are poorest among the poor in the society.
2. By providing security of tenure to the tenants and sharecroppers and by regulating rent payable by tenants in urban areas, so that they may work with peace and more hard work can be rendered by them resulting into more production or output to the kitty of the society and the state.
3. By protecting interests of the indigenous people in land through the community management and to give them right in forests and its fringe or degraded areas and to protect their lands against alienation and encroachments by non-tribals.
4. By pooling the landholdings of marginal small and government allottees (*pattadars*) including their waste lands to make their lands more productive through government help by means of various anti-poverty schemes undertaken by the government.
5. By development of public land and pastures for providing better access to the rural poor for fuel, wood and fodder.
6. By regulating various money-lending practices and providing alternative sources of credit or government grants.

7. By providing equal access to women to land or house so that needs of families of rural and urban poor of education and health are taken more care of.
8. By providing homestead rights of the rural and urban poor on lands possessed by them for long time say twenty years or so and providing them grant, subsidy or credit for construction of residential houses to shelter them and their families.
9. The tenants dispossessed by force, or by fraud or due to distress from their land must be restored back in their possession as expeditiously as possible through expeditious justice delivery system.
10. The marginal farmers or government allottees of vested land should not be allowed to sell or mortgage their land due to distress. Rather they should be provided social security for health and education. At least, in case of critical diseases in their families, they should be given free or concessional treatment so that they may not have to alienate their lands.
11. The poor are given passbook or identity card mentioning their ownership right on parcel of land so that their land cannot be easily taken over by outsiders through process of land tribunals or quasi judicial authorities or judicial courts. These land passbooks should reflect their updated records-of-rights. There should be legislative mandate to update and maintain land records in rural as well as in urban areas on urban local bodies.
12. General awareness and reform camps should be organised to educate them about their right to land. At the same time, they will be advised to keep themselves away from vices like drinking, gambling, chewing tobacco, etc., and away from social dogmas, religious superstitions and inculcate saving habit among them to face rainy days in life.
13. Sharecroppers should be legally included as tenants within the tenancy reform laws. Special drive should be launched to identify informal tenants/sharecroppers in all the states who should be conferred occupancy tenant/possession status. In this drive, local peasants' organisations/agricultural labour organisations/voluntary organisations/farmers' committees and other activist groups should be actively associated. They should be permitted to file claim for

the conferment of occupancy right/possession right to sharecroppers before the appropriate authority. In case of a dispute between the landowner and the persons claiming to be tenants/sharecroppers, the burden of proof should be on the landowners to prove the negative.

14. In adequacies in the administrative set-up of LAS should be seriously dealt with. There should be administrative will and the officers who have will to implement land reforms should be encouraged and patronised and duly rewarded. Adequate financial support should be made available by the concerned government.
15. Co-operative farming should be encouraged in villages on the pattern of Egypt. Local *panchayats*, councils, communes or community may be nodal agencies to organise these collective farms. Arrangements for marketing, implements and fertilisers, etc. should be accessible with these local bodies to readily make them available to the farmers for scientific farming and proper marketing of agricultural produce.
16. 'Political Will' should be created. For this landless, marginal and small farmers should be members of local panchayat bodies, councils, communes or communities and also ministries so that they are associated at each decision-making level.
17. Panchayat, local council, commune or community should be given power to dispose of local petty land matters. Until the land tribunals or vilalge courts are established, a small sub-committee of these local bodies may function as judicial bodies to adjudicate local petty cases relating to land dispute or cultivation conflicts.
18. The poor peasants or urban poor may be provided legal and up to the level of highest court of the country. The various stages of a case should be reduced land tribunals may be set up at sub-division, district and state level so that the justice is also decentralised so as to reach at the doorstep of the poor person. However, there should be watchdog of interest of the poor either or NGO or local responsible person in courts or tribunals so that lawyers do not take one sided stand against the poor persons in courts/ tribunals.
19. State or government should implement anti-poverty schemes to provide work during lay off period in rural areas, because

generally farming depends on rains and majority of farmers take one crop in a year. Rest of the time, they are unemployed. They should be provided guarantee of employment at least for 150 days in a year. Similarly, government should have sound financial/ economic situation, then only, the state can provide compensation for the surplus land expropriated from the landowners. Secondly, when the excess of land is not available, the government may purchase land from the open market and distribute up to 16 decimal of land.

20. There is no better security of right of the peasants than to organise themselves. Most of the actors in the welfare of the poor are active if the poor themselves are activated and are mobilised. The administration has so many problems at hand that they tend to forget the dumb majority of peasants in rural areas and the homeless or jobless workers in urban areas. Most of the members of the administration and legal profession can't be relied upon. Even, the judiciary slowly turns deaf ear to the voice of the poor under the influence of big lawyers and advocates who appear on behalf of big landowners and their capitalist associates in cities, due to receipt of fat fees from them. Therefore, Marx suggested for withering away of the state including judiciary. However, the poor cannot wait for unlimited period with hungry stomach to see that the blood revolution is started by the industrial workers. In their struggle they will find their lot of supporters and activists among elite bureaucrats, intellectuals, writers and enlightened politicians. Ideally, there will be integration between rural and urban societies. A deprivation or injury to a rural poor will find reaction among urban populace and *vice-versa* also.

Karl Marx says "by the prevalence of monopoly prices in many cases, particularly through the most shameless exploitation of poverty and the monstrous power wielded by landed property, when united hand in hand with industrial capital, enables it to be used against labourers engaged in their wage struggles as a means of practically expelling them from the earth as dwelling place."[2]

He further proves that the big fish eats the small fish in the agricultural field as well. According to Marx, "even the enclosure of waste lands bears hard on the poor, by depriving them of part of their subsistence and only goes towards increasing farms, already too large. This land gets into the hands of a few great farmer, the consequence must be that the little farmers will be converted into a body of men who earn their subsistence by working for others and who will be under a necessity of going to market for all they want. Upon the whole, the circumstances of the lower ranks of men are altered in almost every respect for the worse. From little occupiers of land, they are reduced to the state of day labourers and have things and at the same time, their subsistence in that state has become more difficult."[3]

He gives example of England where medium size farms were reduced or merged into a few large farms. Even the community lands cannot do great welfare of the poor. Even law cannot bring revolution. In sum and substance , the peasants have to fight their own battle for realisation their just and reasonable right on land or share of produce. In rural areas, the rights of farmers can be realised by way of implementation of land reforms to a large extent. Yet many intellectuals question this thesis. "Most of the rural poor, as Minhas (1974) points out, are made up of agricultural labourers without land, agricultural labourers with very little land, other rural labourers without land and small land holders, who usually have less than five acres."[4] In urban areas, the poverty is caused mainly due to lack of opportunities for employment, trade or industry. The growth creates opportunities despite increasing inequality. Employment income is between two-thirds and three quarters of total income and this share tends to be even larger for poor households with little income from non-labour-related sources. Countries with relatively low levels of GDP per capita tend to have most employment concentrated in agriculture, but as productivity in that sector rises and non-agricultural activities expand, the work force shifts out of agriculture, and into attractive informal and formal employment in industry and services."[5]

Lifting infrastructure constraints to improve market access, as well as increasing access to electricity and education in high density rural areas and small towns, may raise non-agricultural earnings for the poor. But inspite of market access, the farmers are exploited there by the traders and middlemen, who charge fixed commission to facilitate the sale of their crop produce. The government officials managing the market places, connive with traders and both of them exploit the farmers. Of course, this is less than the ones who directly purchased from the farmers. In all cases, the farmers take loans from the traders or seeds before the crops are sown. Naturally, after the crops are raised, they become morally bound to sell their crops to him at the dictation of the trader or the middleman. When there is either crop failure due to drought or flood or otherwise, he will not be able to pay off debts. And he takes the path of running away from the struggle. In India alone one farmer in every 32 minutes commits suicide. More than 1,00,000 farmers have taken their lives since 1997 in India. About 86.5 per cent of farmers who took their own lives were financially indebted apart from indebtedness due to medical emergency or daughters' marriage. Their average debt was about $835. Vidarbha, the cotton belt of Maharashtra, India is especially famous for suicides by farmers along with arid zone, of Bundelkhand in Uttar Pradesh. Bank credit crop insurance and simultaneously punishment to moneylenders can extricate the situation to large extgent."[6]

However, the international scene of suicides by farmers is equally damning. It is better that these farmers die while fighting for their rights in an unequal society. They give the message: Let the peasants in rural areas and the homeless and jobless workers in urban areas unite and fight for their rights.

Professor Gunnar Myrdel, Nobel Laureate correctly forecasts that "it is in the agricultural sector that the battle for long-term economic development will be won or lost."

It is agreed that "poverty is borne primarily by those with little or no access to land; one solution is to redistribute land. But this is not the only solution to alleviate poverty. Another is to increase sources of non-farm employment through agricultural growth."[7]

Karl Marx found that legal enactments like land reforms laws cannot remove obstacles nor unemployment problem can be solved in urban areas. The steps suggested can only shorten and lessen the birth pangs. Let us shorten the misery of the peasants and homeless working class in urban areas as far as possible with the help of measures suggested in this work with scientific study and practical experience. However, none can prevent the development of the society as per economic law of motion. If the violent revolution is the only solution, we have simply to welcome it. However, we should see that minimum injury is caused to the human life because a revolution is made of brick and mortar of human beings.

References

1. FAO, Voluntary Guidelines on the Governance of Tenure – At a glance by F&AO, *Viale della Terme di Ceracalla*, Rome, Italy, p. 4, 2012.
2. Marx, Karl, *Capital*, ed. by Engels Friedrich, Vol. 3, Andhra Vignana Samithi, Abids Hyderabad, p. 273, 2009.
3. *Ibid.*, 2, pp. 679-680, Vol. 1.
4. Singh, Inderjit, *The Great Ascent, The Rural Poor in South Asia*, World Bank, p. 35, 1990.
5. Besley, Timothy, Cord, Loisez, *Delivering on the Promise of Pro-Poor Growth*, World Bank and Palgrave, MacMillan USA, p. 12, 2007.
6. Shiva, Dr. Vandana and Jalees, Kunwar: Farmer Suicides in India, Research Foundation for Science, Technology and Ecology, New Delhi, p. 49, 2014.
7. *Ibid.*, 4: p. 95.

Bibliography

Agrawal, P.K. (2010), *Land Reforms in States and Union Territories in India*, Concept Publishing Company Pvt. Ltd., New Delhi.

______, (1993), *Land Reforms in India, Constitutional and Legal Approach*, M.D. Publishing Pvt. Ltd., MD House, New Delhi.

______, (2010), Naxalism: Causes and Cure, Manas Publications, New Delhi.

Agrawal, P.K. and Bhatt R.K. (2011), *Globalisation, India and the World*, Concept Publishing Company Pvt. Ltd., New Delhi.

Bardhan, Pranab K. (1984), *Land, Labour and Rural Poverty*, Oxford University Press, New Delhi.

Besley Timothy, Cord, Delivering on the Promise of Pro-Poor Growth.

Louise J. (2007), *Insights and Lessons from Country Experiences*, World Bank and Palgrave MacMillan, New York, NY.

Binswanger, Hans P, Bourguignon, Mkhize, Brink, Rogier Vanden (2009), *Agricultural Land Redistribution, Towards Greater Consensus*, The World Bank, Washington, DC.

Das, Chandreyee and Ghosh Dipankar (2006) (ed.), *Eye on Development, SAMPARK*, Kolkata 700089.

Datta, Gaurav and Ashwani Mahajan (2011), *Indian Economy*, S. Chand and Company Ltd., New Delhi.

Deininger, Klaus (2003), *Land Policies for Growth and Poverty Reduction*, The World Bank and Oxford University Press, NW, Washington DC.

Deininger, Klaus, Selod Harris and Burns, Anthony (2012), *The Land Governance Assessment Framework*, (Identifying and Monitoring Good Practice in the Land Sector), the World Bank, NW, Washington DC. (www.worldbank.org).

Ghimire, Krishna B., ed. (2001): *Land Reforms and Peasant Livelihoods*, ITDG Publishing London UK.

Griffin, Keith (1976), *Rural Poverty*, The Macmillan Press Ltd., London and Land Concentration and Madras.

Gupta, Asha (1987), *Socialism in Theory and Practice-Narendra Dev's Contribution*, Gitanjali Publishing House, New Delhi.

Marx, Karl, Engels, Frederik (2009), *Capital, Critique of Political Economy*, Vol. 1, 2 and 3, ed. Visalaandhra Vignan Samithi, Hyderabad.

Mende, Tibor (1961), *The Great Revolutions, The Chinese Revolution*, Thames and Hudson, London.

Janvry Alaindle, Gordillo. Guslavo, Platteau Jeen Phillippene, Sadoulet Elisabeth (2001), *Access to Land, Rural Poverty and Public Action*, Oxford, University Press, Oxford Ox2 6 DP.

Kesari, UPD (1975), *Lectures on Administrative Law*, Central Law Agency, University Road, Allahabad.

Hanstad, Tim and Lokesh, S.B., (2002): *Allocating Homestead plots as Land Reforms: Analysis from West Bengal*, India, by Rural Development Institute, New York, U.S.A.

Sen, Ashok (1968), *Das Kapital, Centenary Volume* ed. Sen, Mohit, Rao MB, People's Publishing House (P) Ltd., Delhi.

Shiva, Dr. Vandana and Jalees, Kunwar (2013), *Farmers Suicides in India, Research Foundation for Science*, Technology and Ecology, New Delhi.

Singh, Inderjit (1990), *The Great Ascent (The Rural Poor in South Asia)*, World Bank, The Johns Hopkins University Press, Baltimore, Maryland, USA.

Singh, Tarlok (1969), *Poverty and Social Change*, Orient Longmans, New Delhi.

Williamson, Enemark, Wallace and Rajabifard (2010): *Land Administration for Sustainable Development*, ESRI Press, California.

Reports, Newspapers, Periodicals and Official Publications

All India Reporter (1986), Supreme Court of India, p. 180.

Department of Land Resource, Ministry of Rural Development, Government of India: Nirman Bhawan Annexe, New Delhi , Annual Report.

Indian Institute of Public Administration (2011), India Chronic Poverty Report, Towards Solutions and New Compacts in a Dynamic Context by Aasha

Kapur Mehta, Andrew Shepherd, Shashank Bhide, Amita Shah and Anand Kumar, Indian Institute of Public Administration, Indraprastha Estate, Ring Road, New Delhi.

Food and Agriculture Organisation of the United Nations (2012): Voluntary Guidelines on the Responsible Governance of Tenure (of Land, Fisheries and Forests in the context of National Food Security), FAO, Viale delle Terme de, Caracella 00153 Rome, Italy, www.fao.org.

Ministry of Rural Development, Government of India (2014): Enhancing Sustainable Livelihoods of the Poor through Convergence of MNREGA with various schemes, pp. 1-2.

Ministry of Rural Development, Government of India (2013), Annual Report 2012-13, Krishi Bhawan, New Delhi.

United Nations Human Settlements Programme UN-Habitat: Secure Land Rights for All, and UN-Habitat Global Land Tool Network, 2008, UN-Habitat, Nairobi , Kenya.

UN-Habitat: Tapping the Potential, The Role of Grassroots in Land Policy Implementation, Report 3/2012, 2012, UN-Habitat Headquarters, Nairobi, Kenya..

UN Habitat: Innovative Urban Tenure in the Philippines, Challenges Approaches and Institutionalisation, Securing Land and Property Rights for All, Report 2012, 2012, UN Habitat, Nairobi, Kenya.

World Bank (2007): India Land Policies for Growth and Poverty Reduction, Report No. 38298-IN, the World Bank, Washington DC, USA.

World Bank (2013), Abstracts of Papers at Annual World Bank Conference on Land and Poverty, The World Bank, Washington D.C, April, 8-11, 2013.

Khwaja Mohammed Vs Muhammad Ibrahim, 1904, ILR 26, ALL 490, p. 493.

Ram Saran V. Harihar Prasad: 1961 ILR AP 314.

Mahdav H. Rao Hoskt Vs. State of Maharashtra, AIR 1978. Supreme Court, p. 1548.

Olga Tellis Vs. Bombay Municipal Corporation, AIR, 1986, SC, p. 180.

Economic and Political Weekly.

The Pioneer.

Index

K

L

O

P